THREE DAYS

The Search for the Boy Messiah

CHRIS STEPIEN

DynamicCatholic.com
Be Bold. Be Catholic.®

THREE DAYS
THE SEARCH FOR THE BOY MESSIAH

ISBN: 978-1-937509-92-7

Design by Jenny Miller and Leah Nienas

For more information on bulk copies of this title or other books
and CDs available through the Dynamic Catholic Book Program,
please visit www.DynamicCatholic.com or call 859-980-7900.

The Dynamic Catholic Institute
5081 Olympic Blvd • Erlanger • Kentucky • 41018
Phone: 1–859–980–7900
Email: info@DynamicCatholic.com

DEDICATION

For my family and friends and all those throughout the world
who have shown me how much God loves us.

GLOSSARY

ADONAI:
Hebrew for My Lord (God)

MIRIAM:
Hebrew for Mary

SHLAMA:
Aramaic for peace

YAHWEH:
Hebrew for the sacred name of God

YERUSHLEM:
Aramaic for Jerusalem

YESHUA:
Hebrew for Jesus

YOSEF:
Hebrew for Joseph

PREFACE

JESUS WAS JUST 12 YEARS OLD WHEN HE FOUND himself alone in Jerusalem, separated from his parents. As the father of two sons, I have often wondered about that preteen experience. What did Jesus do to survive on his own in Jerusalem for three days? What did he eat and where did he sleep? Who did he meet? Was he ever in jeopardy? How did his parents cope with his disappearance?

Jesus encountered an intense and bustling metropolis — a global trade center — with the most magnificent Temple on earth. Caesar's Roman army occupied the territory, including its capital city, Jerusalem. It would have been an exhilarating, yet dangerous environment for a youngster. Surprisingly, all we have to describe that adventure are 12 verses in the second chapter of Luke's Gospel.

This novel is based on that account, my imagination, and love for God and His Word.

I hope it helps you contemplate the Holy Scripture and this event in the boy Messiah's life.

It's a story for the child in all of us.

THE JOURNEY TO JERUSALEM

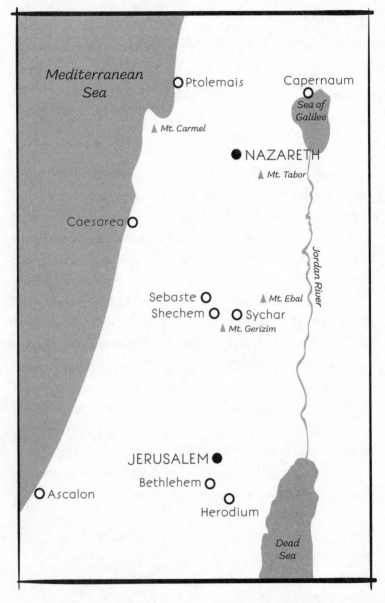

The Boy in the
TEMPLE

EACH YEAR HIS PARENTS WENT TO JERUSALEM for the feast of Passover, and when he was twelve years old, they went up according to festival custom. After they had completed its days, as they were returning, the boy Jesus remained behind in Jerusalem, but his parents did not know it. Thinking that he was in the caravan, they journeyed for a day and looked for him among their relatives and acquaintances, but not finding him, they returned to Jerusalem to look for him.

After three days they found him in the temple, sitting in the midst of the teachers, listening to them and asking them questions, and all who heard him were astounded at his understanding and his answers. When his parents saw him, they were astonished, and his mother said to him, "Son, why have you done this to us? Your father and I have been looking for you with great anxiety." And he said to them, "Why were you looking for me? Did you not know that I must be in my Father's house?"

But they did not understand what he said to them. He went down with them and came to Nazareth, and was obedient to them; and his mother kept all these things in her heart.

And Jesus advanced [in] wisdom and age and favor before God and man. (Luke 2:41-52)

chapter
ONE

YESHUA SMILED.

He loved to sit on the roof of his mud brick house after dinner. He'd carve small wooden shapes and toys with his knife, whenever he had time. His father had let him hang out on the flat roof, ever since Yeshua helped repair it last year. They used sycamore branches and covered them with clay plaster. Their fix was holding up well, so far.

Almost every time he climbed the ladder, Yeshua had to promise his mother not to sit on the roof ledge. For safety, it was 18 inches high and ran along the perimeter of the home. Standing at his favorite perch, he had a bird's-eye view of the surrounding hillsides. The highest point in his hometown, Nazareth, was 1,300 feet above sea level.

There was a nice breeze that skipped along the rooftops. The hot sun would set in an hour or so. Yeshua welcomed the relief. His skin was a deep, dark brown, even under his shirt, which he carefully took off, rolled up, and set on the ledge. He pulled back his dark, curly hair and cinched up his tunic around his hips to cool off. His rich tan made him look even more muscular. The more wood and stonework he did with his father, the more he looked like him, a seasoned carpenter and mason. But his face clearly resembled his mother's.

Facing north, Yeshua sat down and leaned back against the ledge. He could see snow atop Mount Hermon on the horizon. The Sea of Galilee was about 15 miles to the east. Mount Carmel stood due west, stretching to the Mediterranean Sea. When he faced east, there was Mount Tabor to his right. And as Yeshua looked over his shoulder and gazed south, he imagined mighty Yerushlem. It was about five days away on foot, across a sprawling plain.

He often waved to travelers in the distance, as they walked along the caravan route to and from Egypt. Occasionally, someone would spot him on the roof and wave back. The path wound its way through the hillsides of Nazareth. Yeshua could sling a stone and almost hit the trail from his roof. That's where he saw his first horses. Roman soldiers riding them. Rugged. Muscled. Yet, they were gentle and beautiful animals. Horses were his favorite toys to carve.

Yeshua chewed on an olive pit, while he craftily whittled and smoothed a chunk of sycamore wood with his new blade. He had saved the scrap piece from his father's shop. He was getting really good at making toys. His father, Yosef, had sold a couple recently. But this one was special. It was a gift for his friend, Ezra. They were headed to Yerushlem together for the Passover. How amazing it would be to visit the Temple for the first time. Just thinking about it made him laugh and shout for joy from the rooftop, "Ye-ru-shlem!"

Thousands and thousands of people would be traveling to celebrate the festival in the Holy City. He and Ezra would both turn 13 later this year. Each would make his formal dedication to Judaism in front of Nazareth's whole Synagogue community. But the rabbi had said their first trip to Yerushlem would be incomparable. They would join Hebrew pilgrims from across the world, see the Temple High Priest, and perhaps meet some of the greatest thinkers anywhere — brilliant Jewish minds. Awesome.

Yeshua's mom and dad made the Passover pilgrimage every year, but until now, he had been too young to go. It was a little scary and intense at festival time. For every visitor, there was a highwayman, a pickpocket, a professional beggar, or a street hawker. Younger children were vulnerable in big cities. So, every year, Yeshua had stayed behind with his grandmother or one of his great-aunts. They would celebrate the Seder dinner, eat lamb with neighbors, and pray for the safe return of his parents and everyone from the village making the journey.

But this year would be profoundly different. Yeshua would travel to Yerushlem and experience it with his friend. The city would overflow with pilgrims from places like Egypt, Africa, Persia, and Greece. Every Jew dreamed of observing Passover in Yerushlem, and reveling in the festival. There were more than a million Hebrew believers spread across the Roman world, and hundreds of caravans would follow the four roads that led to Yerushlem. And, of course, armies of Roman sentries would stand on duty. Some soldiers would mount battle-tested chargers to better manage the enormous crowds.

Yeshua carved Ezra's horse with flaring nostrils like the one in the book of Job. He knew the Scripture passage by heart, and recited it as he scraped at the wood with his knife.

> *"Do you give the horse his strength,*
> *and clothe his neck with a mane?*
> *Do you make him quiver like a locust,*
> *while his thunderous snorting spreads terror?*
> *He paws the valley, he rejoices in his strength,*
> *and charges into battle.*
> *He laughs at fear and cannot be terrified;*
> *he does not retreat from the sword.*
> *Around him rattles the quiver,*
> *flashes the spear and the javelin.*
> *Frenzied and trembling he devours the ground;*
> *he does not hold back at the sound of the trumpet;*
> *at the trumpet's call he cries, "Aha!"*
> *Even from afar he scents the battle,*
> *the roar of the officers and the shouting."*
> *(Job 39: 19-25)*

As he said the words, he sculpted the steed in his hands. He could easily picture the majestic animal in real life, almost dancing with excitement. He had seen a horse dance once. Hearing the music from a wedding celebration, the stallion pranced in time with the rhythm. The thought made Yeshua's heart skip with excitement.

When he closed his eyes to imagine the scene again, he saw several horses pressing against a large crowd. There was a man riding a donkey, and people waved palm branches and cheered for him.

"Yeshua!"

He opened his eyes, as if startled from a nap. It was his mother, Miriam, calling him to come down from the rooftop before it got too dark. The sun was setting now, as he put on his shirt and tucked the knife and carving into his belt for the climb down the ladder. He was still too young to sleep on the roof by himself. In the scorching summer months, he would follow his father up the ladder and spend the night under the starry sky. One time, Ezra had been allowed to join them. But it wasn't quite warm enough to convince his parents to let them sleep outside tonight.

Besides, maybe he could do a little more carving before bed. He had to finish the horse soon if he hoped to give it to Ezra on their trip to Yerushlem. Putting wheels on the toy horse would be the hard part. But he had an idea about how to make them. He had watched his father craft wagon wheels many times. Yeshua would create the horse as if it had reared up on its hind legs. He'd attach its hooves to a wooden, wheeled platform that could be pulled on a string or pushed along by hand. Ezra and Yeshua were very competitive at board games and jacks. They both played to win. The horse would give them something to enjoy together just for fun. No winners and no losers.

Yeshua pulled down the ladder and stowed it inside his father's shop. Yosef was about to latch the door for the night. His tools were valuable. He had axes and hatchets; an adze for shaping wood; an awl and drill to bore holes; nails; hammers for stone and wood; knives; chisels; wedges; saws; planers; a spoke shave; a rule; plumb-line;

and compass. Each one took hours, even days to craft by hand. To make them, Yosef had ordered some of his metal components from a blacksmith in Ptolemais on the coast. The tools had to be carefully secured. The noisy bell on the wood door clanged as he shut it. Yeshua had helped his father fix the leather-strapped hinges. The door hung better now and would frustrate prowlers. Yosef couldn't afford locks for the shop, but he tied and knotted a strap around the latch. For the most part, Nazareth was a very safe little village.

The family's donkeys, sheep, and goats were already resting for the night in the outer room of the house, as Yeshua and Yosef ducked their heads to enter through the narrow door. Yosef bolted it. They hurried to step up into the inner room, leaving their sandals at the threshold. Yosef dipped his cup into the water bucket and took a long, slow drink. He sat away from the fire, near his wife to watch her work. Miriam was in the corner near the window, quietly singing while she wound flax on a spool. When the cooling breeze blew through her long, black hair, she leaned back and closed her eyes to savor its comfort. Her oil lamp flickered in the wind. She put down her work to brush her tresses. Miriam had brought the brush back from Egypt years ago. The wooden handle, once decorated with shells, was worn, but the flint bristles still did their job. Yosef put his hand on his wife's shoulder and offered her some of his water.

Yeshua had settled down in the kitchen area, near the faint glow of another oil lamp. He worked a little more on the wooden horse, his knife reflecting the light.

When Yosef had finished his water, he crossed the room to Yeshua, leaned down and took the carving from his hands. He picked up the lamp and then carefully turned the toy over in the flickering light, inspecting the craftsmanship, smiling and nodding with approval.

"Like father, like son," said Yosef. He beamed as he handed the toy back. Yeshua blushed at the compliment and smiled.

Yosef wasted no time walking over to his bed with the lamp, and took off his tunic. His body was ruggedly muscled, his hair long and greying. He knelt down at his mat to say his bedtime prayer. Yeshua closed the door to the outer room, and then he and Miriam joined Yosef.

> *"Praised are You,*
> *Adonai, our God,*
> *Ruler of the universe,*
> *Who closes my eyes in sleep,*
> *my eyelids in slumber.*
> *May it be Your will,*
> *Adonai,*
> *My God and the God of my ancestors,*
> *To lie me down in peace*
> *And then to raise me up in peace.*
>
> *Let no disturbing thoughts upset me,*
> *No evil dreams nor troubling fantasies*
>
> *May my bed be complete and whole*
> *in Your sight.*
>
> *Grant me light*
> *So that I do not sleep the sleep of death,*
> *for it is You who illumines and enlightens.*
>
> *Praised are You,*
> *Adonai,*
> *Whose majesty gives light to the universe."* [1]

As Miriam put out the lamp, Yeshua said, "Amen." The room was now totally dark, but for the dim orange glow of the coals in the kitchen. Yeshua could sense the light and warmth of His heavenly Father. He was in the breeze that blew in through the window, caressing Yeshua's face as he drifted off to sleep.

chapter

TWO

THE AROMA OF FRESH BREAD BAKING IN THE outdoor oven woke Yeshua. His mom was a good cook. He loved to dip Miriam's warm, soft bread in the olive oil she had pressed. She would make her loaves from barley, and when they could occasionally afford it, from wheat. Miriam would mix the coarse grain meal with water and salt, adding just a little sour dough from yesterday's yeasty batch. That would make the bread rise.

"Mmmm!" Yeshua would say at the first bite of a warm and fluffy round loaf. But his favorites were her fried honey cakes. His grandma had taught Miriam how to make them. Every once in a while, she would cook up the sweet, doughy pastries. They would sizzle in the oil of the hot pan. But honey was expensive, so they didn't have it often. Yeshua's grandma always made the cakes when he visited.

He could hear Miriam grinding grain to make more flour with the millstone in the courtyard. The sun was barely up, but Miriam always rose with the rooster. She had already been to the well, fed the chickens, gathered eggs, and milked the goats. Later she would make cheese curds, tend the garden, and then do laundry in the stone washtub Yosef had made her.

Before Yeshua even opened his eyes he prayed quietly:

"I thank you, living and eternal king.
  For returning my soul within me, in compassion.
  Great is your faithfulness."[2]

The first thing he saw that morning was his knife and the shape of the toy wooden horse he had been crafting. It looked pretty impressive in the early morning light. He would have liked nothing better than to climb back up on the roof and finish his masterpiece. But it was time to get ready for school.

Like most boys in Nazareth, Yeshua began attending classes when he was five. But Yosef and Miriam had taught him prayers and the stories from the Torah from the moment he could talk. When he was five, they had walked him to the Synagogue for classes that started at daybreak, six days a week. At noon every day, Yeshua met Miriam or Yosef at the door for the walk home.

When he got a little older, he started staying after school. Yeshua often helped classmates with their work. It was not uncommon for him to hang around the Synagogue to tutor Ezra or someone else, or to walk home with a friend to explain the day's lesson.

"Yeshua, you have been fattened with the Torah," his teacher would say, although he was not fat at all. Fortunately, he didn't have a big head either. Most of his classmates really admired him, but he wasn't popular because of his looks. Yeshua was ordinary on the outside, but his passion for the Word of God was extraordinary, and very contagious.

This morning, Yeshua was running a little late. He hadn't heard his mother's first call to wake him. He had been dreaming about the horse he was carving and how much Ezra would like it. When he smelled the bread baking, he knew he had overslept. Yeshua quickly pulled on his tunic.

He was in advanced studies now, and all his classmates were very competitive. Yeshua had morning classes and another session in the late afternoon. The work was demanding. When the boys turned ten years old, the lessons expanded to include both the written law of the Torah, plus the complex Jewish oral law. These were rabbinical, philosophical interpretations about the meaning of the Torah. Many generations of Israel's spiritual minds had left their marks on Jewish tradition. These insights on the Torah were written down and were eventually compiled hundreds of years after Yeshua was born. They became the Talmud.

Secretly, Yeshua enjoyed these lessons because his teacher often used Midrash, like parables to explain them. Rather than simply raise a question and then refer to the law to answer it, his rabbi told stories. And the stories helped the students understand his teachings. At least it worked for Yeshua.

It was not uncommon for Yeshua to close his eyes and envision the story he was hearing. He had a vivid imagination. Maybe that's why he was so good at carving. But every time he closed his eyes in class, Yeshua took a risk. The rabbi sternly punished daydreamers, sleepers, and slackers. Sometimes there were even spankings. Yeshua cringed at the thought. Arriving late was not recommended.

Yeshua quickly cleaned up at the water basin behind his home, near the garden. The beans and cucumbers were coming along. When he was done, Yeshua poured the water from the basin into the vegetable patch. He ran around the house and through the courtyard, shaking his hands dry before he grabbed a loaf at the oven. Miriam gave him a date from her apron, and he kissed her on the cheek.

He bowed his head and paused to give thanks as his stomach growled. The loaf had cooled, but it was still a little warm in his hand and would be delicious on the walk to school. Chickens cackled as he ran past them toward the road. Yosef was nowhere in sight, and his wagon and one donkey were already gone. The shop door was closed.

Fortunately, Synagogue school wasn't far, but Yeshua had to run through the marketplace to take the shortcut. There was always something going on that could slow down a 12-year-old boy. A visiting merchant might be hawking pepper from India or fine olive oil from Palestine. A beggar might have news from a distant town. Maybe the fishmonger had both fresh and dried catch to sell. Everybody had stories. Many of them knew Yeshua because Yosef was the village's chief carpenter. His father had been a carpenter, too. So had Yosef's grandfather and his great-grandfather. But Yeshua had other plans. Although he really liked to work with his hands, he was following his heart. He wanted to be a rabbi.

While he munched his breakfast and walked to school, he thought he might be able to do both jobs. After all, the Synagogue always needed repairs and improvements. He could teach and preach on the Sabbath, and then find time to practice his craft between classes during the rest of the week. But as he considered the possibilities, he realized there probably wasn't enough time in a day to do both jobs well. Yeshua was growing wiser.

Approaching the schoolroom, he noticed there was no one standing outside the door. He ran as fast as he could, his sandals slapping the dirt path. When he looked inside the door, the classroom was empty. What was happening?

Through the window, Yeshua could see his rabbi sitting under the almond tree and the students approaching him. He raced around the building to catch up with them. When he turned the corner, he found Ezra waiting. He had already grabbed Yeshua's wax writing tablet and stylus. Yeshua patted Ezra on the back and thanked him.

"No problem," Ezra replied.

The two boys were as close as brothers. Yeshua had met Ezra before they started school. Ezra had trouble walking. Some of the women in the village said he had been swaddled improperly as a baby. Actually, his right leg was just a little shorter than his left.

When Ezra was about two years old, his mother, Deborah, had come to Yosef and asked him to fashion a little crutch for her son.

Yosef made the crutch, and he brought Yeshua and Miriam with him to deliver it to Ezra and his mother. Deborah was a widow, so Yosef wouldn't think of charging her. Deborah insisted on giving him something in return. Miriam suggested that Yeshua and Ezra play together because Yeshua needed a friend. They became inseparable.

As the two boys sat down for the outdoor class, Yeshua made sure Ezra's cane was in a safe spot. In fact, Yeshua had made it for him, and carved Ezra's name in the handle.

Today's lesson was the Passover celebration, and the foods that were either prescribed or forbidden during the special holy season. Immediately, Yeshua and Ezra shared a smile. They knew they would be in Yerushlem in just a week, celebrating the festival in the Holy City. They would visit the Temple and share the Seder of lamb, unleavened bread, wine, bitter herbs and spices, with a multitude of Jewish people.

"Why is this night different from all other nights?" asked the rabbi.

Yeshua had asked the question every year at Passover, since he could remember. It was tradition for the youngest child to be curious and to ask about the divine events that had freed the Jewish people from Egypt and the Pharaoh's heartless grasp.

Each student in Yeshua's class was well versed in the questions of the Seder and the correct answers.

The rabbi continued. "Why is it that on all other nights during the year we eat either leavened bread or unleavened bread, but on this night we eat only unleavened bread?"

In his head, every boy could hear his grandfather or father respond, "We eat only unleavened bread because our ancestors could not wait for their breads to rise when they were escaping slavery in Egypt. So, the loaves were flat when they came out of the oven."

"Why is it that on all other nights we eat all kinds of vegetables, but on this night we eat only bitter herbs?" the rabbi asked.

He reminded the students that they only eat maror, a bitter herb, to remember the bitterness of slavery the Israelites endured in Egypt.

He posed the next question. "Why is it that on all other nights we do not dip our food even once, but on this night we dip them twice?"

The rabbi explained, "The first dip of green vegetables in salt water is a symbol that says we are replacing our tears with gratitude. The second dip of maror in charoses, a fruity paste, represents the sweetening of our burden of bitterness and suffering."

He continued. "Why is it on all other nights we dine sitting or reclining, but on this night we all recline?"

The answer came from Benjamin, the rabbi's son. "We recline at the Seder table because in ancient times, a free person reclined at a meal and slaves and servants stood."

Finally, the rabbi posed the fifth question: "Why is it that on all other nights we eat meat either roasted, marinated, or cooked, but on this night it is entirely roasted?"

He looked directly at Ezra, who was quick to respond with a confident smile. "We eat only roasted meat because that is how the Passover lamb is prepared during sacrifice in the Temple at Yerushlem."

Yeshua closed his eyes and imagined the aroma of lamb and goats sacrificed at the Temple. Meat was not part of everyday meals. But the Passover festival was a unique celebration, and food had always been an important element of the tradition. It honored God's glorious salvation of His people. He had rescued them from the Egyptians and their oppressive and stubborn ruler.

When he was very young, Yeshua and his family had spent several years hiding in Egypt. Ironically, instead of running from a Pharaoh, they had to elude the King of Israel who wanted to kill baby Yeshua. That's how Yosef and Miriam had explained it to their son. He had been born in Bethlehem, his father's hometown. Yosef and Miriam had travelled there from Nazareth to obey the Roman law and to report for the census. Jews hated the idea of a census. It suggested they were being counted as servants and controlled by men, instead of being God's people. But most complied.

In fact, there were so many people in Bethlehem when Yosef and Miriam arrived that they couldn't find a place to stay. And Miriam had already begun to experience labor pains. Yeshua was her first child, so they had a little time. Her labor would likely last all day. However, she had ridden a donkey for days, all the way from Nazareth. The bumpy motion only hastened the process.

When traveling, people stayed with family whenever possible. Everyone knew that roadside inns were risky places. Proprietors were often shady characters, squeezing the most they could out of their patrons. In return, travelers received little food and only basic accommodations. The Romans had adopted a special set of laws designed to protect weary travellers from greedy innkeepers.

Yosef had stopped in on relatives, but their homes were filled with other guests and some were sick. The couple didn't dare have their newborn where people were ill. The inns overflowed. Every floor mat was taken. The baths and latrines were jammed. Tent cities popped up everywhere. People packed the eateries, so folks had to buy food from street merchants, dining anywhere they could find a little cover. Yosef was parched and beyond hungry, but he could only think about finding a comfortable place for Miriam to rest and have their baby.

As they approached the edge of town, Yosef became concerned for their safety. The sun was setting, and with so many visitors in Bethlehem, a man with a very pregnant woman to protect would be easy prey for robbers. Yosef gripped his staff tightly as he led the donkey past a group of men entering the town from the south. They had camels, so they were likely from Egypt or another desert region.

Bethlehem was a short distance south of Yerushlem, so there were plenty of people moving through, looking for any space near the major city to rest for the night. In fact, Yosef and Miriam had journeyed through Yerushlem just a few hours earlier, stopping for a quick snack on the street. The crowds were enormous, and the traffic was snarled with animals, vehicles, and Roman soldiers. Census takers were lined up, but there were too many heads to count quickly.

The young couple from Nazareth had to register in Bethlehem, but they made time to stop at the Temple gates and pray. It was a little while later that Miriam's contractions had started.

Now, after traveling through the Holy City, they arrived at Bethlehem's southern gate; their last hope was an inn near the livery. The inn was always busy because it was so close to the Temple. It hosted caravans, and many people rented two-wheeled and four-wheeled carts and carriages from the livery stable.

Those fortunate enough to be rich traveled in private carriages and parked them under the inn's few private rooms. Yosef hoped someone would be kind enough to squeeze them in. Oftentimes, many travelers shared a single space, but with the census, plus the typical traffic near the big city, the young family would have to rely on the grace of God to see them through.

Yosef knocked hard at the door, but no one answered. He knocked again, and then again even harder. No answer. But there was plenty of noise coming from upstairs, inside the innkeeper's apartment. Miriam shrugged her shoulders. Yosef led the donkey with Miriam aboard around the side to stand under the apartment window. He began to shout, "Anyone home?"

Splash!

Water came pouring out of the window above. The innkeeper's wife had emptied a huge basin, soaking Yosef's feet.

"Hey, watch what you're doing!" Yosef yelled, startling the woman.

"Well, it's hard to find an open piece of dirt in this town tonight," she shouted. "Why didn't you come to the door?"

"I did, but no one answered. And I knocked plenty," Yosef said. "My wife is about to have our son. Can you help us get a room?"

"How do you know it's a son?" she asked.

"We know. God's messenger told us it's a boy," Miriam responded.

"Well, he should have told you we're full," the woman chuckled. "Besides, this is no place to have a baby tonight. Much too crowded and crazy. You'll be better off in one of the stables. You can use the one here, under our apartment. Of course, I'll have to charge you for your animal and the price of a room.

"There's plenty of fresh straw there, and I'll bring down some water in a few minutes. My sister, Chaviva, is our town midwife. I have some cloth for swaddling," she offered. "My name is Adina."

And a few hours later, that very night, Yeshua was born under a heavenly, starry sky. He loved to hear his parents tell that story and many other exciting details of his birth. People had come to visit him that evening, including some from the roads. Others were shepherds from the fields who had heard about his birth. Chaviva and Adina proved to be very helpful. They were astonished to see so many people coming to visit Yeshua. The shepherds said angels had told them of a savior's birth. He was the long promised Messiah, they claimed. The angels had pointed to Bethlehem, and encouraged them to find the swaddled baby there, lying in a manger. It was "a sign from the Lord," they rejoiced. Adina remembered what Miriam had said about God's messenger – how she knew she was going to have a son. Adina was a little shaken by the coincidence.

But there was also a terrifying part of the story. Shortly after Yeshua's birth, King Herod the Great had ordered his guard to slaughter all male children in and around Bethlehem who were two years old or younger.

It was an unthinkable, evil command. The king was insanely jealous, all because he had heard a prophecy from three travelers. They said that the Messiah, a king sent by God himself, had been born in Bethlehem, the city of David. Herod felt threatened. He had already been forced to share his power with Roman occupiers. And now three wise men, who studied the constellations, were telling him that a brilliant star had stopped over Bethlehem to mark the birthplace of God's anointed ruler. And Yeshua was that child!

Herod was an enormously proud person. He wanted to be remembered as a greater king than Solomon. Not because he shared Solomon's love for wisdom and justice. The king was hungry for power and wealth. Herod had actually dismantled much of the Temple and was building anew on its foundation. His objective: a renovation that was even larger and grander than Solomon's Temple.

Hundreds of years earlier, the Babylonians had destroyed Israel's first Temple, the one built by King Solomon. Fortunately, after a time, the Babylonians no longer ruled Israel, and the people had been able to construct a new Temple. This second sanctuary was much simpler, but a fitting house of God where everyone could worship.

Hundreds of years later, when Herod became king, he was unsatisfied with the simple house for Yahweh. He set out to create a Temple so large and opulent that it surpassed imagination. Herod really had no idea what Solomon's Temple had looked like, but he was convinced his would be unparalleled.

Just how big was Herod's Temple? He had 1,000 wagons built to haul stone. Ten thousand workers and craftsmen were assigned to the job. Among them were 1,000 priests that the king had trained as masons and carpenters. Herod wanted priestly hands to build his majestic house of worship.

But the thought of God sending a new baby boy king made Herod's blood boil. How could God do this to him? After all, wasn't he building a magnificent Temple for Yahweh? Of course, Herod's Temple wasn't really for God. He was constructing a monument to his own pride. And if he had to kill dozens of babies to defend his throne, so be it.

Yahweh had other plans. He sent an angel to Yosef in a dream, warning him that the evil king was plotting to find and murder baby Yeshua.

So, Miriam and Yosef followed the angel's instructions and escaped safely to Egypt. Frustrated, Herod would order the slaughter of the innocents in Bethlehem, in hopes of killing the newborn king. Yeshua's family remained in hiding among the Egyptians until Herod the Great died. That's when they were able to return to the Holy Land and the town of Nazareth, and to introduce their family and friends to young Yeshua.

Finally, in just a few days, Yeshua would be headed back to Yerushlem. He hadn't been there since he was a tiny baby, but not much had really changed. At first, Herod's son, Archelaus, had taken over after his father's death. He was every bit as evil and oppressive, but unable to maintain peace in the capital. After one Passover riot, Archelaus called in troops. The battle led to 3,000 deaths. Rome took over, and assigned the first of their many military leaders to stabilize and rule Yerushlem with force. As an adult, Yeshua would meet one of Herod's other sons, Antipas, and the Roman governor, Pontius Pilate.

It didn't matter who was in charge of the Holy City. Yeshua wasn't afraid. He knew his heavenly Father would be watching his every step on the road to Yerushlem.

chapter

THREE

EZRA WAS SICK. VERY SICK.

In just a few days, the caravan from Nazareth would begin its Passover pilgrimage, but Ezra wasn't in school. When Yeshua came home, he immediately ran to see his friend. Deborah met him at the door.

"Your friend is too sick to visit, Yeshua. He has a very high fever," Deborah warned. "And a terrible headache. The doctor has been here already, but the balsam sap hasn't relieved his pain. I tried mustard oil, but he's still hurting so much."

Yeshua could see Deborah was distraught. She had been crying. He touched her hand to console her, and he told Deborah they should go inside and pray for Ezra. She was grateful for his compassion, but reluctant to allow him to see Ezra. She couldn't bear the thought of him getting sick, too.

Yeshua reached into his satchel and pulled out the horse he had carved for Ezra. For a moment, a smile lit up Deborah's face. She knew Ezra would appreciate the toy. The carving was impressive, and it might distract Ezra from his pain. She nodded approval and touched Yeshua's face to thank him. Quietly, they slipped inside the house.

Ezra lay on a mat in a darkened room, near a small crock with embers burning inside. Flushed with fever, he shivered. As soon as he caught a glimpse of his mother entering the room with Yeshua, he sat up. Yeshua put out his hand and urged him to lie down.

Tears started to run down Ezra's face. "I'm sorry, Yeshua. My mom says I can't go to Yerushlem for Passover. I'm too sick. But I think I'm gonna be better after the Sabbath," Ezra said as he wiped his eyes.

The Sabbath would begin at sundown, in just a few hours. Yeshua and Ezra both knew he would never feel well enough to leave for Yerushlem on Tuesday. The trip would be too demanding, even if he rode in a cart the whole way. He could become a burden for the entire caravan. Even a healthy Ezra would be challenged by the long trip because of his limp. But weakened by fever, Ezra could die.

Yeshua knelt down next to his friend and reached into his shoulder bag. When he pulled out the horse, Ezra could hardly believe his watery eyes. Yeshua handed it to him; then he moved over to the window to remove the shade Deborah had draped over it. The sunlight was a bit too bright for Ezra, but now he could really see the detail in the horse. He lit up and reached for his cane to stand. His mother intervened.

"What a wonderful horse," said Ezra. "It's so real!"

Ezra made the sound of a rearing steed. He coughed as he laughed.

Squinting with pain from his headache, and with one eye closed, he said, "The wheels are excellent." Ezra turned them with his fingertips, admiring their smooth rotation. He set the horse on the dirt floor and pushed it with his hand.

"A rich boy's father will pay you a whole shekel for this toy in Yerushlem," he exclaimed. It was a quite an exaggeration, and it made both boys laugh. Ezra loved to joke about becoming rich. His late father, Abram, had been a merchant. Since his death, Ezra and Deborah had been just getting by. The widow and her son had to rely on the generosity of others. Abram had no brother to marry his widow, as was the custom. Fortunately, Abram had saved some of his earnings, but as the years went by, that inheritance grew smaller and smaller.

Yeshua knew just what to say to make Ezra feel a little better. He told him the toy horse was for him. He explained he'd been working on it for a month, and had hoped to give it to Ezra on their journey to the Temple.

"I don't know what to say," Ezra responded. "No one ever gave me anything like this. You're a brother to me, Yeshua."

Deborah was overwhelmed by the genuine love between the two boys. There was something inspiring, even spiritual about it. It was rare to see such unselfishness and concern between two young men. But she was worried that Ezra was getting too excited, and that his fever might become worse.

In his heart, Yeshua knew he could heal Ezra. He could call on his heavenly Father, and He would grant him any request. But he also knew it was not his time to act as the Messiah. He understood it was not God's will that he behave like a little magician or a medicine man.

As much as Yeshua loved his dear friend, Ezra, he would not ask his heavenly Father for a miracle to instantly end his suffering. But he would ask for a blessing that would heal his friend, if that healing were his Father's will.

Yeshua helped Deborah calm Ezra, and then he asked that together they recite the Mi Sheberakh. It was a traditional healing prayer recited at Synagogue after a reading of the Torah. Since Ezra was too sick to attend Synagogue, perhaps Deborah or a friend like Yeshua would be called up to the Torah, and then the rabbi would offer the prayer.

But today, Yeshua stretched out his arms, and raised them to pray as he knelt at Ezra's side.

"May the One who blessed our ancestors —
Patriarchs Abraham, Isaac, and Jacob,
Matriarchs Sarah, Rebecca, Rachel, and Leah —
bless and heal the one who is ill —

Ezra son of his late father, Abram and his mother, Deborah.
May the Holy Blessed One
overflow with compassion upon him,
to restore him,
to heal him,
to strengthen him,
to enliven him.
The One will send him, speedily,
a complete healing —
healing of the soul and healing of the body —
along with all the ill,
among the people of Israel and all humankind,
soon,
speedily,
without delay,
and let us all say, Amen!"[3]

Both Deborah and Ezra said, "Amen." But Deborah didn't know what else to say after that. She was grateful for the powerful prayer, but so surprised Yeshua had said it outside the Synagogue. He had demonstrated such confidence, reciting it from memory. It was as if he had written it — as if he were having a personal conversation with Yahweh.

Then she noticed Ezra. He was sleeping comfortably. All the excitement must have been too much for him. She touched his face and forehead. They were very hot, but it was good to see him finally relax and rest.

Yeshua helped Deborah up from her knees. She showed him to the door, and offered him cool water and some dried figs for his walk home. Otherwise, she was speechless. The experience had been so calming and yet so untraditional.

"Thank you for your kindness, Yeshua," she said finally, with a warm smile. "I'll never forget this day."

He touched her arm and nodded, asking her to be sure to tell Ezra he'd stop by before leaving for Yerushlem. Yeshua spoke as if he knew Ezra would feel better soon.

This was the journey both boys had been dreaming about their whole lives. If Yeshua had to travel without Ezra, he had to know his friend was well.

FOUR

IT WAS VERY EARLY TUESDAY MORNING.
Yeshua called to Ezra through the open window. The sun had barely
risen, but a shaft of light brightened the inner room.

Ezra opened his eyes and saw Yeshua in a shadowy silhouette.
He quickly sat up and smiled. No blinding headache. No chilly
feeling. No shakes. No sweating. No fever.

"I feel a lot better," Ezra exclaimed. He picked up the toy horse
that had been standing at his bedside.

"I spent the whole Sabbath sleeping," he said. "Every once in
a while, I'd wake up and drink something and eat a little bit. My
mother let me play with the horse after sundown. That's when I felt
stronger. The fever broke."

Yeshua laughed with joy. His friend Ezra grabbed his cane, and
hobbled over to the window, holding the horse in his free hand. He
set it on the sill in front of Yeshua. They both admired it.

"I have a name for the horse," said Ezra. "I'm calling him Thunder."

Yeshua liked the name. He was happy to see his friend enjoying
his gift, but he was far more grateful that Ezra was healthy. And
then Yeshua reached through the window, and put his hands on his
friend's shoulders. He began to quietly sing a Psalm of thanksgiving
from memory:

"Shout joyfully to the LORD, all you lands;
  serve the LORD with gladness;
  come before him with joyful song."

Yeshua's singing voice was about average, but his praise was strong and true. After a few verses, Ezra joined him. His mother heard the boys and stepped into the inner room, as well. They sang together in gratitude for Ezra's recovery.

"Know that the LORD is God,
  he made us, we belong to him,
  we are his people, the flock he shepherds.
  Enter his gates with thanksgiving,
  his courts with praise.
  Give thanks to him, bless his name;
  good indeed is the LORD,
  His mercy endures forever,
  his faithfulness lasts through every generation."
  (Psalm 100:1-5)

As they concluded their prayer, Deborah said, "you will make a fine rabbi one day, Yeshua." Ezra agreed.

Yeshua blushed. He told them that he and his family had gone to Synagogue on the Sabbath, of course. The whole congregation had prayed for Ezra's health. They would all be delighted to know he had recovered.

Yet, this was a sad moment. Yeshua would have to leave behind his best friend and travel to Yerushlem without him. Ezra was not well enough to make the trip. It would be risky. He needed time to fully recover, to prevent a recurring fever. The trip was out of the question. The friends wouldn't see each other again for three weeks, with no way to communicate. There were private couriers for the wealthy, but no mail service. Of course, Caesar Augustus and the

Roman army had their messengers, but the masses relied on the kindness of strangers to carry their letters. Yeshua might be able to find a friendly traveler headed past Nazareth to deliver a note, but there would be thousands of people in Yerushlem looking for willing messengers. And what would he write on? He couldn't really afford to buy parchment, unless it was an emergency.

Ezra would be thinking about Yeshua, and Yeshua would miss Ezra. They had planned to enter the Temple together for the first time, hand in hand. Since Ezra's father was dead, Yosef would give both boys a tour. Next year, they would come of age in the Israelite nation, and be full members of their Synagogue in Nazareth. And then they could make the Passover pilgrimage to the Temple as men. They would be old enough to fully participate in the worship services. In fact, in just a few years, they could even take wives and marry.

In those days, the men of the family typically arranged marriages. Two fathers would get together and negotiate a match between one father's son and the other's daughter. The bridegroom was usually between the ages of 17 and 18. His father would approach the bride's father, and they would haggle over a price for the woman. Most times, the bride was a little younger than her husband, as young as 13.

A daughter had real value because a groom would pay for her hand in marriage. A father expected to be compensated for the loss of a woman in his family and all the work she could do.

Although neither Ezra nor Yeshua was considering marriage at the moment, they were planning their futures. And the time together on the road was going to be invaluable. Ordinarily, they just didn't have the opportunity to talk like they would on a three-week journey. They were busy with school and work around their homes.

From sun up to sun down, there was always something to do. Life was a full-time job. Everyone in the family had to participate because everything had to be made or built from scratch. And there was very little money to buy things they needed. If you couldn't make it or grow it, you might have to barter. Yosef could trade his work to make a set of wagon wheels for four pairs of sandals, a few chickens or several jugs of Sabbath wine. Between Yosef's paying carpentry and masonry jobs, he always had a side project for Yeshua.

Miriam was constantly busy cooking; cleaning; nurturing the garden; spinning fibers and making garments; washing and mending clothes; building fires; fetching water at the well; trimming wicks; and filling lamps with oil.

When Yeshua wasn't under Yosef's wing, Miriam would find something for him to do. Even if it was just running to the well for more water, or fixing the doors on the chicken coop. And because there were no bright lights, most work had to be done while the sun was up.

Time with friends was precious.

In those quiet moments together, sometimes Ezra would tell Yeshua he worried nobody would marry him because of his handicap, and because he was poor. He didn't have a father to teach him a craft or business. Yeshua would tell Ezra not to worry about tomorrow; he should simply do his best today and leave the rest to God. But it was easy to understand Ezra's situation. And now, being left behind again might make Ezra feel somewhat hopeless and depressed.

Yeshua felt sorry for his friend. He knew some of their classmates made fun of Ezra. Like most kids, they could be cruel. But Ezra had a sharp mind, and Yeshua was confident he would one day follow in his father's footsteps, and become a respected, successful merchant.

Ezra looked forward to the Passover pilgrimage for many reasons. He had heard people talk about the enormous, bustling marketplaces in Yerushlem. The Promised Land of the people of Israel was the only good pathway between the Mediterranean Sea and a vast desert. The dry region produced a limited number of goods for export, but it was a fulcrum for the levers of commerce — serving as an ancient, strategic highway for products entering and exiting the trade channels of the Mediterranean. In Yeshua's day, Syria, Rome, and Egypt transported scarce, valuable glassware through the Promised Land. Egypt enjoyed a monopoly on papyrus trade, and also sent its vast grain shipments to that shore. Countries as far east as China also sent their silk and exotic products through the west coast of the Israelite nation. White cotton arrived from India. The Romans built reliable and durable stone roads across the region. From this territory, merchants could transport goods throughout the Roman Empire and beyond, either by road or by sailing ships. Exporters could reach destinations as far west as Cadiz, Spain, above the tip of Northern Africa. They could travel as far north as Britain and the North Sea, and as far eastward as the Bay of Bengal and the China Sea. Spain shipped fancy foods like artichokes, pickled fish, hams, and other meats. Italy exported wines. Oil pressers around the Mediterranean profited from their wares. In Mesopotamia and at the Dead Sea, merchants acquired bitumen, a petroleum tar, popular with shipbuilders to ensure watertight seals for their vessels. Balms, perfumes, and spices came from Somaliland and Arabia, while the rich bought African and Indian ivory. Miners dug up gold, silver, copper, tin, iron, and lead in Europe and Africa. In Asia Minor, prized timber met the lumberman's saw.

Traders from around the known world shipped their products by land and sea through Judah and past Yerushlem. Ezra hoped to see the impressive markets first hand, and to rub shoulders with major merchants, the kind rarely seen in a tiny town like Nazareth. Now, he would have to be satisfied with hearing his best friend describe the experience.

"Do me a favor, Yeshua," Ezra requested. "Bring me some kind of souvenir from the Temple."

Yeshua promised he would find something special to bring home. He was relieved to see his friend's upbeat attitude. The two boys embraced through the window. Ezra forced a big smile through his tears.

"Yeshua!"

It was Yosef calling him from the wagon, which was loaded with all the provisions they were taking on the trip, as well as his mother. Deborah was there, wishing his parents God's speed.

Quickly, Yeshua hugged Ezra again and then ran to help his father lead the donkeys on their way.

It was time for the family to join their neighbors from Nazareth, and leave for Yerushlem in a caravan that would unite them with all of Israel for the Passover. There were over a million Hebrew believers worldwide!

chapter
FIVE

THE MOOD WAS LIKE ONE, GIANT PARTY.
This is what the Israelites must have felt like when they fled Egypt
during the first Passover. Everyone in the caravan was excited to be
leaving on a trip and escaping the drudgery of Nazarene life, even if
it was for just a few weeks.

Plus, they would be visiting the Temple, the Holy of Holies. For
all believers in the one God of Israel, it was the center of the universe. And they would be celebrating one of their great triumphs as
a nation, and perhaps the single most dramatic example of God's
love and mercy for his people — the Passover that led them to freedom from slavery in Egypt.

The thought made Yeshua's spirit dance with joy. Some pilgrims
played flutes and drums as the caravan left town. It was a little like
a fall wedding celebration on a beautiful spring day.

Friends and family who stayed behind waved goodbye and
shouted blessings as the pilgrims passed. Not everyone could go.
Some were too old or feeble. Others had to tend to the animals and
farms of those who would make the Passover journey. Neighbors
and family would take turns going on the annual pilgrimage. One
year they'd see Yerushlem; the next, they'd remain home to manage
their households.

For those who stayed behind, the traditional saying at the Seder supper was always, "next year in Yerushlem."

Yeshua already missed Ezra, but he had to admit, he looked forward to seeing his cousin, John. He was just six months older than Yeshua. John's mother, Elizabeth, and Miriam were cousins. Elizabeth was considerably older than Miriam. Her husband, Zechariah, had been a Temple priest, so John was raised to be a priest, too. They didn't see each other often, but when they did, Yeshua savored his time with John.

He had been looking forward to hanging out with Ezra and John in the camp, at the Temple, and in the streets of Yerushlem.

John was filled with the Holy Spirit, and Yeshua looked up to him. He was a powerful speaker with a deep voice for his age. And he was tall, with an impressive physique. Destined to be a spiritual leader, John had all the physical tools for the job.

Yeshua's cousin would be waiting to visit the caravan from Nazareth when it set up camp along the Mount of Olives, just outside Yerushlem. John's family home was in a small village, Ein Karem, nearby. Zechariah had made the walk every day to perform his devout priestly duties in the Temple. He had long passed away, and Elizabeth was quite old now. But every year, John and his mother met the caravan from Nazareth. They would welcome Yosef and Miriam to the grand Passover festival and celebrate the Seder together. And now, Yeshua was old enough to join them.

As a member of a priestly family, John would have special access to the Temple. Having an insider as a guide could make the whole experience even more rare, especially with the enormous crowds during Passover festival. Throughout its history, estimates of Yerushlem's population ranged from 50,000 to a half million people. Regardless, the number inside the city's walls could triple or quadruple during Passover.

Fortunately, the Temple guards would certainly know John as the son of a priest, and perhaps let him hang out in the Temple at night. Without John, they wouldn't know Yeshua. He would be just another pilgrim, and a kid at that.

For now, Yeshua would have to imagine his adventures with John. The journey from Nazareth to Yerushlem was five days on foot. And with the caravan, it would take every bit of that time, plus a day of rest for the Sabbath. Getting dozens of people to move together as a group is never easy. Certainly Moses discovered that when he and the Chosen People wandered the desert for 40 years in search of the Promised Land.

Yeshua, Yosef, and Miriam would travel the same road they took to Bethlehem some 12 years earlier. The caravan would follow a very direct route, almost a straight line across the Jezreel Valley. Later, they would climb the hilly regions beneath the peaks of Samaria that scraped the sky at some 2,500 to 3,000 feet. Below, along sculpted terraces, the Samaritans tended their olive and fig trees and grapevines. In the fertile valley, they grew barley and wheat. From there, the terrain became more arid as it rose toward the Holy City. At that point, most of the traffic would be heading south for the Passover.

On the first morning of their trip, the caravan quickly came to a major fork on the trail. One well-traveled path turned right, due west toward the Mediterranean Sea. It led to the highway that ran the shoreline of the Promised Land to Egypt; the same one Yeshua and his parents had walked when he first came to Nazareth. Along the shore, travelers would meet fishermen and merchants. They might spot sailing vessels from around the world. The late King Herod the Great had built the kingdom of Israel's first seaport, a short trip from Nazareth to the southwest. It was a grand, artificial port and a magnificent city. Herod had dedicated it to Caesar Augustus. He called it Caesarea.

Yeshua, Yosef, and Miriam had traveled past the port on their journey from Egypt to Nazareth. It was indeed impressive, but a sinful city.

The things Herod did there would have triggered riots and a revolution in Yerushlem. Not only did he build a wealthy seaport with two massive breakwaters, he also erected a pagan temple in honor of Caesar, complete with altars and statues of false gods. Herod had a likeness carved of Augustus, and it stood right alongside the altars. The Romans regarded their rulers as divine.

Just the thought of this violation of God's commandments should have caused the Jewish priests to tear their vestments and lead protests. But they didn't dare. Herod was ruthless. If he'd murder babies, what would he do to old men? The misguided King of Israel had invested enormous wealth in securing favor with Caesar, his court, the Roman Senate, and the military. This unholy alliance had been the source of his power and riches. As long as Herod kept the people in line and the taxes flowing to Rome, he had been free to do as he wished.

After all his spending and efforts to win Roman favor and secure his power, imagine how enraged Herod was to learn that God had sent a baby Messiah to one day rule Israel. Fortunately for Yeshua, Herod the Great died a few years after his birth.

The Nazarene caravan headed due south past the fork in the highway. The route would be easy for the first day, as they worked their way through the Plain of Esdraelon. They had planned to set up camp at night in the valley, as there were no major towns until they reached the area near Sebaste, about a third of the way to Yerushlem. Sebaste was another one of Herod's creations. In Greek, the name meant Augustus, as in Caesar. It was another lavish city with another pagan temple. Herod had even granted land to local militiamen who volunteered to protect the city whenever necessary.

He had built Sebaste on the ancient capital of Samaria. It had been demolished in war, and the king was all too happy to mock the Samaritans by burying their city under the name of Caesar. Besides, the Israelites and the Samaritans had a long-standing feud. They stayed apart.

Because of Herod's infamous hedonism, the Nazarenes would spend minimal time around Sebaste. But they needed to replenish essential supplies on the trip, so they'd have to stop there very briefly to stock up on dairy products.

Every mother on the pilgrimage had prepared and bought food to last a week. There were wines and grains to eat. Miriam had dried dates and figs and fruitcakes with raisins. She had packed salted sheep and goat cheese, almonds and olives; she even bought dried fish. The sundried catch from the Sea of Galilee was one of Yeshua's favorite meals. Of course, he liked fresh fish best.

The Sea of Galilee wasn't a sea at all. It was a fresh water lake fed by the Jordan River, just about 15 miles northeast of Yeshua's home. He had enjoyed fishing trips there with his father; the 30-mile round trip was worth the hike.

But walking 15 to 20 miles a day for five days would make anyone very, very hungry and thirsty. Water was the most prized resource. Each family kept a covered tub of water in its wagon, and most men carried a sheepskin or two filled with water. Fortunately it was spring, so the temperatures were in the 70's and 80's. In May, 90-degree weather would be common. But it was still hot enough now to require gallons of water each day for people and beasts of burden; some had to be saved for ceremonial washing.

The pilgrims would watch for animals in the valley in order to identify various sources of water. There were many creeks that meandered through the plain, and mountain gazelles and their footprints often led the way. Where there were gazelles, there were cheetah and other wildcats, like leopards, that stalked the desert region. The foxes, hyenas, and jackals fought over the prey as well.

Someone would have to keep guard at night to protect the donkeys, oxen, and sheep in the caravan. A wild boar might come searching for food scraps near the campfire and attack the animals. That was life on the open road through the wilderness.

Yeshua looked up at the vultures circling overhead. They marked the site of a recent kill. The honey buzzards might get a scrap or two in the spring. In the fall, there were hundreds of thousands of honey buzzards, and they got a better share of the grub on the plain and in the foothills below the peaks of Samaria. Yeshua hoped to see cranes and other large birds. The Promised Land had been blessed with hundreds and hundreds of winged species.

Yeshua and his father took turns leading their donkeys, Mo and Mazel. Mo was strong, but slow, the son of the beast the family brought with them from Egypt. Like his father, Mo liked to stop and graze. Mazel was spirited and a perfect partner for Mo. He kept Mo moving forward.

The sweet smell of flowers filled the air. Bees hummed on the rolling, lush and colorful countryside. Butterflies skipped across the wildflowers, and, blue flax blossoms carpeted parts of the valley in dazzling displays. Galilee was known for flax that women spun to make fine, sturdy linen that priests wore at the Temple.

Yeshua took it all in as he guided the donkeys in sync with the caravan. They were yoked together. His father and mother rode behind in the cart and shared a smile about their son. How he'd grown up to be such a fine young man – strong and unselfish.

For Yeshua, the journey through the Jezreel Valley was a fitting tribute to his heavenly Father and the glories of His creation. After all, this was the land of milk and honey, and in Hebrew, Jezreel means "God will sow."

And Yeshua was His seed.

chapter SIX

A BLAZING CAMPFIRE LIT THE HAPPY FACES
of the Passover pilgrims. Miriam played her lyre nearby in a tent
filled with women. It was a mysteriously pleasant and much-needed,
relaxing melody. The Nazarene caravan had made some 20 miles on
the first day. The trip to Yerushlem was about 95 miles, so they had
about four days to go.

The pilgrims had plenty of energy for the first day on the trail,
so the caravan made great time and they managed to avoid serious
mishaps. No real injuries, no trouble with highwaymen, and no
animals pulled up lame.

Yosef and Yeshua were able to repair a neighbor's wagon wheel,
and the local sandal maker and his son were kept busy fixing footwear. In fact, they were still mending sandals by the campfire.

Yeshua had just started whittling a piece of sycamore. He had
brought a small stash of good wood for carving in a satchel on his
belt. He also kept a shoulder bag on the wagon for situations when
he needed to carry more stuff. Yeshua planned to carve a little boat
for his cousin John. It was something he could easily do by the fire.
His young eyes were very keen and his imagination endless.

Everyone wanted to hear Yosef tell stories because he was very,
familiar with Yerushlem. He had been born in Bethlehem, the town
where the prophet Samuel had crowned the great King David. Yah-

weh, God Himself, had commanded Samuel to make David king. Yosef was a direct descendent of David, as was his wife, Miriam.

Not only did Yosef grow up in David's city, but he had also learned to be a carpenter and mason there. He was born at the right place and time for that profession — because Bethlehem was only five miles or so from Yerushlem. That was considered a short walk for a man who wanted a job. And there were plenty of jobs while King Herod was rebuilding the Temple and his colossal fortress, Herodium.

Herodium was part palace and part fort. For its time, it was an amazing architectural and engineering masterpiece. Herod had built himself a four-tower citadel and desert retreat more than 2,400 feet above sea level, a few miles south of Bethlehem. Invaders might mistake it for a volcano, but it was entirely man-made. Even the Romans considered it a formidable challenge. Some secretly thought it was impenetrable because the man-made structure sloped up 45 feet to form a crater with steep, smooth walls. They were very difficult to scale.

At the top were the four towers joined by a double-walled corridor. Three of the towers were six stories high. The tallest spiraled another 60 feet, and housed Herod's luxury apartments. Two hundred rock-hewn steps were the only entryway.

From Herodium, the king's guard could see for miles, and if necessary, defend their ruler.

"There were so many carpenters and masons and slaves working on the Temple and Herodium it was insane," Yosef said. "I'm sure that's what it was like when our ancestors built the pyramids in Egypt. Only Herod was oppressing his own people!

"He hired Roman engineers and Greek architects. I spent two years working at Herodium, before I was able to persuade my foreman to let me assist at the Temple. Whenever I visit, I feel like a part of me is there in those massive cedar timbers."

Yeshua was fond of listening to his dad talk about his work, especially the role he played in building the Temple as a young carpenter. He never grew tired of the tales, especially since he'd never been to Yerushlem. Tonight, Yosef was talking about some of the craftsmen who worked on the Temple.

"The double doors of the sanctuary are two stories tall," Yosef exclaimed passionately, using his hands for emphasis. "They are covered in gold and the artisans carved huge vines with enormous clusters of grapes into the gold. Each cluster is taller than me."

When Yosef talked about the Temple construction, he was as enthusiastic as a schoolboy. Miriam and the women would peek out of the nearby tent, and occasionally, Miriam would pause her strumming, so she could eavesdrop on the storytelling.

She was always grateful for the man Yosef was. Unless he was talking about his work, he was actually a very quiet, gentle man. She enjoyed his enthusiastic outbursts.

The happy couple had met quite by accident.

Yosef came to Nazareth at 19. He had toiled in Yerushlem on Herod's projects as both a carpenter and mason. His muscular shoulders and arms were sculpted from all the rigorous hammering, planing, and sawing. He caught the eye of many young women in the village, but it was his personality that was the most attractive.

Ironically, Yosef also had a delicate touch and an artistic side. He settled in Nazareth to pursue an opportunity to do more meaningful work with stone and wood, and help improve people's lives. Yosef's jobs at the Temple and at Herodium were backbreaking. They paid steady wages, but his work was rough and offered little satisfaction, besides the fame and scale of the projects. In Nazareth he could make a living crafting farming tools like wooden implements: sickle handles; winnowing forks; wheels; carts and wagons; plows, yokes; and heavy threshing sledges. He would fashion everything for the home: from tables, chairs, spinning wheels, spindles, and storage boxes — to doors, posts, beams, and window frames. He'd also use his powerful hands to cut down trees, split rock, and create stone mills, cisterns, and basins.

So Yosef traveled north, leaving behind his aging father and older brother. They ran the family carpentry business in Bethlehem. Yosef's father had a friend, Nathan, who was the town carpenter in Nazareth. But he had no sons to inherit his business. Yosef arrived at Nathan's door with an endorsement letter from his father and an offer to be his apprentice.

Nathan was overjoyed by the possibilities. "You look just like your papa," he exclaimed as he embraced Yosef. Now, Nathan had a helper he felt close to, almost like a son. And there would be another man around the house. Nathan and his wife had four daughters. Perhaps Yosef might even marry one of them. For Nathan it was a blessing.

For Yosef, it was a chance to eventually own a business. He would buy into Nathan's carpentry shop by taking significantly lower wages, and performing all the tasks Nathan preferred not to do. And the extra, younger hands meant Nathan could finish jobs faster and even take on work from surrounding villages. When a traveler's wagon broke or a farmer's plow failed, he could respond more quickly. Nathan's family would earn more, plus Yosef would pitch in for room and board.

That was some 15 years ago now, and Nathan had died of an illness about five years back. But not before he had taught Yosef all he knew, and Yosef had demonstrated his special gifts and attention to detail.

Yosef was excellent at crafting curved shapes with both stone and wood. He made bowls and wagon wheels, and spindles. In fact, he met Miriam while delivering a set of spindles for spinning threads.

Yosef had finished working on the spindles about an hour before sundown on a Friday. The Sabbath would start soon. Nathan suggested he deliver them to Hannah, Yoachim's widow, so she would have the spindles when the Sabbath ended and her daughter could use them. Yoachim's family was wealthy, and

Hannah had already paid for the job. The delivery would end Yosef's workweek. He would simply return to Nathan's home for the Sabbath dinner.

Yosef packed the spindles in a sack on his back. He'd assemble them in the rack he'd crafted when he arrived at the customer's home. As he approached Hannah's house, he could hear the alluring melody of a lyre from within. The chickens scattered in the courtyard, as he walked toward the outer room of the house.

"Hello ... I have your spindles from Nathan's shop," Yosef called.

The music stopped.

From a nearby window, Yosef heard a sweet, young voice. "You can just leave them right there."

"But I'd like to show you the work and assemble them in this box I built," Yosef responded, with a puzzled look on his face.

"No worries. My mother and I will put it all together when she returns," the voice said.

"I see," Yosef responded. The young woman was obviously home alone, and didn't want to have contact with a man, especially a stranger.

"Thank you for your business," Yosef said. "If you have any problems, I'll be glad to come back after the Sabbath and make any adjustments. Most of them are new, but I was able to repair a few of your older spindles."

"And thank you for your kindness," said the lovely voice. "Good Sabbath and God's Peace."

"Good Sabbath," he responded. Yosef couldn't help but wonder what the young woman looked like.

As he turned on his heels, the lovely lyre music resumed. It was a classic melody, beautifully played. It made his walk a little lighter and carefree. He smiled as he looked back over his shoulder, and made up his mind he'd come back after the Sabbath. Just to make sure Hannah was completely satisfied with the work, of course.

Walking a little further, he recognized Hannah coming up the road. As they approached, Yosef said, "Hello, Hannah, I just dropped off the spindles at your doorstep."

"Oh, good! Thank you, Yosef. We'll be able use them on Sunday," she replied with a smile.

"If you don't mind, I'd like to show them to you to make sure you're perfectly satisfied," Yosef requested.

"But the Sabbath is coming," Hannah said.

"It'll only take a moment. I just want to be sure you're happy," Yosef explained.

They walked together the short distance back to Hannah's home. Yosef offered to carry the jug of Sabbath wine Hannah had bought. She was grateful for the courtesy.

But when they reached the house, the spindles were nowhere in sight.

"I set them right here," Yosef said with a puzzled look.

"Miriam must have taken them inside," Hannah reasoned. "Come in, please."

Yosef held the door for Hannah and then entered with the jug. He immediately noticed the perfectly set Sabbath table in the inner room. He put the jug down nearby. The home was simple, but furnished with many nice things like pottery and glassware. It was obvious Hannah's late husband, Yoachim, had been prosperous.

The lyre music continued from the adjacent room. Hannah found the spindles on a table by the door.

"These are exceptional," she said excitedly.

"I thought they were, too," said the voice from the other room.

"Thank you," said Yosef. "I hope the box keeps them organized."

The music stopped. Miriam came out from around the corner. She was a beautiful 12-year-old girl. And she was carrying her lyre.

"This is my daughter, Miriam," Hannah said. "Miriam, this is Nathan's apprentice, Yosef."

"You play very well," Yosef said with a genuine smile.

"And you're a good carpenter," Miriam replied cheerfully. She cast her eyes to the floor.

"These designs on the spindles are wonderful. I never expected any artwork," Hannah said.

"If you like, I could carve flowers into your lyre sometime," he said to Miriam. "With your mother's permission, of course," Yosef added as he acknowledged Hannah.

"I'd like that very much," Miriam said as she glanced at her mother. Hannah smiled back.

"I could even add a little color, if you want," Yosef explained. "Red, like real pomegranate flowers."

There was an awkward moment, and then Hannah said, "Thank you for your amazing work, Yosef. Miriam, here are the new Sabbath candles."

"Oh, yes! I must be going to my own Sabbath dinner. Good Sabbath!" Yosef said, as he quickly stepped out the door and ran up the road.

The sun would be setting soon, and he had to get home and wash up by then. At Sabbath dinner that night, Yosef had many questions about Yoachim, Hannah, and Miriam. Nathan's oldest daughter was amused because she was already engaged. But the three younger women were disappointed. Each one hoped Yosef would ask Nathan for permission to marry her, and the conversation about Miriam was a threat to their dreams.

Everything Nathan told Yosef about Miriam's family was complimentary and appealing. Years earlier, Hannah had been unable to conceive a child, and her husband, Yoachim, became depressed about it. The couple had prayed for children, and Yoachim hoped for a son to share his business. He was a landowner and many people rented farms, orchards, and vineyards from him. His investments included a small share in a trade company that shipped oils, olives, spices, and other goods from the eastern shores of the Mediterranean all the way to Tomi on the Black Sea.

As the couple grew older, Yoachim became desperate. He had wealth but no heir. He went alone into the desert for days and prayed for a child. He would gladly accept a son or a daughter, whichever God preferred. It would be the ultimate blessing that he and Hannah would cherish in their old age.

After a few days, upon his return home, Hannah told Yoachim she might be pregnant! Soon she was certain. They were so excited, yet Yoachim was very fearful. The thought of a miscarriage was paralyzing. Hannah finally told Yoachim, "If you believe that it is God who has given us this child, we must trust Him." And so they did, despite the fact that miscarriages were extremely common, and many children never saw adulthood due to infections and illnesses like Ezra's fever. At the time, for every ten pregnancies, three children died by age 14.

When their baby girl was born, Hannah and Yoachim named her Miriam. The name has Egyptian roots and means "beloved" or "wished for child."

Yoachim would have spoiled her, but Hannah wouldn't allow it. Despite their wealth, Miriam learned to cook and clean, tend a garden, spin, and sew.

Hannah taught Miriam how to play the lyre, and she encouraged Yoachim to teach her the Scriptures, as if Miriam were a son. The family was devout, and Miriam was an obedient daughter who could read and write. By the time she was ten, Miriam was not only beautiful, but she was well liked by people in the village. Although she came from a privileged background, she was humble. Talented, she sang as well as she played the lyre. She was a natural.

Hannah had become a little protective of her since Yoachim's death. Two men had already attempted to negotiate matches for their sons. But Hannah insisted she would wait, and deferred the offers to her brother-in-law. He honored Hannah's wishes and resisted the engagements, but as Miriam approached 13, that would become more difficult.

Yosef next saw Miriam at a bris, a party to celebrate a baby boy's circumcision and dedication to Yahweh. They had both been invited to the party for the newborn. Miriam had offered to play and sing for the event. Yosef was smitten when he heard her voice with the music.

After performing for an hour, Miriam finally took a break. Yosef rekindled the conversation about decorating her lyre. He had a couple of knives in his belt, and he demonstrated how quickly he could inscribe the lyre with a geometric pattern that resembled flower petals.

Miriam enjoyed watching him work. His powerful hands managed the tools with a delicate touch, and the images came to life in the wood almost as if by magic. Hannah was in conversation nearby, and occasionally glanced over at the two of them. She gave Miriam a smile to let her know she approved of her contact with Yosef.

Although he was much older than she, he was a gentleman in every way.

"That's just a start," Yosef said as he showed her the completed pattern in one corner of the lyre. Miriam secretly hoped this was also the start of a relationship. Little did she know it would be the beginning of a scandal.

chapter
SEVEN

YOSEF CONTINUED TO COURT MIRIAM IN THE MOST appropriate and traditional ways, under the watchful eye of her mother and her uncle. After about six months, following Miriam's thirteenth birthday, he asked for permission to marry her. He didn't have much of a purse to offer, but it was clear to Hannah that Yosef loved her daughter. And Miriam didn't need money. She needed a good husband who would cherish her for a lifetime.

Miriam was delighted to hear the news. She and Yosef had talked about getting married, but she wasn't certain her mother would permit it because she was so young. Yosef was now 20, and he would want to start a family soon.

Hannah threw a splendid engagement party for the young couple, and all of Nazareth was invited. And then it happened. Miriam became pregnant, and it would soon be obvious. But Yosef was not the father.

If he had been, the child would have been considered legitimate because the couple was already betrothed and planned to marry in a year. However, if word got out that the baby wasn't Yosef's, Miriam could be stoned. That was the law of the Chosen People. The punishment for a convicted adulteress was death — the town's people would throw large stones at the woman until she died in the barrage.

But Miriam was no adulteress. She hadn't been unfaithful to Yosef or Yahweh's laws. God had given her this child, and His Holy Spirit was the Father.

It all began as she was quietly playing her lyre late one evening, shortly after Yosef left for home. She liked to look up at the starry sky through her bedroom window. Suddenly, Miriam felt like someone was standing behind her holding a light.

As she turned to look, she expected to see her mother holding an oil lamp, and urging her to say her prayers and go to bed. But it wasn't her mother; it was a man — sort of. Light poured from his face as he spoke. It was the angel Gabriel, God's messenger.

"Hail, favored one! The Lord is with you," Gabriel said. (Luke 1:28)

Miriam became very frightened. Who is this man? Why is he acting like he knows me? How did he get into our house? "Momma!" Miriam yelled. But Hannah was sleeping deeply.

"Do not be afraid, [Miriam], for you have found favor with God," the angel proclaimed joyfully. (Luke 1:30)

"He knows my name!" she thought. Miriam wanted to talk, but she was too nervous to speak.

"Behold, you will conceive in your womb and bear a son, and you shall name him [Yeshua]," Gabriel declared. (Luke 1:31)

Miriam's head was spinning.

"He will be great and will be called Son of the Most High, and the Lord God will give him the throne of David his father, and he will rule over the house of Jacob forever, and of his kingdom there will be no end," Gabriel added. (Luke 1:32-33)

This was unbelievable news. Miriam had to find her voice. What the angel said was impossible. She was a virgin.

"How can this be, since I have no relations with a man?" Miriam stammered. (Luke 1:34)

And the angel said to her in reply, "The holy Spirit will come upon you, and the power of the Most High will overshadow you.

Therefore the child to be born will be called holy, the Son of God."
(Luke 1:35)

The light from his face grew brighter.

Miriam was shaking now. Was this a dream? Did the intruder have her in a trance? She didn't understand. How? Why was this happening to her?

But then the angel Gabriel said something very personal. It was information only a Higher Power could know.

"And behold, Elizabeth, your relative, has also conceived a son in her old age, and this is the sixth month for her who was called barren; for nothing will be impossible for God," he added. (Luke 1:36-37)

How did he know Elizabeth was her cousin? She was too old to have a baby! If Elizabeth was pregnant, then indeed the angel was from God. Miriam could visit her cousin and verify the story.

The angel looked at her, as if waiting for a response. Inside her head, Miriam experienced a small, quiet voice.

"Do you accept this calling, my child?"

Miriam paused. This was not Gabriel's voice. She heard nothing with her ears, but felt it in her heart. She was moved to respond truthfully.

Miriam said, "Behold, I am the handmaid of the Lord. May it be done to me according to your word."(Luke 1:38)

At that, the angel vanished. Miriam was exhausted from the heavenly visit. She was exhilarated, yet terrified. How would she explain this to her mother? Suddenly, she fell asleep.

The morning sun cast a warm glow on Miriam's face, but she slept right through it. Hannah thought Miriam might be sick because she was an early riser; it wasn't like her to oversleep. Ever since her father had died a few years ago, Miriam felt compelled to wake up early with her mom and help around the house.

Hannah entered the room and placed her cool hand on Miriam's forehead. No fever.

The touch woke Miriam. Her mother smiled.

"You are sleeping in like a queen," Hannah joked. "Yosef will not wait on you when you marry, your highness."

"Sorry, momma," Miriam said, as she jumped up from the mat totally refreshed. "But I have some amazing news."

"More plans for the wedding feast?" Hannah teased.

"Momma, Elizabeth is six months pregnant!" Miriam exclaimed.

"What are you talking about?" Hannah responded with shock. "Where did you hear such a thing?"

"She is. An angel told me last night," Miriam blurted.

"Child, you have been dreaming," her mother said, shaking her head. "Elizabeth is too old for children."

"No momma, it's true. Let's go visit her. You'll see," insisted Miriam.

Hannah thought about her lonely cousin and her husband. Like Hannah and Yoachim, they had been unable to have children for too long. The two women prayed for each other. Elizabeth had been overjoyed when Miriam was born. Could it be true that God had heard their prayers, and given Elizabeth and Zechariah a child in their old age?

And how could Miriam possibly know about it?

"Come on, Miriam. Let's go. We have work to do," Hannah ordered.

Miriam listened to her mother and began her day. She was paralyzed by the thought of telling Hannah she was also pregnant. Obviously, she wouldn't have to divulge anything immediately, but it would be apparent soon enough. How would she tell Yosef? What would he say? What would he do? Would she have to run away to avoid a stoning?

For now, she would concentrate on the good news about her cousin's baby. Miriam prayed God would tell her the right time to reveal her own situation. She knew the unwed pregnancy would create so much confusion and heartache, especially for Yosef.

There was a knock at the door. Hannah opened it to discover a stranger. He was a traveler.

"I'm told this is the house of Yoachim and his widow, Hannah. Is that correct?" the man asked. He was a peddler headed to Capernaum with fishing nets.

"I am Hannah," she replied.

"I have a message for you from your cousin in Judah," the man said. He handed Hannah a small scroll of parchment.

Surprised, Hanna thanked the traveler, and put the scroll in her pocket. She offered him some cool water, which he gladly accepted. Hannah gave him freshly baked bread, some dried figs and dates. The traveler was very grateful, but left quickly. He was in a hurry to reach Capernaum before the end of the day.

Miriam watched from the doorway of her room. When Hannah came back into the house, after saying goodbye to the peddler, Miriam asked, "Who sent the message?"

Hannah smiled awkwardly as she took the little papyrus scroll from the pocket in her apron. It was tied with a string and a wax seal secured its privacy.

Her hands shaking, Hanna broke the seal and unrolled it. "It's from Elizabeth and Zechariah," she said. When she pulled the string the wax crumbled, and she walked over to the table to sit down and read.

"Dear Hannah and Miriam: we have wonderful news. A miracle! Elizabeth is six months pregnant. We waited to tell you because we wanted to be sure Elizabeth would not miscarry.

"An angel appeared to me in the Temple, near the altar when I was burning incense. He told me the baby is a boy. His name will be John!

God's Peace, Zechariah."

Hannah dropped the scroll. She was incredulous. She looked up at Miriam, who had crossed the room to stand at the table.

"You were right," Hannah stammered. "Elizabeth is six months pregnant."

Miriam smiled with joy and relief, but said nothing as she picked up the scroll and read it.

"An angel appeared to Zechariah in the Temple and named the child. It will be a boy," she said.

And suddenly Miriam blurted out her news. "My baby will be a boy, too, momma. The angel told me to name him Yeshua!" Instinctively, she knew it was the right time to share the news. It was as if God had nudged her and told her, "Speak up, Miriam. Don't be afraid of the truth."

Hannah sat stunned.

"This is not Yosef's baby. It will be God's baby. He gave it to me. I am still a virgin. Please believe me, momma," Miriam pleaded.

Hannah's expression was pained. She lowered her head for a moment, and when she looked again at her daughter, a tear rolled down her cheek.

"I want to believe you, Miriam," she replied. "It had to be God. How else would you know Elizabeth was precisely six months pregnant? But how will Yosef feel? This will break his heart. He may disown you. You could be stoned!"

"I trust God," Miriam said. "He helped me tell you, and you believe me. He will help me convince Yosef that I have been faithful to him."

Hannah was astonished by her daughter's remarks. Miriam spoke with such wisdom and conviction. Hannah was suddenly humbled. Her tense expression changed to real joy. She realized she was going to be a grandmother, and God had chosen to work a miracle through her daughter.

"We must tell Yosef, immediately," Hannah said.

When they arrived at the carpenter's shop, Nathan and Yosef were repairing their workbench. Yosef saw Miriam and put down his planer. He had been smoothing a timber they would use as a replacement in the bench.

"Good morning!" Yosef said with pleasant surprise.

"Good morning, Yosef. Good morning, Nathan," Hannah said, as she briskly entered the shop. "Miriam and I have some wonderful news to share. Our cousin, Elizabeth, and her husband, Zechariah, in Judah, are going to be parents!"

"That is wonderful news," Nathan said. "Praise the Lord."

"Praise the Lord, indeed," Hannah replied. "They are an older couple with no other children. Miriam and I will be going to visit them immediately to help prepare for the birth."

"I will take you there," Yosef offered. "It will be safer that way."

"Thank you, Yosef. I knew you would offer to help. That's why I love you so much," Miriam said.

"And I have more exciting news to share with you," she added.

chapter
EIGHT

YOSEF HAD TO GET BACK TO WORK. HE PROMISED Miriam he'd visit her when he and Nathan closed shop for the day. Hannah invited Yosef to dinner.

The two women headed home, and the two carpenters went back to repairing the bench. Yosef couldn't help but wonder what Miriam's special news was. Maybe she would be performing with her lyre at another event for the Synagogue. Or perhaps some wealthy person from another town had hired her to sing at a celebration.

Yosef was also anxious to work on the little house he had been renovating. He had bought it recently, and the couple would move in after their wedding. Yosef started in the shop before dawn each day, so he could quit work early and have a few hours each evening to remodel the modest house.

It was located just one street away from Nathan's place, closer to the center of town and the market. That would be perfect, once he and Miriam were married. He could be at Nathan's shop at a moment's notice. In fact, he could hear Nathan if he shouted from his rooftop.

The project was really coming along. Miriam said she'd meet him at the house that evening, and they could walk to dinner together.

Yosef was proud of the work he'd done so far. Hannah had offered to pay to build them a new home, but he wouldn't have it. It wasn't about pride. Yosef was a simple man, and he wouldn't be able to furnish a fancy home. He wanted a place he had earned, and a home he and Miriam could make together with their hands, sweat, and love. Miriam agreed. She was no ordinary rich girl.

The day dragged for Miriam at home. Her mother knew she was bursting to share the news, to see Yosef's face, and hear his voice. Hannah gave her plenty to do around the house to distract her as much as possible. Neither Miriam nor her mother felt much like talking. The silence was awkward. Finally, about two hours before sunset, Hannah suggested Miriam go to the house a little early, to see if she could drag Yosef away from his work.

When Miriam arrived, Yosef was surprised, but happy. He was hanging a new door on the inner room of the house, and had just finished lashing the leather hinges.

Miriam opened and closed the door to test it. Then she knocked on it and asked, "Is this the house of Yosef the carpenter and his wife, Miriam?"

"It is, indeed," Yosef said. "Please come in." They laughed.

"So, what is this big news you can't wait to tell me?" Yosef asked.

"I don't know the best way to say it. I'm nervous and afraid… but I'll just have to put it in Adonai's hands," Miriam replied.

Yosef realized this was not going to be a conversation about a musical performance. Perhaps, Miriam wanted her mother to move in with them. There wasn't a lot of space in the little house, but he could always build an addition.

"Trust God," Yosef said, encouraging her to speak.

Miriam swallowed hard. "I had a visitor last night," she finally said.

"What kind of visitor? The messenger with the news about your cousin?" Yosef asked.

"Why, yes!" Miriam said with surprise. "He was the first of two messengers."

"What do you mean?" asked Yosef.

"It was an angel who first told me Elizabeth was six months pregnant. And then, this morning, a traveling peddler came to our door with a note from Zechariah," Miriam added. She reached into her apron pocket and handed Yosef the little scroll. There was still a small piece of the wax seal on it.

"An angel?" Yosef wondered. Then he read the note.

"This is miraculous news, Miriam, but what's all this about an angel visiting you?"

"While I was playing my lyre last night, after you left, he came into my room and told me all about Elizabeth and her baby. Then, this morning, we received Zechariah's note. I knew she was six months pregnant before we even broke the seal on the scroll," Miriam explained.

"Was it a dream? You interpret dreams! Are you like Yosef, son of Jacob? Where's your coat of many colors?" he said half jokingly.

"This isn't a joke. It's true," Miriam replied.

Yosef realized this was a sensitive issue for Miriam, and he nodded.

"I'm sorry," he said.

"It was not a dream. The angel spoke to me, and when I spoke to him, he answered my question," she added.

Yosef was intrigued. "Unbelievable!" he said. "What did you ask him?"

"I asked him how I could be pregnant, if I hadn't been with a man," Miriam said as she looked at Yosef.

His brown eyes grew large, and he furrowed his brow. He shook his head.

"I … I thought you said Elizabeth was pregnant," he stammered.

"She is. But the angel said I will be, too. And the baby will come from the Holy Spirit. It will not be your baby," Miriam explained.

"I'm confused. Are you pregnant or will you be pregnant?" Yosef said, in a low voice so no one passing by could hear.

"I won't know for certain for a little while, but I think I'm pregnant," she responded quietly. "I told the angel, let it be done to me according to your word."

Yosef began to pace around the worksite. His head was swimming. Miriam stood in the center of the outer room as he walked around her.

Finally, he took a deep breath and quietly said, "Miriam, I love you, but if you have been unfaithful to me, I will not pretend to be the father of another man's child."

"I have not been with any man," she said in a very low voice. This was more than gossip or a neighborhood scandal; it was a life and death matter for her. She was at risk of execution by stoning. "You've got to believe me. My mother will confirm everything I've said. I told her Elizabeth was six months pregnant a half hour before the messenger arrived at our home."

"Miriam, if I were to tell people my wife is a virgin and she's pregnant, they would call me a fool, or crazy … or both!" Yosef said, in an angry whisper.

Miriam paused, stared at the floor and prayed in silence. "Please God, tell me what to say." Then she replied, "I understand, Yosef. I'm so sorry this is happening to us. I love you so much, but I can't change what happened. I didn't ask for this. God chose me. We're leaving to visit Elizabeth on Sunday morning, if you want to come with us."

Miriam turned and started to walk away. Yosef let her go.

chapter
NINE

IT WAS THE SABBATH AND YOSEF WENT TO SYNAGOGUE as usual. He saw Hannah and Miriam as he walked past their home, but avoided eye contact. He hadn't slept in days. He was tormented and exhausted.

Earlier in the week, at work, he had pretended nothing was wrong. When Nathan asked about Miriam's news, Yosef said she had told him about a dream that had to do with their wedding.

All he could think about was Miriam and his disappointment. How dare she sleep with another man, get pregnant, and then try to convince him she was still a virgin! Did she think he was that gullible? Obviously, she did, and so did her mother. On the other hand, Miriam had come to visit him alone at the house, so maybe Hannah wasn't in on it. Otherwise, they were setting a trap for him to raise some other guy's kid. Not him.

It would have been different if Miriam were a widow and needed someone to adopt her baby boy. Yosef loved her and would gladly be a stepfather. But this was a question of adultery.

After Synagogue, Yosef decided he would wait until Miriam and Hannah left town. Then he would quietly visit the rabbi and divorce Miriam. But he would conceal the alleged infidelity because he loved her too much to put her at risk. Yosef would simply say they came from two dissimilar worlds – upper class and working class, and their realities were different. They were incompatible. He would send her the witnessed divorce papers by messenger.

That way, Miriam would be safe. Elizabeth wouldn't have her baby for three months. By then, Miriam's pregnancy would be showing slightly. She could stay with her cousin and have her baby there. Thinking about the whole thing made Yosef angry and crazy.

He had a little wine with his lunch, and felt lazy on that Sabbath afternoon. The sun was hot, and it was a perfect day for a nap. He lay down under a tree behind Nathan's house. The leaves danced in the breeze, and the sun flickered between the branches. Watching them and the birds above made him drowsy. Thank God. He ached for some rest.

Suddenly, a brilliantly lit face overpowered the bright sun. Yosef couldn't make out the features, but the face was atop a body, and its eyes stared right at him.

> *"[Yosef], son of David, do not be afraid to take [Miriam] your wife into your home. For it is through the holy Spirit that this child has been conceived in her. She will bear a son and you are to name him [Yeshua], because he will save his people from their sins." (Matthew 1:20-22)*

Yosef tried to speak, but the words wouldn't come. In his head, he repeatedly heard an echo of the angel's last words, "… name him Yeshua; because he will save his people from their sins." Again and again and again he heard that proclamation.

When Yosef finally opened his eyes he was looking up at the moon. He had slept for hours. The sky was filled with stars. Although it was cool, Yosef was soaked with sweat. He remembered the dream with the angel, and what he had said. And then his mind was filled with a Scripture verse from the prophet Isaiah. He had heard it many times in the Temple and in Synagogue.

> *"Therefore the Lord himself will give you a sign; the young woman, [a virgin], pregnant and about to bear a son, shall name him Emmanuel." (Isaiah 7:14)*

Could this be the fulfillment of the prophecy? Oh, how the chosen people of Israel had waited – thousands of years for the Messiah. Was the angel Yosef had seen in his dream Miriam's angel?

He couldn't be sure about the Messiah, of course, but he could learn more from Miriam.

At daybreak, Yosef headed for Hannah's house. But when he arrived, there was no answer at the door. The neighbor's servant came out across the road. "There's nobody home," he said.

As Yosef turned to listen, the servant crossed the road and continued his account. "The runner took Hannah and Miriam on the road to Yerushlem; they are going to Judah. I'm paid to care for their home. They'll be gone for three or four months. How can I help you, Yosef?"

"When did they leave?" Yosef asked.

"It was early. Before sunrise, maybe an hour ago," the servant figured as he looked at the sun on the horizon.

"Thanks!" Yosef yelled. He ran up the road, his sandals slapping dirt all the way. When he arrived at Nathan's shop, he quickly unhitched the donkey that had been drinking water.

"I'll be back!" shouted Yosef, as he jumped on the animal and urged him to gallop up the road.

"I hope so," laughed Nathan. Yosef was a very hard worker, so Nathan knew he must have had a good reason to leave in a hurry. And besides, he was a young man. They're always in a hurry.

Because Hannah and Miriam were riding in a carriage, they would be traveling a lot slower. The roads and trails were bumpy. The faster the cart, the rockier the ride. Yosef could make better time on the young donkey. He and Nathan had bought the colt a year ago, and it had plenty of spirit.

As he raced down the road, Yosef realized how unprepared he was for his journey. He hadn't taken any supplies. Not even a goatskin of water. "What a fool," he thought. "I was going to travel with Miriam and Hannah to make sure they were safe, and I can't even take care of myself," he laughed.

The donkey sped up as two gazelles raced across the path in the early morning sun. There wasn't much traffic, other than a few people on foot, probably making day trips to nearby villages. Yosef glimpsed dust churning on the road ahead. That might be Miriam's carriage! He kneed the donkey a couple more times, and shouted for him to go.

"Balaam, Faster!" Yosef yelled.

Nathan had named the young donkey after the prophet Balaam who had a talking animal. He responded to Yosef's command, almost tossing him off his back as he went into a full gallop. Yosef had been in such a hurry that he had neglected to slap a saddle on Balaam. Now, he struggled to stay on his back. He slid up and down as Balaam ran, while holding onto a short rope attached to the animal's bridle. The tether wasn't really designed for a rider. Balaam typically pulled a wagon or a two-wheeled cart, and Nathan or Yosef led him along by the cord.

Yosef laughed as he bumped along on the road. He felt silly as he passed a couple of walkers. They laughed, too. This ride was a little more than Yosef had bargained for. The trail was reliable and solid, but there were plenty of ups and downs in the valley, and Yosef had no idea how fast Balaam could go. He was used to pulling a heavy cart, so the donkey must have felt truly free. He jaunted on the trail through the open wilderness.

Soon the carriage was in sight. Yosef was certain it was Miriam's. He began to call her name. "Miriam! Stop! Miriam, please stop!"

The carriage clipped along, and every time Yosef yelled, Balaam would startle, making the ride even a little more crazy. Although it was really tough to hang on, Yosef kept gaining ground, until he and Balaam were about one hundred yards behind the carriage.

Fortunately, the runner managing the vehicle turned to look back at it, as the wheels rolled over a serious bump. He noticed someone rapidly gaining on him. The traveler and his donkey were really kicking up a dust storm. Yosef shouted again, "Miriam. Miriam, stop!"

The runner halted the two donkeys he was leading, abruptly stopping the carriage. He pointed to Yosef. Miriam and Hannah poked their heads out from under the sun cover.

As soon as she caught a glimpse of Yosef, Miriam reached out to her runner to help her climb down from her seat.

"Joel, please help me. It's my betrothed," she exclaimed.

As Miriam worked her way off the carriage, Yosef and Balaam whizzed right past her.

"Whoa, whoa! Stop, Balaam. Balaam, stop!" Yosef pleaded.

Joel, the cursor, ran after them, but to no avail. There was no way he could catch them.

Yosef was not in a laughing mood now.

"You stubborn donkey," he shouted, as he pulled hard on the rope with all his might. Instantly, Balaam reared up and stopped. Yosef slid off the animal's bare back, flopping with a thud onto the road.

"Well, that's one way to dismount," Yosef thought as his bruised body throbbed from the impact.

Joel scurried up behind him. "Are you hurt? Are you OK?"

Yosef was embarrassed, but uninjured. He nodded and stood up. "It would have helped if I had saddled him up before we took off," he said. "Thanks for stopping."

By now, Miriam had run up to join them. Hannah was still seated in the carriage, but she waved to Yosef. He waved back.

"Yosef, what a surprise to see you. What's wrong?" Miriam said.

"Forgive me. I'm sorry that I interrupted your journey. But I have to ask you something really important," Yosef explained. "It can't wait."

He looked at Joel, who got the message, and walked back to the carriage to give the couple some privacy.

Yosef stepped off the road and reached out to help Miriam walk into the nearby field. As they strolled, Yosef said, "I had a dream last night, Miriam."

She said nothing and looked up at him.

"I saw an angel in my dream just like you did," he continued.

"But I wasn't dreaming, I actually saw the angel," Miriam replied.

Yosef nodded. "The angel told me about your baby. He told me not to be afraid, and that the Holy Spirit had given you this child."

Miriam stopped walking. She smiled at the man she loved. "What's your question, Yosef?"

"The angel gave me a name for the child. Did he tell you the name?" he asked.

"Why, yes, he did," she replied. "He said, 'you shall call his name, Yeshua.'"

Yosef was stunned. There was no way Miriam could have known the name, unless the angel had also visited her.

"You are to name him [Yeshua], because he will save his people from their sins," Yosef said, smiling. (Matthew 1:21)

"You believe me!" Miriam exclaimed.

"I do, now," Yosef replied. "I wanted to believe you before, but it just didn't seem possible."

"The angel told me nothing will be impossible for God," Miriam said.

Yosef reached out and hugged Miriam. The couple walked back to the carriage, and whispered the happy news to Hannah, while Joel watered the three donkeys.

Within a few minutes, Yosef was on Balaam's back again for the return trip to Nazareth. He had work to do, and a house to rebuild for his future wife and her baby.

Miriam and Hannah headed the other way to visit Elizabeth and to celebrate their joyful blessings. The good news would make the long road ahead seem shorter.

Miriam and Yosef were getting married, and they would soon have a son.

chapter
TEN

NO ONE IN NAZARETH KNEW ABOUT YESHUA'S
supernatural beginnings. To the travelers in the Nazarene caravan,
he was just another young man, the carpenter's kid. He appeared
very ordinary. He wasn't especially good looking, nor was he tall. At
a glance, Yeshua was quite average.

Right from the start, Yosef made sure the neighbors never suspected anything unusual about his adopted child. They assumed he was
Yeshua's natural father. Yosef had never said a word to the rabbi about
his plans to divorce Miriam. He hadn't told anyone about Miriam's surprise pregnancy, her visit from an angel, or his own supernatural dream.

About three months after Miriam and Hannah went to Ein
Karem to visit Elizabeth, Yosef joined them. A rabbi in that village
married Yosef and Miriam.

Miriam was a sweet, beautiful bride. She wore a new linen robe
and a dowry of gold coins. The precious metal dangled in rows, like
beads of jewelry across her forehead. It was a small wedding, but it
was wonderful. Yosef traveled to nearby Bethlehem and brought his
family to the event. His parents were very old. Hannah had several relatives near Jerusalem, who also attended. Elizabeth was nine
months pregnant at the wedding. It was a joyous family celebration.

Shortly after Elizabeth gave birth to her son, Miriam and Yosef returned to Nazareth. They started to make a home in the little house, while Yosef continued remodeling it.

Soon it was very obvious Miriam was pregnant. When Hannah later returned to Nazareth, they invited their friends to celebrate their new marriage. Yosef and Miriam were a handsome couple and very much in love. Miriam played the lyre and sang at the party. Unfortunately, it wasn't long before they had to journey to Bethlehem again to comply with the Roman census. All men had to return to the city where they were born.

Many years later, the couple finally resettled in Nazareth after their asylum in Egypt. The whole town had been surprised and delighted to see their old friends return home. Miriam had become a woman. Yosef was in his mid-twenties. He explained how they had escaped King Herod's massacre of the innocent babies in Bethlehem, and that they had wanted to be sure their son remained safe. They hid in Egypt until the king died. Because Herod had been a maniacal ruler, no one questioned their fears or their discretion.

Hannah was thrilled to finally meet her grandson. She had worried so much about him. Miriam had sent her mother messages from Egypt, so she would know the family was safe. But they had been afraid to reveal their specific hiding place. That secrecy prevented Hanna from joining them. Now, she finally held Yeshua on her lap. He was smart and happy, and the town of Nazareth welcomed the young family with many gifts. Nathan was delighted to have Yosef to help him again. The old carpenter was ready to retire. Plus, Yosef had saved money from his job in Egypt to complete his purchase of Nathan's business.

Yeshua and the other kids grew up in a close-knit community. It was almost like one big family. Traveling together for this Passover was a moveable feast and rolling party, although it meant a lot of hard work, too.

Before the caravan hit the trail to Yerushlem for the second day of travel, Yeshua and Yosef volunteered for night watch. Both had slept well after the first day on the road, and they would be headed into the lush, green foothills that would lead to the mountains. There were ibex and flocks of wild goats there, so the area would be filled with predators like jackals and leopards. Donkeys and oxen in the camp were easy prey.

Six men would stand guard over the caravan that evening. The second day of travel would end somewhere in Samaria. Samaritans and Jews were fierce enemies, so the Nazarenes would be unwelcome.

The Promised Land had been torn by wars and invasions ever since the Israelites escaped Egypt in 1290 B.C., and had finally found their God-given home 40 years later. Even under Jewish rule, the people were divided, and for a time, so was their kingdom. Following King Solomon's death, the land God had bestowed on them as one nation became Israel in the north and Judah in the south.

The Assyrians, Babylonians, Persians, and Greeks invaded and occupied the Promised Land, dominating the Israelites for hundreds of years. When Israel revolted and finally controlled their destiny again, aggressive Hebrew rulers attacked and pillaged Samaria, desecrating the Samaritan shrine at Mount Gerizim. The Samaritans never forgot the destruction. They believed Scripture proclaimed the mountain God's Holy of Holies. They also believed that Abraham went to Mount Gerizim to sacrifice Isaac; Noah's great flood had not touched their sacred place; and it would survive the end of the world. Samaritans rejected the Temple at Yerushlem.

But the Judeans and Samaritans actually had a lot in common. They both revered the five books of the Torah as the Word of God written down for them by Moses. However, the Samaritans rejected the rest of Jewish Scripture. Each religious sect claimed ownership of the true faith that would one day restore its people's relationship with God forever.

To the Romans, the religious differences seemed trivial, and so they tolerated both Jews and Samaritans. However, Jews and Samaritans stubbornly avoided each other.

The disagreement and rift troubled and frustrated Yeshua. As a young child, he had asked his parents why the Hebrew people were divided. They explained that the animosity was built on the scars of sin, misguided kings who worshiped idols, and vengeance for wrongs and retribution in the past. Samaritan men had also taken non-Jewish, foreign brides, violating the people's commitment to racial purity. Israelites believed these failings cursed their whole nation.

When Herod built Sebaste on the site of the old Samaritan capital, it was as if the Jewish king was flaunting his power on sacred Samaritan soil. The natives returned the favor by intensifying their contempt for the Jews.

Yeshua knew his Father's true Temple was in Yerushlem and not on Mount Gerizim. He knew that some of the ancient people of Samaria had once been idolaters, bowing to golden calves at Bethel and Dan, where the king of the northern tribes erected pagan shrines. King Jeroboam, the Samaritan, had declared:

"You have been going up to Jerusalem long enough. Here are your gods, O Israel, who brought you up from the land of Egypt." (1 Kings 12:28)

Jeroboam's real intention was to prevent his people from traveling to worship in Yerushlem, and shifting their loyalty to the house of David and King Rehoboam, son of Solomon. His move to paganism was political. He had separated the ten tribes of the north from the two of the south.

But whenever Yeshua heard the explanations for the hatred between the two peoples, he would quote Leviticus:

"Take no revenge and cherish no grudge against your own people. You shall love your neighbor as yourself. I am the LORD." (Leviticus 19:18)

He was proud that his parents weren't bigots. In fact, his father had convinced the leaders of the caravan to travel through Samaria to Yerushlem. Most Jews bypassed the region. They would rather journey miles out of their way than set foot in Samaritan territory. To Miriam, Yosef, and Yeshua, this made no sense at all. It was a straight shot from Nazareth through Samaria to the Temple.

"We have to pay taxes to the Romans, and don't believe in their gods, or agree with Caesar, but we use their roads," Yosef had reasoned.

It was hard to argue with that logic, but people don't always follow their heads. Miriam and Yosef had taught Yeshua to be kind to anyone he met, regardless of faith, status, or birthplace. In his heart, he knew it was exactly the right way to live.

After a breakfast of cheese and dried fruit, Yeshua hurried to help his parents hit the road. The trail would be steeper today and the sun hotter. The ascending scenery would welcome them with green, lush terraces. It was home to vineyards and farms. Unlike the semiarid regions of Yerushlem, Samaria was one of the most fertile territories in the Promised Land. Galilee to the north offered both its fresh-water lake and a flatter farming region.

But the rainy region of Samaria was still the largest source of fresh water in Israel. The precipitation made the hills and valleys excellent for farming. The rains ran to the lowlands, where people collected the precious resource in cisterns carved from rock. Yosef had made the stone basins in Bethlehem, Yerushlem and Nazareth.

As the Nazarene caravan rolled south on this partly cloudy morning, they could see two mountains on the horizon. Mounts Ebal and Gerizim defined the region, with the ancient, historic city of Shechem in the valley between them. The highway ran in the open valleys between the mountains, through the rich vineyards and farm fields in the wilderness. The region was appetizing to invaders and easy to access. It was little wonder that the Samaritans battled and intermingled with foreigners.

The caravan's pace was not as brisk as the first day. Despite the beauty, there was still some complaining among the pilgrims. Some resented passing through Samaria. Others barked slurs against the people of the region, as they traversed their homeland. But few could argue that God had blessed the people who tilled these fertile hills.

And the Passover story also had roots in this valley. It all began with the seeds of evil more than 1,500 years earlier. This is where Yahweh's servant and remarkable dream reader, Yosef, took the first steps on his journey down the path of destiny. Yosef's father, Jacob, loved him very dearly — much more than he loved Yosef's brother and ten half-brothers. Jacob gave Yosef a long, ornate coat of many colors. The brothers were jealous and despised Yosef.

Their anger exploded when Yosef told them about two of his dreams. In his visions, harvested crops and heavenly bodies had bowed before him. They represented his family members honoring him.

Jacob and his sons chastised Yosef for his apparent arrogance, but his father was patient with him. One day, Jacob became concerned about his other sons, who were away tending his flocks in Shechem. He sent his favorite son to check on them. But when Yosef arrived in Shechem, he learned his brothers had moved on to Dothan. As he approached the flocks, his brothers spotted him in the distance. They plotted to murder him, but the oldest, Reuben, argued against the idea.

Instead, they stripped Yosef of his splendid tunic and threw him down a dry well. Then, his brothers sold him for twenty silver pieces to slave traders, who peddled Yosef in Egypt. His slave master was an official in Pharaoh's court. Meanwhile, the brothers dipped Yosef's coat in goat's blood and sent it to Jacob. Devastated, he concluded a wild animal had devoured his beloved son.

However, Yahweh was with his enslaved servant, and He protected Yosef. The dreamer would eventually win his freedom by interpreting the Egyptian Pharaoh's nightmares. He predicted seven years of abundant harvests, followed by seven years of fierce famine.

Yosef helped the ruler save his people from starvation. The grateful tyrant appointed him governor of all Egypt, to manage the harvests and sell the grain. During the famine, even Yosef's brothers traveled there to beg for food. Not recognizing the brother they had sold into slavery, they bowed before him and faced the ground. Yosef's old dreams had become reality.

Mercifully, he forgave his brothers. Yosef invited them and his father to join him in Egypt. Their families prospered in the land, and the Israelites grew strong in number. Many years later, after Yosef, his father, and brothers had all died, a new Pharaoh came to power. He feared the large Israelite nation, and forced them into hard labor. Israel would sojourn in Egypt for 430 years. Only Yahweh's Passover and the wrath of his mighty hand could untie the knot of oppression and slavery.

When they fled Egypt, the Israelites had carried Yosef's bones with them, and buried them at Shechem in the Promised Land. As Yeshua and the Nazarene caravan now approached Shechem, local shepherds were raising goats and sheep, just as Yosef's brothers had. Bees collected nectar across ribbons of wildflowers and farmers' blossoms. It was easy for the travelers to daydream, while soaking in the scenery and the Passover history.

Yeshua gazed up at the rocky hillsides and ridges. The contrast to the greenery was striking. The highlands helped the Samaritans keep watch over their territory and aggressively defend it.

Yerushlem would be brown and dusty compared to Samaria. But it had the Temple Mount and the Holy of Holies. And for Yeshua, that was the top of the world.

The caravan made a brief stop for lunch near Shechem, barely pulling off the quiet mountain highway. The women hustled to serve food, mostly yogurt and kefir, dried fruit, and salted olives. The bread was crusty and stale, but it filled many bellies. There were 77 of them, including women and children.

The men kept busy securing cargo on the wagons and repairing wheels and sandals. The animals needed water and rest before they continued.

"Yeshua!" Miriam called. "Take this bucket and find some water."

He left his father to finish double-checking the wheels and yoke on the wagon, and grabbed the bucket from his mother. Yeshua sprinted toward the hillside, looking for a trickle or a puddle. His father had told him there was a main mountain spring near Shechem. In this very place, God had promised Abraham the land, and Abraham built an altar to Yahweh. His grandson, Jacob, had purchased a plot of land in Shechem, and had also built an altar there. Jacob's sons had tended their herds near here, and his well was nearby in Sychar. Yosef had come looking for his envious, resentful brothers in Shechem. The 12 tribes of Israel descended from Jacob. Yeshua couldn't help but feel connected to his ancient ancestors in this place. It renewed his energy after the grueling morning journey.

A herd of sheep grazed below the vineyard in the distance, a few hundred yards away. Yeshua ran toward them, and before long he splashed into a puddle near a little creek. The water gurgled and flowed clean and clear, widening into a pool before continuing down the slope.

The sheep looked up at Yeshua, and then went back to munching on the grass nearby. He crouched down and dipped his bucket in the stream. He watched it slowly fill up. Cupping his hands, he scooped up some fresh water, and splashed it on his face. It was cool and refreshing. "Ahhh!"

Until the caravan arrived in Yerushlem, Yeshua couldn't be sure when he'd have access to this much fresh water on the trip. He took advantage of the opportunity to really clean up. Yeshua grabbed the bucket, and poured water over his head and the back of his neck. He washed his face. It felt wonderful.

Grass rustled on the other side of the stream. Yeshua looked up to see the sheep approaching the water. Suddenly, a young shepherd sat up in the lush valley. He had been hiding in the brush, lying on his back near the creek. He was about Yeshua's age, maybe a little older.

Yeshua and the shepherd stared at each other, but said nothing.

The mountain boy was Samaritan. His staff was short and thick, and he wore a wool shirt. His hair was long and curly. He had a stern look on his face and then he finally spoke.

"What are you doing drinking and bathing in our stream?" he asked sarcastically, pointing to the water.

Yeshua paused and then replied:

> *"God speaks in his holiness:*
> *"I will exult, I will apportion Shechem;*
>   *the valley of Succoth I will measure out." (Psalm 108:8)*

He was quoting the Psalms.

"That is not from the Torah," the shepherd replied with a scowl. "That's not God's word. Those are your words! They mean nothing to my people. We are God's people. This is His mountain!" He pointed to Mount Gerizim.

Then Yeshua said,

> *"Abram passed through the land as far as the sacred place at Shechem, by the oak of Moreh. The Canaanites were then in the land.*
>
> *"The LORD appeared to Abram and said: 'To your descendants I will give this land.' So Abram built an altar there to the LORD who had appeared to him." (Genesis 12:6-7)*

The shepherd grinned again. "Yes, it all began right here. And this is our land," he confidently proclaimed.

Yeshua reached into his satchel. The shepherd grabbed his staff with both hands, and held it out in front of him. He was ready for a fight. But instead of a knife or a stone, Yeshua pulled out something covered in cloth. He held it out toward the shepherd and unwrapped it, revealing the small toy boat he had been carving for John. It was almost finished except for some detail work.

He set it on the water and gave it a little shove. The boat floated down the creek to the pool.

The shepherd's eyes widened. Yeshua gestured to him to pick up the toy.

He did, smiling as he examined it. He put it back on the water and laughed as it moved with the current into the wider pool.

Yeshua stood and quoted God's promise to Noah after the great flood,

> *"God said: 'This is the sign of the covenant that I am making between me and you and every living creature with you for all ages to come: I set my [rainbow] in the clouds to serve as a sign of the covenant between me and the earth.'" (Genesis 9:12-13)*

Hearing the Scripture verse, the shepherd paused. He nodded and smiled, realizing the truth in Yeshua's words. Indeed, they shared the same creator who loved them both and every living creature of the earth. He reached into the satchel at his waist, and pulled out a small sack. He tossed it across the creek to Yeshua.

Yeshua caught the fabric bag, and pulled the woolen cord to open it. He discovered it was full of sweet raisins from nearby vineyards. He sampled one and smiled, nodding his approval.

As Yeshua picked up his full bucket of water and walked away, he turned back to the shepherd. "Shlama," he said, the Aramaic word for peace.

"Shlama," replied the shepherd.

ELEVEN

THAT EVENING AT SUPPER, YESHUA SHARED his story about the young Samaritan herdsman. His father and mother were pleased to hear how he had handled the confrontation. They also agreed with Yeshua that the raisins the shepherd had given him were delicious — plumper and much sweeter than any they normally had in Nazareth.

The night would be cooler in the highlands. Everyone huddled around the fire. The doctor wrapped one man's ankle. He had turned it badly in a rut, while managing his donkey on the trail. During the rainy season, the roads in Samaria had become quagmires, and they dried rough and uneven. The limited Passover traffic hadn't done much to smooth them out. The doctor applied a splint he had made from tree branches and bandages. The swelling was quite bad. The pilgrim would have to ride in a cart tomorrow. His wife would walk alongside their beast. Other people in the caravan would relieve her, so she could rest and ride, too.

Many people developed blisters from walking. Some had become badly infected. The doctor was busy lancing them with his sharp instrument. He used a poultice made from flaxseed to help draw out the infection. Lots of Passover pilgrims would have their feet bound and elevated this evening.

The Nazarenes had walked about 15 miles today; more than one-third of the trip was complete by the end of day two. Although it was cooler in hill country, the highway twisted and turned through the mountains, and there were more problems on the trail. Damaged carts. Animals had sore hooves, and the quality of the food was less appealing than the first day when everything was fresh.

Fortunately, there was plenty of water, so no one, including the animals, went to bed thirsty. The fire crackled big and bright as men tossed more wood scraps and timber onto the flames. Miriam played her lyre more softly tonight. It was like a lullaby. Some weary travelers fell asleep in mid conversation. The cool breeze meant slumber would be deep. They hoped the rain clouds would pass.

Yeshua and Yosef would be on watch tonight, along with four other men. Since he was younger, Yeshua would remain close to the fire to secure the tents, wagons, and livestock. He was grateful for the assignment. Since he would be by the fire, Yeshua would have all night to carve another boat for John.

It wasn't long before Miriam stopped playing her lyre, and the rabbi gathered the whole community to say their evening prayer. As the watchmen walked off to their posts carrying torches, Miriam gently played again and sang "The Travelers Psalm." It was a special musical prayer for those on watch tonight.

"I raise my eyes toward the mountains.
From whence shall come my help?
My help comes from the LORD,
the maker of heaven and earth.
He will not allow your foot to slip;
or your guardian to sleep.
Behold, the guardian of Israel
never slumbers nor sleeps.
The LORD is your guardian;
the LORD is your shade

at your right hand.
By day the sun will not strike you,
nor the moon by night.
The LORD will guard you from all evil;
he will guard your soul.
The LORD will guard your coming and going
both now and forever." (Psalm 121:1-8)

As Miriam's final notes faded into the darkness, the camp grew mysterious. Night sounds replaced human voices and activity. Yeshua heard the nocturnal animals now. Especially the owls hooting. One soared over the camp, pursuing his prey.

Yeshua decided to walk around the camp before resuming his carving. He picked up his torch from the fire, and marched past the animals. They were fast asleep. The tents were quiet, except for the very loud snoring of one man. Yeshua laughed at the sound. He wasn't frightened. He knew his heavenly Father was watching his every step. He just wished everyone else felt the same way about God. Fear was an evil enemy. It made people do foolish, cruel, violent, and selfish things.

Yeshua put the torch back in its hole by the campfire, and sat down nearby to carve. He was just getting started on the boat. With time to think as he worked, he realized that he missed Ezra. They would have shared the watch duty, and had a wonderful time talking by the fire and patrolling the camp. Ezra would have accompanied him during the day and met the Samaritan shepherd. Yeshua would share that story with Ezra when he returned to Nazareth.

He stared into the flaming embers, envisioning the face of his friend. It had been two days since they left Nazareth. By now, Ezra would be feeling much better, yearning to be on the pilgrimage, living in the wilderness.

"Next year in Yerushlem!" Yeshua imagined Ezra saying at his Seder supper. He would truly mean it.

The small boat slowly began to take shape in Yeshua's hands. He had hollowed out the center. He'd look up from his work every few seconds to make sure nothing or no one was approaching the camp. He paused to sharpen the blade on a small stone he kept handy. Soon it would be time to pick up his torch again and check the animals and the tents.

The clouds above parted to reveal the moonlight. For a little while, the glowing moon and brilliant stars brightened the entire camp. It was as if someone had lit a giant lamp in the night sky. Yeshua gazed up at the heavens. He saw Pegasus, the constellation shaped like a winged horse. Thoughts of Ezra raced through his mind, and he could picture the toy he had carved for him. Yeshua chuckled at the name Ezra had given his wooden stallion. "Thunder" was an excellent moniker for the powerful-looking horse Yeshua had crafted.

Suddenly, as he studied the stars, he pictured Roman soldiers riding their handsome mounts past the Temple in Yerushlem. In Yeshua's imagination, the mounted unit pushed its way through a crush of people. Some of the Israelites were forced left and others right as they attempted to get a closer look at someone or something. One horse grew excited and reared up. People screamed in fear of the huge animals, and the soldiers shouted warnings to disperse.

"Yeshua!" Yosef whispered harshly. "What are you staring at, son? The danger is down here. You didn't even see me coming up on you. I could have been a thief or a jackal."

Actually, Yeshua had heard him coming. He told Yosef that he could see the glow of the torch out of the corner of his eye, so he knew it was one of the watchmen.

Yosef had simply come back to check on his son. All was quiet. No intruders of any kind. He took the opportunity to share a serious moment with Yeshua.

"I want you to know that your mother and I are very proud of you. So far, you've been smart about this trip," Yosef said. "I know

God watches over you in many special ways, but I can't help worrying about you in Yerushlem. It can be a dangerous place. You have to pay attention to everything you're doing, everywhere you go, and every moment. There will be so many people there during Passover, it's very easy to get lost in the crowds or to be robbed."

Yeshua listened respectfully, nodding.

"Promise me, Yeshua, that if something goes wrong, or you get lost while we're in Yerushlem, no matter who tries to persuade you, you will not go home with them unless you know the person well. There are people there who could steal you and sell you into slavery. You would be worth 2,000 denarii as a slave. They'd kidnap you and ship you off to another part of the world, and we'd never see you again," Yosef explained.

In response, Yeshua quoted Moses: "I am a stranger residing in a foreign land." (Exodus 2:22)

Yosef laughed with relief. He hugged his clever son, picked up his torch and headed back to his post.

Yeshua resumed carving the boat, as clouds again covered the moon and the starry sky. He moved his mat closer to the fire for warmth and better light. As Yeshua watched Yosef's torch grow fainter in the distance, he felt very grateful he had two loving fathers.

chapter

TWELVE

IT SEEMED LIKE MORNING WOULD NEVER COME. Although Yeshua was enjoying the carving, and John's boat was all but finished, the night had become more overcast and chilly. First light and warmth were slow to arrive.

At one point, Yeshua heard a commotion among the animals. He dropped his artwork, and snatched up his torch. He ran full speed toward them, screaming and scaring off the intruder.

"Arrrh!" he growled.

He couldn't be sure if it was a wildcat or a pack of jackals, but the livestock definitely behaved like they had been threatened. Yeshua remained with them for a while.

After hearing him shout, his father came running back to the camp to check on him.

They walked out into the wilderness together with torches blazing, maybe fifty yards from the camp, but saw nothing. Yosef returned to his post about 200 yards away, while Yeshua circled the tents with his torch, likely scaring off any remaining predators.

The death of any pilgrim's donkey or ox could be devastating, especially on the open trail. It would be that much harder for the caravan to move, if a family had to pull their cart by hand or abandon it. Borrowing another family's second donkey would mean two wagons would move more slowly. And the cost of replacing a strong beast would be steep and painful. Especially if they were many miles away from home, where the breeder would know the pilgrim was desperate to purchase a replacement.

A pilgrimage to Yerushlem for Passover was a very expensive endeavor.

For some families, it was a once-in-a-lifetime journey over land or sea. But a visit to the Temple was a personal, spiritual triumph. It was worth saving for years to join the Hebrew nation in a massive worship celebration.

When morning finally arrived, the women came out of their tents, and began preparing a pot of barley cooked in water. The men who had guarded the camp would eat first. They would enjoy a special treat: salted, dried fish from the Sea of Galilee. Yeshua enjoyed his reward. It was a rare breakfast in the wilderness with one of his favorite foods. He ate heartily.

The caravan of pilgrims would need all the nourishment they could get today because they would face more challenges. As they climbed higher toward Yerushlem, the morning air in southern Samaria grew misty and wet. At first, that made the trail a little slippery. The sun rose higher and the air grew steamier. The closer they would move toward the Holy City, the drier things would become. Yerushlem was certainly not known for milk and honey like Samaria and Galilee. Just south of Yerushlem lay the Judean desert.

One natural spring, Gihon, quenched the entire Holy City. The Pool of Siloam was filled by that spring. More than 700 years earlier, King Hezekiah had a tunnel dug through the Yerushlem limestone to provide a steady flow of water for the Israelites. To the east of the Samarian hills ran the Jordan River, all the way south from Galilee to the super salty Dead Sea. But that water was many miles away, across the elevation. Jericho, east of Yerushlem, boasted fruitful oases, and at En Gedi, there were cool pools where a hot traveler could shower in one of four waterfalls. David had hid there from King Saul.

But those places were days away. The Nazarene caravan would have to capture all the water they could before they left Samaria because it would soon become scarce. They stopped to water the animals and fill up their jugs, skins and reservoirs. You could go without food for a day, but in the heat, water was the difference between vital life and severe dehydration, or even death. This was especially true for the beasts of burden. And the terrain would continue to rise up toward the Holy City, demanding more stamina.

Despite no sleep, Yeshua was full of energy. He was becoming a man, and enjoying the responsibilities that came with it.

"Yeshua, come rest," his mother urged him from the wagon. She offered both Yosef and Yeshua a chance to nap, while she led the donkeys. But the men insisted they would take turns, and Yeshua volunteered to go first.

As Yosef rode onboard with Miriam, she refused to let him sleep.

"Can I ask you a question?" Miriam said, as she shaded Yosef's face with her apron in the open wagon.

"You just did," he replied with a smile, his eyes closed.

Miriam laughed. "I'd like to know if you've thought about a wife for Yeshua?"

Yosef's eyes opened with surprise. "Not really," he replied. "Have you?"

"Well, a mother is always considering who will make a good partner for her son," Miriam said. "But Yeshua is still young."

"Then why are you bringing it up?" Yosef puzzled.

Miriam paused, lifting the apron from Yosef's face. She looked at her husband. "Because Judith mentioned it." Miriam said.

Yosef sat up. It was customary for the fathers to arrange marriages, but everyone understood that mothers influenced their husbands. So did grandmothers and aunts, even sisters. They could put in a good word for a young woman or make an outright plea on her behalf. They could also offer lukewarm praise to cause a father to think again, or say absolutely nothing, making a man feel uneasy about his decision.

Judith had five daughters, but no sons. Her husband, Eli, was an older man who needed help in his farm fields. He had been a tenant of Hannah and Yoachim, and eventually bought his land outright. With five girls, Judith had all the help she needed, but Eli was frequently forced to pay hired hands. A young man like Yeshua would be a blessing to their family. Not only was he strong, but he was also skilled. Yeshua could walk behind a plow and repair it if it broke. Or he could build one from scratch. But he was so young.

"He's just a kid," Yosef said. "Wonderful, smart and talented, but just a kid."

"Of course," Miriam replied. "But I'm talking about the future. He will need a wife in a few years. We should start thinking about that."

"He tells me he wants to be a rabbi. There will be no shortage of fathers who would want a rabbi to marry their daughters," Yosef proclaimed. "Even though he isn't particularly handsome. He is a unique and a very appealing young man."

"Believe me, I know," Miriam replied. "Avigail has a big crush on him."

"Who's Avigail?" he asked.

"You know Avigail! Eli's second daughter. She is a very intelligent girl. A good weaver. A hard worker. Her mother is very proud of her," she said. "And I'm teaching Avigail to play the lyre."

Yosef nodded as he raised his eyebrows. He could see that Miriam liked Avigail as much as Avigail liked Yeshua.

"And that was the other thing I wanted to tell you, Yosef," Miriam explained. "I invited Avigail to join us after we stop for lunch. She would like to ride along, so I can give her another lesson on the lyre."

Yosef laughed and shook his head. Yeshua turned around to see what was so funny, but his parents weren't ready to share their conversation.

Yeshua liked girls. He liked everyone. He was one of those kids who could strike up a conversation with a total stranger. He talked to all types of people. Older and younger. Men and women. As the town carpenter's son, he met virtually everyone. He made deliveries and accepted orders when his father was away. In fact, in the last year, Yosef had allowed Yeshua to make estimates on carpentry and masonry jobs, and even to collect payments.

Many young girls in the community were familiar with him, although not from school. Young women were educated at home. Cooking; spinning; making clothing; gardening; mending; laundry; raising children; midwifing; and family psychology. Plus, in the Hebrew faith, children inherited their birthright from their mothers. As they grew up, their mothers played very vital roles in nurturing their spirituality. It was the mother who set the Sabbath table, and prepared young girls to be Hebrew wives and raise their own families.

Yeshua was that friendly kid who showed up on doorsteps, hefting his father's handiwork — like tables, ladders, and stone mills. People throughout Nazareth and nearby towns hired Yosef to make things and do repairs. He occasionally helped people build or remodel their homes and fix roofs. Yeshua began assisting him as soon as he was old enough to hand his father a tool, or hold a rule in place so Yosef could chalk a line. He joined him on larger orders and helped Yosef pick up broken plows, yokes, and furniture. Everyone in town who knew Yosef had met his eager and diligent son, Yeshua.

Avigail had first set eyes on Yeshua when he came to her farm with his father to do a job. She offered both of them some cold well water on that hot day. Yeshua had shown her one of his carvings. He had been making a wooden flower as a gift for his mother.

She was so impressed. He was strong, yet artistic. Not many Israelite boys had time to learn art. It wasn't taught in school nor emphasized in their society. Egyptians, Greeks, and Romans were artists, but Jewish boys devoted their time to learning about the Torah, plus ancient rabbinic writings and oral traditions that later became the Talmud. Of course, they studied the Hebrew language, too. The people spoke Aramaic on the street. Hebrew was the tongue of the Scripture and the Temple.

Yeshua was a natural when it came to sculpting and carving. These were skills his father had perfected on the job. But Yeshua also had a good eye. He could carve a pomegranate or a lily out of wood after looking at it once. A few years earlier, shortly after he met Avigail, Yeshua fashioned a wooden wildflower for her. She had been carrying flowers the day he saw her at her farm. The gift stole her heart. It really wasn't a romantic gesture. It was just the kind of thing Yeshua did, but to Avigail it was a precious memento. She kept it in her apron.

Yeshua had dyed the wood purple. He had borrowed a tiny bit of coloring from the town dyer. She let him scrape the residue from her vat. The pigment came from the murex sea snail, produced at Tyre in Lebanon, and it was very popular with the wealthy. Herod and other royalty were known for wearing purple robes.

The dyer, named Shifra, had finished some work for the rabbi, and she was all too happy to help Yeshua. She appreciated his craft and enjoyed his visits. Shifra was a widow with no children. She welcomed guests, especially youngsters.

Yeshua used a little of the purple dye to fill in the detail of the wildflower he had scratched into the wood. That was two years ago. Now Avigail was blossoming. The beautiful young woman was the same age as Yeshua. Neither of them had shared any feelings for one another, but Avigail was full of questions about him. She asked Miriam all about Yeshua in the women's tent the night before.

"Does Yeshua play the lyre? How old is Yeshua? Does Yeshua want to be a carpenter like his father? How did Yeshua learn to carve so well?" She probed Miriam with query after query. Her mother, Judith, and the other women smiled at each other. This was part of the courting process in a marriage tradition where fathers arranged the unions, but mothers had sway.

Finally, to relax Avigail, Miriam offered to teach her to play the lyre. She was a quick study, and the women nodded their approval and encouraged her.

"My Avigail can do anything she puts her mind to," Judith said proudly. "Just like her sisters," she added. The lyre was a favorite instrument of the Israelites. David had played it to soothe King Saul's anger.

The caravan from Nazareth was blessed to have Miriam play music and sing so well. And she was all too happy to pass it on to the next generation. She had no daughter of her own, and Yeshua preferred to listen to music rather than play it. But he could sing.

When the caravan stopped for lunch on the third day, Yeshua was dead on his feet. The group would pause about an hour. Beasts guzzled water and their masters stretched out on the roadside. Since they were making their way out of Samaria, the terrain was dustier and less grassy. Yosef immediately volunteered to help a few pilgrims make minor repairs to their wagons, yokes, and reins. He was really going through his supply of nails and leather straps.

Miriam gave Yeshua a cucumber she had been saving in the bottom of one of her straw bags. It quenched his thirst, along with the water. Sheep cheese and crisp bread crusts helped revitalize him. He climbed into the wagon and lay down at the rear, prepared to nap. With his stomach full, Yeshua quickly drifted off. He had found some space in a corner amidst straw, bags packed with supplies, Yosef's wooden toolbox, clothing, and goatskins of water.

After two-and-a-half days of travel, the caravan was a little more than half way to Yerushlem. The sun was high overhead and it would get hotter in the afternoon. As the Nazarenes neared the Temple, the roads would grow much, much more crowded. If they made good time today, perhaps they could complete the trip in less than five days. They prayed no one had an accident or a major breakdown.

Their provisions grew thinner. But the pilgrims had planned for the shortages. By the end of the third day, the caravan would reach small villages with roadside inns near Tephon. They would pitch their tents outside an inn set up to accommodate caravans. Although the place would be overflowing, with many people sleeping in the courtyard, the Nazarenes would be able to purchase meals and supplies for at least another day of travel.

There would be sufficient well water for the animals and the people. Water was the number one issue for everyone, especially on the road. Even King Herod the Great understood severe thirst. He and his family had suffered it, while hiding in Masada to escape their enemies. When he later assumed the throne, he made certain all his palaces were equipped with ample water storage. In fact, his Hanging Palace at Masada had an ingenious system that stored over 10 million gallons. During the rainy season, the king's servants dammed up two ravines. Water flowed through an aqueduct and drained into huge cisterns that masons had carved into the rock. Slaves and beasts would carry jugs of water up to the fortress for the king, his guests, and hundreds of others who did his bidding.

The Passover pilgrims from Nazareth would experience nothing as sophisticated or as abundant, but the inn would be ready for them with refreshment from cisterns and a well. Their goal was to arrive there before dark. Many wanted to cut lunch short, but once you stop a caravan, it's not an easy task to get it moving again. By the time the last family was aboard its wagon and back on the road, Yeshua was sleeping deeply in the corner of the cart. He had shaded his face with a towel, so he didn't notice when Avigail climbed aboard with his mother. Yosef helped both women up into the wagon and the donkeys lurched forward.

Within minutes the lyre lesson began.

"So, why don't you show me what you learned last night?" Miriam suggested to Avigail.

"Won't we wake Yeshua?" Avigail replied with a nervous glance toward the rear of the wagon.

"He can sleep through a rooster crowing and the sheep bleating," Miriam said. "Don't worry, the music is relaxing. I just hope he doesn't snore."

The two women shared a laugh. The beautiful Avigail strummed the strings with her nimble fingers. At first she was a little tentative, but soon she gained confidence, and began playing a soothing melody often used for the Psalms of David. The great Hebrew king had written Psalms to the music of his lyre.

Avigail glanced at the corner when Yeshua rolled onto his side, but he showed no real signs of waking. With a nod, Miriam encouraged her to continue playing.

"Very good! You remembered what I taught you yesterday. Now, why don't you sing something, like a Psalm … you will see how the words fit with the music," Miriam suggested.

Avigail shook her head as if to say, "I couldn't possibly sing, I am too shy."

"I'll start," Miriam said, as Avigail continued to strum the simple melody she had learned the night before.

"I am a flower of Sharon,
a lily of the valleys,"
Miriam sang in a sweet voice. *(Song of Songs 2:1)*

The words were from King Solomon's "Song of Songs." He was David's son.

Then Yosef responded in his deep baritone, as he led the beasts along the road.

"Like a lily among thorns,
so is my friend among women." (Song of Songs 2:2)

Miriam gestured for Avigail to sing, and so she did. Her voice was faint at first, but then rose stronger with Miriam's smiles of approval. Avigail chanted very naturally:

"Like an apple tree among the trees of the woods,
so is my lover among men.
In his shadow I delight to sit,
and his fruit is sweet to my taste.
He brought me to the banquet hall
and his glance at me signaled love.
Strengthen me with raisin cakes,
refresh me with apples,
for I am sick with love.
His left hand is under my head
and his right arm embraces me.
I adjure you, Daughters of Jerusalem,
by the gazelles and the does of the field,
Do not awaken, or stir up love
until it is ready.
The sound of my lover! here he comes
springing across the mountains,
leaping across the hills.
My lover is like a gazelle
or a young stag.
See! He is standing behind our wall,
gazing through the windows,
peering through the lattices." (Song of Songs 2:3-9)

By now, many in the caravan were commenting on Avigail's singing. Other women aboard their carts had joined in, as if in a chorus. But they sang quietly. No one wanted Avigail to stop.

Yeshua opened his eyes and quietly sat up in the wagon behind her. Her voice impressed him, and he smiled broadly. Yeshua knew the words well from his Scripture studies. He waited eagerly for the next set of verses. They were the young man's part in this beautiful love song about the tender covenant between God and his people.

"My lover speaks and says to me," sang Avigail.

"'Arise, my friend, my beautiful one, and come!'" Yeshua and Yosef chanted the response in unison.

Yosef turned around and smiled at his son, surprised to hear him singing. He let Yeshua finish the verses alone.

> *"'For see, the winter is past,*
> *the rains are over and gone.*
> *The flowers appear on the earth,*
> *the time of pruning the vines has come,*
> *and the song of the turtledove is heard in our land.*
> *The fig tree puts forth its figs,*
> *and the vines, in bloom, give forth fragrance.*
> *Arise, my friend, my beautiful one,*
> *and come!*
>
> *"'My dove in the clefts of the rock,*
> *in the secret recesses of the cliff,*
> *Let me see your face,*
> *let me hear your voice,*
> *For your voice is sweet,*
> *and your face is lovely.'"* (Song of Songs 2:10-14)

Avigail blushed. She didn't dare look at Yeshua, but inside she was very excited to know he was awake, and actually singing with her. Her voice shook a little as she continued, but she quickly found her confidence again. She performed beautifully, never missing a beat on the lyre.

"Catch us the foxes, the little foxes
that damage the vineyards; for our vineyards are in
bloom!
My lover belongs to me and I to him;
he feeds among the lilies.
Until the day grows cool and the shadows flee,
roam, my lover,
Like a gazelle or a young stag
upon the rugged mountains." (Song of Songs 2:15-17)

Avigail finished the verses and stopped playing. Miriam and Yeshua applauded. Yosef cheered. Other people in the caravan shouted out to Avigail, "Sing more! Play more!"

"You are a natural musician," Miriam said joyfully. "Don't you think she's very good, Yeshua?"

He nodded with a warm smile, and applauded again, "Amen, Amen!"

Avigail blushed at the praise. Yeshua encouraged her to play again. He apologized for falling asleep.

Avigail was eager to learn, and Miriam was very happy to teach her. More than that, she was glad to see Yeshua treat the young woman so politely and generously.

The beautiful music had lifted the spirits of the Nazarenes. Their hearts were light, and the afternoon heat didn't seem quite so oppressive, nor did the day feel quite as long.

Avigail was in love with the carpenter's son. But she would have to wait patiently to see how Yeshua really felt about her.

chapter

THIRTEEN

THEY MADE IT.

The Nazarene caravan arrived at a village near Tephon, just as the sun was setting. This would be a lot more civilized than staying in the middle of the wilderness. But from a security standpoint, they had traded wild predators for two-legged versions — thieves with sinister plans and wily ways. The open road was filled with con men and crooks, especially at Passover time, because there were wealthy travelers and inexperienced, vulnerable country souls with plenty to steal. And, of course, there were also beggars, people who were crippled, sick, or unemployable for some reason. A crowded inn meant many opportunities to find merciful, devout Jews who were willing to share their blessings. But most of the wealthy class felt little responsibility for the poor.

Yeshua hadn't been around rich people other than his pious grandmother. But the roadside inn would give him a real taste of the upper crust, before he experienced the full force of materialism in Yerushlem. As they approached the building and courtyard, he saw a man and his wife reclining on two litters. Six muscular slaves carried each of them. These Gentile servants had been shouldering the load the entire trip. A third group of six litter bearers hefted their luggage. Perhaps they had traveled in from Joppa on the Mediterranean coast, or Jericho to the east, where Herod and his wealthy court had once wintered in his majestic palace.

The couple wore fine, flowing mantles over their tunics. The woman's was silk, imported from the far, far East. Both wore masterfully crafted anklet boots made of exotic skin. The wife's footwear and belt were made of something Yeshua had never seen — hyena hide. Rouge and paint dramatically adorned her face. She wore her hair piled up high on her head, and Yeshua got the sense not all of it was hers. Her husband was clean-shaven and his hair was henna, a reddish color that was most obviously dyed. It was a look that was very foreign to Nazareth, where every man wore a traditional Jewish beard in his natural color, and women covered their heads while they worked from dawn to dusk. Yeshua couldn't imagine when his father would find time to shave. Yeshua himself was just beginning to sprout some faint whiskers, and he looked forward to sporting his own classic Hebrew mane.

Under the rule of Herod the Great, Yerushlem and the entire Promised Land had become less Hebraic and more worldly. The king had adopted the style of the Greeks and Romans, even featuring gladiator games of competition at a theater just outside the Holy City, with a hippodrome for chariot races. The nearly naked bodies of the athletes clashed with the modesty prescribed by Jewish law, and it angered many traditional believers. But Herod was stubborn and merciless. He had put thousands to death, so few were willing to openly oppose him — although there had been a failed plot on his life, and others were rumored. After his death, Herod the Great's legacy was a more hedonistic Israel, and for all the compromises he'd made, his nation was really no safer. If Caesar wanted to rule the Hebrews with an iron fist, he could and would.

In these times, people were pretty much either rich or poor. There wasn't really a middle class. About five percent of the population could be considered wealthy. They lived in beautiful homes carved from native limestone with courtyards, gardens, and baths with hot water. There were servants to wait on their dinner parties and style their hair. Some families had their own barbers, who kept the men clean-shaven, bleaching and dyeing their hair. Others piled tresses atop women's heads, securing them with nets, jeweled headbands, or a maze of combs and hairpins decorated with tortoise shell and ivory.

But most people worked very hard for a living. Even a beggar's days were busy. You might be a farmer, a tailor, a stoneworker or carpenter, a charcoal burner or a dyer. Anything needed had to be crafted by hand from raw materials. Potters threw bowls, plates, pitchers, and jugs. There were copper smelters, tanners, and even dung collectors. The animal dung was used to tan hides. Some had jobs that created quite a stench. In fact, one of the very few reasons a Hebrew woman could divorce her husband was that he stunk. Even if she knew about his smelly occupation prior to the wedding, she was legally permitted to end the marriage. She could claim she had no idea just how badly he would actually smell when he came home after a long, hard day smelting or collecting dung.

Big cities like Yerushlem had jobs unique to urban living, like water carriers, because it had to be brought from wells and stored in cisterns. Yerushlem was famous for its Valley of the Cheesemakers. Between the Temple Mount and the Upper City where the wealthy lived, a commercial district of artisans flourished. The spinners and carders generated miles of wool thread. Butchers and bakers prepared fresh, scrumptious foods; merchants sold all varieties of supplies — from oil that came from the Gethsemane olive oil presses — to wicks for the lamps. There were jewelers, glass blowers and glassmakers, souvenir craftsmen, even those who made the incense for the Temple and sold animals for sacrifice.

Yeshua had no idea what lay ahead in the Holy City. For now, the commotion at the roadside inn made his head spin. As Yeshua watered the two donkeys and prepared to tether them, Yosef headed to talk to the innkeeper. Miriam joined the women to help prepare a place for the fire. She grabbed a bundle of dried wood they had scavenged in Samaria and stowed in the wagon.

Yeshua patted Mo and Mazel while they drank from the trough. Suddenly there was a tug at Yeshua's tunic.

"Young man, young man, can you spare something for a cripple?" A beggar, who had come up behind him, startled Yeshua. The wealthy couple and the line of animals taking a drink had distracted the young Nazarene. "Adonai be praised. He has brought you to me," the beggar proclaimed hopefully.

As he turned to face the beggar, the first thought that went through Yeshua's mind was his friend Ezra. The man had a cane like Ezra's, but it was very old and worn. His clothes were tattered, and his hand shook with palsy as he stretched it outward. He held a small wooden cup. Perhaps he ate his meager meals in it.

Yeshua was moved with pity, and immediately began fumbling through his shoulder bag. Suddenly, there was another beggar standing at his side, crowding him and looking into the bag. Yeshua was surrounded, and although it was a little intimidating, he continued to rummage in his bag.

"Please, I haven't eaten today. Adonai has blessed you with a healthy body. Can't you help me?" the second beggar pleaded. He was a very old, feeble man, and his eyes met Yeshua's. For a moment, they stared at each other, and then Yeshua smiled at him. The man instinctively smiled back and then looked down. He wasn't used to having people respect him. In fact, in Yerushlem, these beggars would be considered the ha-aretz or people of the land. Pharisees and Sadducees, the religious elite, regarded them as social outcasts based on religious precepts. Their lower class lifestyle prevented them from tithing food and earnings to the Temple. It was also more difficult for them to follow the prescribed rituals, such as carefully cleansing their bodies before meals. They often grabbed a morsel wherever possible. The Temple ruling classes generally kept their distance from those on the lower rungs of society.

Yeshua dropped the donkeys' reigns to free up both hands, stepping on the tethers to make sure his animals didn't stroll off. He fished inside his shoulder bag for his tiny goatskin purse. He had been saving for this Passover pilgrimage for years. Some was money from his grandmother for the trip. He had also earned a little by selling a few of his carvings; occasionally someone would tip him a very small amount for delivering carpentry or masonry work that was particularly heavy.

Yeshua took out two coins, one for each beggar. As he handed them the money, he comforted them with one of his favorite Psalms.

"Because he clings to me I will deliver him;
because he knows my name I will set him on high.
He will call upon me and I will answer;
I will be with him in distress;
I will deliver him and give him honor.
With length of days I will satisfy him,
and fill him with my saving power." (Psalm 91:14-16)

The cripple kissed Yeshua's hand. "The Lord has indeed shown me his salvation today! Thank you; thank you. Shlama!"

"Shlama!" echoed the second beggar as he toddled off toward the inn. Now he could buy something to eat. He stopped after taking a few steps, and turned to look back at Yeshua.

"Thank you. You are a merciful young man," the grateful beggar said. Then the man joyfully proclaimed:

"You who dwell in the shelter of the Most High,
who abide in the shade of the Almighty,
Say to the LORD, 'My refuge and fortress,
my God in whom I trust.'" (Psalm 91:1-2)

Yeshua recognized the Scripture passage. He smiled at the beggar, and waved to him to acknowledge his gratitude and his unique response.

"For it is loyalty that I desire, not sacrifice,
and knowledge of God rather than burnt offerings," Yesh-
ua replied. (Hosea 6:6)

There was dramatic irony in the verse the man had chosen to recite, and in Yeshua's response. Little did the beggars know that Yeshua was the long promised Messiah, and that when the man thanked him, he was thanking the Son of God. He was the Savior the lower classes had been waiting for, while they were ground down by the challenges of daily life. Without health and wealth, living in these times was demanding drudgery, unless you had a firm hope in God, and the kind of peace that only He could offer. That alone could give people the strength to endure a lifestyle that required everything be done by hand, the sweat of the brow, and the tired, strained muscles of their backs.

Yeshua would have loved to heal the cripple and restore the health of the other beggar, but he knew it was not yet his time. His first job was to do his heavenly Father's will, as a human. He was the Word of God in the flesh, and his every action of compassion and mercy glorified his Father. Unfortunately, most of his people thought they had to follow more than 600 rules and laws in order to obey God. They knew these laws well, and had many debates about their interpretation and implementation. This frustrated Yeshua; he knew what his Father really wanted from his people was their love and forgiveness for each other — and not ritual, ceremonial washing, and burnt offerings.

On his way back from the innkeeper's quarters, Yosef had witnessed Yeshua's generosity. He walked over to his son, placing a hand on his shoulder while Yeshua tethered the animals.

"My son, I'm pleased to see you giving to the poor, but remember what I told you. When you get near the city, you're going to meet a lot of people who look friendly, but they're really thieves," he cautioned.

Yeshua nodded as he finished cinching the donkeys at the hitching post. All the animals were gathered around the trough. Other boys poured water in from jugs that had been brought from the well by the water carrier. The innkeeper had hired him for the Passover festival.

The Nazarenes scurried to set up their tents in the large courtyard. The wealthy people stayed inside the building. The sounds of partying poured from the dining hall. Some from the caravan sauntered inside to enjoy some wine, a few laughs, and an evening away from the outdoors. But most were too tired to bother. They bought food supplies from what was left at the tiny market outside the inn. Kefir, goat cheese, olives, fresh bread, dried fruits, and nuts would be dinner and breakfast in the morning. A few of the men would stay by the fire to keep watch all night. But at least the walls of the courtyard would help limit the danger.

Yosef, Miriam, and Yeshua enjoyed the dates and figs they'd bought along with some almonds. Miriam poured wine from a goatskin, and it went well with the music she strummed on her lyre.

Tomorrow they would be ascending toward the Temple Mount of Yerushlem. The excitement would swell. They were within two days or less of the Holy City. And even though the temperatures would be hot, perhaps they could walk the distance in less time.

After they said their evening prayer, Yeshua and Yosef reclined, exhausted. Miriam sat at the opening to the tent, and strummed her instrument as she sang a Psalm of Ascent. It was the traditional hymn many Passover pilgrims chanted as they climbed the terrain toward the Temple Mount. Miriam crooned in a soft, soothing voice as the camp drifted off to sleep in the moonlit courtyard.

"I wait for the LORD,
my soul waits

and I hope for his word.
My soul looks for the Lord
more than sentinels for daybreak.
More than sentinels for daybreak,
let Israel hope in the LORD,
For with the LORD is mercy,
with him is plenteous redemption,
And he will redeem Israel
from all its sins." (Psalm 130:5-8)

The camp was quiet as Miriam stopped playing and lay down for the night. She would need her rest tomorrow.

FOURTEEN

YESHUA WAS UP EARLY.

Even before Miriam stirred, he slipped out of the tent, slid into his sandals, and headed toward their wagon in the blue-grey morning light. He reached into the wagon, where he found one of the walking sticks he had brought along for the journey. He picked up a few tools and smoothed one end to prevent slivers and to create a more comfortable handle.

Quietly walking along the wall of the courtyard, he found the two beggars asleep in the corner. Yeshua set the new walking staff next to the cripple's old worn one. Then he reached into his tunic, and pulled out a loaf of the bread Yosef had bought the night before. He broke the bread and looked up to his heavenly Father to give quiet thanks.

"Abba. Blessed are You, O Lord our God, King of the universe, Who brings forth bread from the earth." [4]

Then he knelt down and wrapped the bread in a cloth between the two men. A dog sniffed around them and headed toward the food. Yeshua shooed the pup away. There were plenty of scraps to be had around the tents. He moved the bread under their blankets. If the dog came back, they would feel him poking his nose around inside their beds.

Yeshua smiled joyfully as he studied the faces of the beggars while they slept. They were exhausted from the heavy routine of panhandling for their daily bread. Today they would awaken and find that God had been very merciful. He had used a humble servant to bless them and answer their prayers.

Before anyone could see him, Yeshua slipped away, back toward his tent. One of the men standing guard at the fire stopped him. His name was Samuel.

"Yeshua, what were you doing over there?" he asked.

Out of respect, Yeshua stopped and said good morning. He explained that he had noticed the men when he woke up. He was curious about the old men.

That was the truth. He was eager to see how the men had fared through the night. But he was also being humble. Yeshua meant to downplay his generosity, not wanting to boast about his charity, or even reveal he had done a good deed. He was always mindful of the advice of Proverbs.

"When pride comes, disgrace comes;
but with the humble is wisdom." (Proverbs 11:2)

"You are a good boy, Yeshua," said Samuel the guard. "But be careful with these beggars. It's not like at home in Nazareth where you know everyone. All is not always what it seems. One minute you're giving, and the next, they're taking!"

Yeshua thanked him and headed back to the tent. By now, the sun was cracking open the horizon, and its light was piercing the gaps in the fabric at the flap of every tent. He found Miriam and Yosef already sitting up. They were surprised to see him awake and outside. Yeshua rubbed his hands together in the chilly morning air.

"Oh, my! You're already up and cooking. What did you make for breakfast?" Yosef joked. Miriam laughed loudly. That would be the day! Yeshua was rarely up first.

"I know you're hungry, Yeshua. You're always hungry. There's still bread and cheese in my bag from yesterday," Miriam said.

After washing, Yeshua reached in for the cheese, explaining that he had already helped himself to some bread this morning. He didn't tell his parents that he'd shared it with the beggars. He paused to say a prayer, and then began to eat the salty, delicious goat curds. He peeked out the flap of the tent to see his two friends standing in the distance. The crippled man was using his new walking stick, and the two beggars seemed to enjoy the bread as they plodded along the path. The sight warmed Yeshua's heart.

As he popped the last chunk of cheese into his mouth and licked his fingers, Yeshua told his parents he would get the cart ready. He was anxious to hit the road, and he reminded them they were less than two days away. Finally, Yeshua would see Yerushlem.

"You're a young man, Yeshua," Yosef mused. "You have a lifetime of Passovers to spend in Yerushlem." But he understood his son's excitement.

Yeshua hustled to organize the supplies onboard the wagon. He signaled the water carrier, who brought him a large jug, almost the size used for purification at wedding feasts. With the man's help, Yeshua hefted it aboard the wagon and filled several containers. It would be a scorcher of a day as they moved up the elevation and closer to the desert. The Judean sands ran both hot and waterless for miles south of the Holy City.

Next, Yeshua shook out the blankets and cushions. His mother had brought a small broom, which he used to sweep the dust out of the wagon. Then he rearranged the cushions.

By this time, Yosef had packed up the tent and was heading over to the wagon to help. Yeshua led their two donkeys, Mo and Mazel. He had already watered them for the day's trip. They looked happy to be untied, free to roam and walk on the trail ahead. Mo always made Yeshua laugh. He had a kind of knowing look on his face, like "Here we go again! I know where we're headed. I've been down this road before. You hitch me up, and I pull you along. Then we eat, and you hitch me up again, and I pull you along."

Yeshua greeted the animals with a rub on their snouts as he and Yosef yoked them together. It wasn't a heavy wooden yoke like oxen wore. This was a single wooden pole that rested on their shoulders, attached to leather and cloth harnesses that went around their necks. Mo and Mazel also wore a pair of blinders to keep them focused on the road ahead, but Mo always had a way of looking around corners, up in the air, down on the ground, and anywhere but straight in front of him. Curiosity was his trademark. They had joked about changing his name to "Hah-Tsee-dah" which means sideways in Hebrew. From time to time, Yeshua would call him that just for fun.

Miriam was busy buying supplies for the next two days. Barley loaves, yogurt, olives, fresh fruit, dried fruit, and nuts. The other women haggled with a fishmonger who had brought a cart-full of freshly dried fish. These were Mediterranean saltwater fish, and they would be delicious at dinner. They struck a deal to buy nearly half his cart. It would be enough for all the Nazarenes to enjoy at Sabbath supper that evening.

The caravan would rest for a day, and then, barring emergency, they would arrive in Yerushlem during the fifth day of travel. The big question was the traffic. Would they reach Yerushlem at nightfall on the fifth day – or could they enjoy the afternoon in the Holy City?

Soon the caravan was on its way with renewed enthusiasm and energy. Sleeping at the inn had been more comfortable. Water and food were plentiful there, and everyone felt safer. They slept soundly, rather than with one eye open. The pilgrims were on the main north-south highway to Yerushlem. The Romans had paved it with stone, so footing was sure and travel was faster. When the caravan had decided to take the shortest route through Samaria, they were on the wilderness trail, where traffic was very light. Most of the people they passed were Samaritans; since most Jews avoided the region they considered a land of heretics.

Today would be different. It didn't take long for other caravans and travelers from nearby inns to merge into the traffic.

"Coming through, coming through," the litter bearers shouted as they jogged along behind the Nazarenes. It was the wealthy couple and their luggage. Their 18 slaves were Africans. They were very tall and very quick. Each litter was topped with a canopy to protect its passenger from the sun. Nets helped keep out the bugs and offered a bit of privacy. The litter bearers kicked up dust as they briskly moved up the road, running to a repetitive rhythm they sang. It was a real example of teamwork.

Yosef insisted on managing the beasts this morning. He warned Yeshua it would be a hectic day.

Suddenly, the Africans accelerated to pass the Nazarenes. Within seconds they had run by the entire caravan and were a good 20 yards ahead. As the litters swept by, the animals lurched. Instinctively, Yosef muscled them back in line, but he rolled his ankle on the edge of one of the Roman stone pavers. It was a serious sprain and he hobbled about in obvious pain.

Yeshua quickly jumped out of the wagon to help his father. Other men came over, too. One of them ran down the caravan and came back with the doctor.

"I can walk, I can walk," Yosef insisted.

"Let's get him up in the wagon and off the road," one man said.

Before Yosef could protest again, two men lifted him and put him in the cart next to Miriam. Yeshua had already grabbed the tether to control Mo and Mazel. The doctor climbed aboard the wagon and was soon wrapping Yosef's ankle. He tied the cloth bandages very tightly. Yeshua continued to pull the wagon along. The caravan had to keep moving; this was too small an incident to stop their progress.

"Keep that foot propped up on the side of the wagon," the doctor commanded Yosef. "That's your best hope to reduce the swelling. Those bandages are snug. As soon as we take them off, that ankle will grow like a melon at harvest."

"Here's a cushion to put under your foot," Miriam said as she lifted his leg and placed it on the board that framed the side of the wagon. "Now lie back and relax, if you want to enjoy the Passover."

"Fine. Fine. I'll rest it for the morning," Yosef replied. "After lunch, I'm sure I will be able to walk on it." The doctor shook his head. "Yosef, you have a capable, healthy son. It's fortunate you have Yeshua along, so Miriam won't have to lead the cart to Yerushlem. Maybe if you rest all day today, you'll be able to walk after the Sabbath. It's a bad sprain," said the doctor, as he carefully slid off the moving wagon.

Yosef wasn't convinced the injury was that serious, but between Miriam and the doctor, he found no support for his diagnosis. Besides, he could help Yeshua by spotting traffic from up on his perch in the cart. From time to time, he would sit up and look to the rear to see who was coming along to pass them.

People converged on Yerushlem from all around the known world. This was the most famous city in the East. The Hebrew world came to worship at the Temple three times a year: Passover in March or April; Shavuot, the Festival of Weeks in late May; and Succoth, the Festival of Tabernacles in late September. But no festival compared to Passover.

On the sea and on the roads, there were Jews from the entire Holy Land, but also Parthians, Medes and Elamites, and those of Mesopotamia, Judah and Cappadocia, Pontus, and Asia. There were visitors from Rome, Egypt, Phrygia and Libya, Arabia, and the island of Crete.

The rich came on fancy chariots, carriages, and litters. Some commoners walked the entire distance. Others rode beasts, and some, like Yeshua's family, traveled by cart or wagon. The ravens and kites soaring above witnessed hundreds of thousands of pilgrims flowing over the four roads to Yerushlem. They would fill the Holy City with a mass of humanity united by a belief in one God, greater than all other gods. Even more powerful than the gods of the Romans, the people who occupied their land.

Yeshua felt a sense of great responsibility as he piloted the family wagon on the highway. The pace was brisk and unrelenting. It seemed as if they were traveling twice as fast today, despite the climb toward Yerushlem. The anticipation was palpable. Everyone wanted to be part of this historic event. There was always a sense of hope in the air, hope that this Passover might mark the coming of the Messiah, the promised one to free Israel of her burdens. Certainly he would drive out the occupiers, ransom Yerushlem, and restore her to full glory in the name of Yahweh. That was a typical interpretation of the Messiah and his reign. Yeshua knew it would be different.

"It's the Romans! Romans are coming!" Yosef sounded a warning from atop the wagon, and he wasn't talking about Roman Jews. These were soldiers. Yosef had scooted to the rear of the wagon, and sat atop the backboard to gain a better vantage point.

A legion of Roman soldiers was moving at a high speed, forcing the caravan to make room for them on the road. Yeshua steered his donkeys to the right so the troops could pass on the left. They rode magnificently powerful horses. Mules, bred from male donkeys and female horses, pulled their supply wagons. Mules were typically faster than donkeys and more sure-footed than horses. These were heavyweights, perhaps the offspring of workhorse mares. Yeshua had never seen anything like this Roman military parade. It roared by like some kind of machine with thundering hooves, spinning wheels, clanging armor, and other noises that were frightening and exhilarating at the same time. The horses were beautiful blacks, mahoganies, and browns. Yeshua laughed as they passed. It was as vivid as one of his dreams.

And then it happened.

One of the Roman carts clipped the wagon behind Yeshua, breaking its axle. The Romans continued their march, unfazed by the crash, but the pilgrims were devastated. A husband and wife and mother-in-law now had a disabled cart. And the town carpenter had only one working leg. Everyone stopped. Yeshua and others ran to assist the startled trio.

Instantly, a young Roman centurion pulled up on his horse. He pointed at Yeshua.

"You, hold my animal!" the soldier commanded. Yosef had already slid down off the cart. He stood on one leg and grabbed the tether to Mo and Mazel. Yeshua stepped over toward the Roman, and took a firm hold of the horse's bridle as the centurion jumped down out of his saddle. He began barking orders and pointing in different directions. The Roman legion continued to march past as if nothing had happened.

"Yeshua, be careful!" Miriam shouted.

"Who has room for these people? Who can take their goods? Their animals?" the centurion cried. He spoke fluent Aramaic. He was focused on public safety. The disabled cart was a hazard to the troops that needed to pass the pilgrims. He ran up and down the caravan, and within minutes had placed the stranded travelers and their luggage aboard various carriages. However, most of the Hebrews refused to make eye contact with him, focusing on his feet when he spoke to them. Their body language seemed to say, "We might have to obey you, but you're not welcome in our land."

A limping Yosef volunteered to tether the couple's donkey to his wagon, and said he'd be sure to water it. Several men helped pull the broken wagon off the road. Perhaps the family could recover it on the return trip if it was still there, but there was no time to repair it now.

The Roman's horse mesmerized Yeshua. It was jet black and its mane was braided with metal accents. The steed's eyes were dark and deep, yet alert. The animal moved his head up and down in a rhythmic cadence, and his hindquarter muscle spasmed as he settled down. Yeshua patted the horse's nose, and reached into the bag on his belt for one of the treats he kept for his donkeys. He found a piece of sweet, dried fruit, and the horse nibbled it off his palm. The intricately crafted saddle was cinched tightly on its back. Leather stirrups were bolstered with metal sheaths. Everything about this horse and his tack was precise and sturdy.

Yeshua marveled at the quality and craftsmanship of the materials. He also noticed everything about the creature, storing it in his memory for future artwork. With this new perspective, he could make so many improvements to the horse he had carved for Ezra. He had mostly seen horses from a distance. He closed his eyes for a few seconds, and said a prayer for his friend back home. He wished that Ezra could have been with him to share this moment. This would be an exciting tale to tell him when Yeshua returned to Nazareth. He could see Ezra's wide-eyed expression. The thought made him grin.

Whenever the centurion walked past, the horse followed his master's voice. Yeshua was impressed; it reminded him of the way sheep and goats know their shepherd's voice.

This Roman soldier talked fast, and was dead set on keeping the Passover traffic moving. He had two jobs: get his men to Yerushlem in time to police the enormous crowds during the festival, and make sure he kept the Hebrew people pacified. The Roman governor, and for that matter Caesar, wanted an uneventful Passover. There would be lots of taxes to collect after the pilgrims poured money into the economy of the Holy City.

Festivals always heightened the political intrigue. The city brimmed with Hebrews, many longing for the days when Israel ruled the Promised Land, and had determined its own destiny in line with the laws of the Torah. Revolutionaries had constantly waged insurrections during the Roman rule and occupation. The Zealots had launched a major rebellion when Yeshua was about six years old, but their leader, Judas of Galilee, died in battle. Some of his followers survived and turned hilltop caves and mountain crevices into secret forts. From there, they continued to pursue stubborn guerilla attacks, and ambushed Roman troops throughout the Holy Land. To some Israelites, these rebels were patriots and heroes. Although they had limited, real impact on the mighty Roman forces, they were a serious nuisance.

Caesar's domain was sprawling. He governed some 30 provinces across two million square miles. The last thing he needed was a major uprising in Yerushlem near critical roads and seaports, which would threaten the world's trade passing through the region. He wanted the economy and tax revenues to keep flowing. Force his hand, and his governor would crucify hundreds, even thousands, to quickly quell a rebellion. That had happened just a few years earlier, when a power struggle ensued after the death of Herod the Great. Varus, the Roman governor of Syria, squashed the insurrection and viciously crucified 2,000 captives. The carnage was so overwhelming, some people thought it was the end of the world. In reality, it was the end of the challenge to Roman power, at least for a while.

The centurion was young, strong, tall, and handsome. He wore a steel breastplate and a polished helmet with a plume of red bristles at the top. His sword was short and shiny, snugged in the metal sheath on his right hip. He was left-handed. In his native language, Latin, "sinister" meant left. It was a military advantage. Most people were right-handed and wore swords on their left hips. A left-handed swordsman could appear to be unarmed if his enemy failed to notice the weapon on his right side.

The soldier also had a dagger in his belt on the left. On the back of his belt hung a small pick ax, used for digging and cutting trees when his troops built fortifications in the field. Because he was an officer, his ax was clean and barely used. His kilt was made of metal-covered leather, woven in a mesh to protect his legs, while offering free movement, especially on horseback. On his shins he wore brass greaves, and straps from his sandals crisscrossed up his calves under the greaves. The soles of his footwear were studded to grip the turf.

Yeshua studied his physique and his armor. They were intimidating. But his personality wasn't. He was a confident professional with a job to do, and right now, this task was finished. The centurion turned on his heels, snatched up his horse's reins, and saddled up quickly. He nodded to Yeshua, acknowledging his brief service, but he did not smile. Yeshua smiled and nodded back at him. Then the Roman rode off to join the column of soldiers and supplies snaking their way up toward Yerushlem.

"That's the Tenth Legion!" Yosef called to Yeshua. "They occupy the Holy City. I'm sure those are reinforcements for the Passover festival. They will be all over the city, except in the Temple."

"They came all the way from Rome?" Miriam asked.

"Who knows?" Yosef replied. "They could be from anywhere in their empire. But every year at Passover, we've seen the Roman ranks in Yerushlem really grow. They double or triple the guard." He remembered it well, having worked there for a few years, building the Temple and maintaining Herodium.

The caravan followed behind the Roman legion shortly after it passed. But the soldiers were out of sight within a minute. The stop for lunch today would be cut short to make up for the time lost with the crash. Many of the travelers grumbled about how careless and uncompassionate the Romans had been, damaging a wagon. Only the centurion had stopped to see if anyone was hurt. They hated their occupiers and their taxes. Incidents like the crashed cart only rubbed salt into their wounds. Yeshua knew he and his nation had to forgive the Romans and pray for them, but few would listen to that advice from a 12-year-old boy. It was not yet his time to preach. But he would soon share his wisdom and understanding of God's will. That day would come much sooner than Miriam and Yosef ever imagined.

chapter

FIFTEEN

EVEN YOUTHFUL ENERGY HAS LIMITS.

As the fourth day on the road ended, Yeshua sighed with exhaustion. He had walked from sunrise until late afternoon, leading two donkeys as they towed the family wagon and another animal up the trail. His mother had offered to spell him several times, but he urged her to take care of his father aboard the wagon. Yeshua continued to prove he was truly capable of stepping up when needed.

The Sabbath started at sunset, so it was critical they arrived long before dusk to set up tents, build fires, and cook their meals. No work was permitted after the start of the sacred seventh day of rest, which began at nightfall on Friday and ended at nightfall on Saturday. The Israelites defined each day from sunset to sunset.

Despite the traffic and the encounter with Roman troops, the caravan had made surprisingly good time and pulled up for the night at an inn just north of Gabaon. The name means "hill city," and it was less than 10 miles from the Temple Mount. This area was famous in the Holy Scriptures. Before the Temple was built, the Israelites had set up the Tabernacle at Gabaon. It was also a temporary seat of government after Nebuchadnezzar and his Babylonian warriors had destroyed Yerushlem.

Pilgrims packed the inn well beyond its capacity. Although they had only about a half-day of travel remaining to get to the Holy

City, the road would be slower. They expected heavier congestion after the Sabbath because the Passover festival was very near.

Dead on their feet, the Nazarenes set up camp in the late afternoon sun. Miriam and Yosef purchased food, and Yeshua tied up the donkeys and watered them. Yosef hobbled along with the third animal he was managing for his neighbors whose cart had crashed. Ephraim, the donkey's owner, met him at the hitching post. He thanked Yosef profusely.

"After the Sabbath, I will buy a yoke and hitch my beast with Gideon's donkey. His animal is old and tired," said Ephraim. "I'm glad to know my loss is a blessing to someone," he added.

"You're a thoughtful man, Ephraim. Don't worry," Yosef said to console him. "If we can't repair your cart on the way home, then you and I will build another as soon as we get to Nazareth." Ephraim smiled broadly and embraced Yosef. He was relieved; now he could enjoy his Sabbath and Passover.

Several women were baking bread inside the inn, and the aroma was heavenly. They made enough for two days. Tomorrow was the Sabbath, and there would be no work in the kitchen until after sundown.

Back at the cart, Yeshua guzzled water. Miriam and Yosef quickly set up their tent. Yeshua helped them pound in the stakes.

Miriam unwrapped her husband's ankle. It was swollen and throbbing. She had Yosef soak it in a bucket of ice-cold well water; he struggled to keep his foot submerged for a long stretch of time. Miriam pushed down on his knee to encourage him to deal with the cold. Many farmers in the region used well water for refrigeration. They would lower a bucket of milk, or a chunk of cheese deep into the well, allowing the container to float in the icy ground water. It would chill the bucket, helping to keep its contents fresh. This was a great way to firm up and preserve a bowl of freshly churned butter on a hot day.

"Good work, Miriam," said the doctor as he passed by. He had given her his prescription at lunchtime. Not coincidentally, he had pitched his tent near Miriam and Yosef so he could keep a watchful eye on the carpenter's injury. He wondered if Yosef had broken a bone.

The camp was particularly congested because the innkeeper welcomed several caravans onto his land. One of his watchmen urged people to squeeze in tightly.

"Closer, closer," he barked. "Pitch your tent as close as you can to your neighbor's. Don't waste space. You can get closer. Don't worry, everyone smells and every one snores."

The pilgrims laughed at his jokes. It was a festive atmosphere. Even though they were road weary, it was good to be in a safe place with fresh food to purchase and only one more day to travel to Yerushlem. Tomorrow they would rest on the Sabbath. There would be more time for sleep, salving wounds, worship, and prayer.

As the sun dropped in the sky, every family in the Nazarene camp prayed and enjoyed a quiet Sabbath meal at their tents. Miriam, Yosef, and Yeshua dined on fresh bread and fish, dipping the still-warm loaves in the newly pressed olive oil. Then they ate honey, as well, with cheese, dates, and figs. All around the camp, fathers and mothers could be heard saying the various Sabbath prayers, including this one over the wine:

> _"And there was evening and there was morning, a sixth day. The heavens and the earth were finished, the whole host of them and on the seventh day God completed his work that he had done and he rested on the seventh day from all his work that he had done and God blessed the seventh day, and sanctified it because in it he had rested from all his work that God had created to do._

> _"Blessed are You, Eternal our God, Ruling Presence of the Universe, Creator of the fruit of the vine._

> _"Blessed are You, Eternal our God, Ruling Presence of the_

Universe, who has sanctified us with commandments and finds favor in us; giving us the holy Sabbath as a heritage in love and favor, a remembrance of the creation, that day being also the first among all the holy occasions, a reminder of the Exodus from Egypt. For You have chosen us and hallowed us above all nations giving us Your holy Sabbath as a heritage in love and favor. Blessed are You, Eternal One, who sanctifies the Sabbath."[5]

After he drank a little wine and finished his dinner, Yeshua crawled inside the tent and went to bed. He began nodding off while he said his evening prayers.

Miriam and Yosef sat in the opening to their tent, taking in the night air.

Miriam very quietly sang Sabbath hymns, but she couldn't strum her lyre after sundown because work was forbidden on the Sabbath. She often puzzled over that prohibition. It wasn't that praising God with music was outlawed on the day of rest, but it was feared that a musician might break a string or other part of an instrument and have to work to repair it. That work was unacceptable. This was an interpretation of God's law that had been changed about the time of the second Temple.

As she sang, Miriam listened to the bleating of sheep and goats in a corral near the inn. Sunday morning, after the Sabbath, Yosef would buy one of the animals for their Passover sacrifice. It would be more affordable here than in the Holy City. The innkeeper knew he had a sales advantage, so he had a large flock of animals available. This was another reason travel would be slower when they hit the road again. Many people would be towing or carrying lambs and kid goats.

Yeshua listened to his mother's singing, and he was asleep almost instantly. Soon he was dreaming about the horse he had met that day — a big, sleek, black stallion. It was such a magnificent, powerful animal. In his dream, he followed the horse, as if in a parade.

People lined the road on both sides, and they shouted and chanted, but he couldn't hear them.

Suddenly, the steed stopped right in front of him, and whipped his tail back and forth. Yeshua tried to lean back out of the way, but couldn't as the horse backed up toward him. When Yeshua turned his head to look away, the faces in the crowd were angry and shook their fists at him.

When he looked down, he could see his wrists were tied to a rope in front of him. As he glanced up, suddenly, the horse ran away, and two Roman soldiers stood in its place. Each had a short whip in hand. The Roman flagrum was a wicked device with leather straps that held tiny lead balls and sharp fragments of sheep's bone. Two soldiers wielding these weapons could shred their victim's flesh within minutes.

Yeshua felt powerless, as one of the soldiers raised the whip and swung it to scourge him across the back and side.

"You're dreaming, Yeshua! It's only a dream!" Miriam said as she shook her son to wake him. He had been calling out in the night. The only light in the tent was the very faint glow from the campfire outside.

"Give him some wine," Yosef suggested. "It will calm him."

Yeshua was sweating. His garment was soaked. Miriam groped around the corner of the tent to find the goatskin vessel. She gave him a sip of wine and helped him remove his shirt. She toweled the sweat off his neck, chest, and back and covered him with her blanket.

"What were you dreaming about, Yeshua?" Yosef asked in a quiet, soothing voice.

Yeshua explained he had a vision with a black horse and Roman soldiers.

"I told you he worked too hard today," Yosef said. "Too much sun! I will lead the wagon from now on."

"Let's all sleep now," Miriam said, as she smoothed Yeshua's hair with her hand, and kissed him on the cheek. "We will need our rest after the Sabbath. God willing, we will leave the camp early on

Sunday. We don't want all of Nazareth waiting for the carpenter's family on Sunday morning."

They lay down their heads, and Miriam continued to stroke her son's hair to help him fall back to sleep. She knew he had a vivid imagination, and hoped he could avoid another nightmare. Yeshua had troubling dreams from time to time, and told his mother stories that fascinated and frightened her. She was happy he would confide in her, but she suspected his nightmares were more than just stories. She had very good reason to be concerned.

Forty days after Yeshua was born in Bethlehem, and just over a month after his official naming and circumcision, Miriam and Yosef took him to the Temple in Yerushlem to follow God's law as handed down by Moses.

> *"Consecrate to me every firstborn; whatever opens the womb among the Israelites, whether of human being or beast, belongs to me." (Exodus 13:2)*

They offered a pair of doves as a sacrifice, also in keeping with the law. And there in the Temple was a devout man named Simeon. He told Miriam and Yosef that God had made a marvelous promise to him. God revealed that Simeon would not die until he had seen the Messiah. Simeon said that God's Holy Spirit told him to go to the Temple on this day. When he saw Miriam and Yosef arrive carrying the newborn Yeshua, he heard a voice in his heart telling him he had seen the Christ!

> *"Now, Master, you may let your servant go*
> *in peace, according to your word,*
> *for my eyes have seen your salvation,*
> *which you prepared in sight of all the peoples,*
> *a light for revelation to the Gentiles,*
> *and glory for your people Israel." (Luke 2: 29-32)*

Miriam and Yosef were filled with excitement and bewilderment at these words. Only they and a few family members knew of Yeshua's virgin birth and its purpose. And now Simeon had approached them, and independently confirmed that God had sent their new baby boy to fulfill an almighty mission. He was indeed the Messiah. Oh, what a miraculous blessing! They were unworthy of this heavenly gift, which had been promised to generations for thousands of years.

Simeon could read the emotions on their faces. He blessed Yeshua's parents. Taking Miriam's hand, he said,

"Behold, this child is destined for the fall and rise of many in Israel, and to be a sign that will be contradicted (and you yourself a sword will pierce) so that the thoughts of many hearts may be revealed." (Luke 2: 34-35)

The old man's words haunted Miriam. What could he mean by his warning that a sword would pierce her? Obviously, he didn't mean she would die by the sword, but something would happen that would shake her very faith and trust in God. How could this be when God had blessed her so? Why did God want her to endure this pain and sorrow?

Yosef was also dismayed by Simeon's prophecy. So much about this child had been trouble from the moment of conception. Little did he know they would soon be running for their lives to Egypt — to protect Yeshua from the wrath of a maniacal King Herod.

Simeon held the tiny infant in his hands, and raised him up in the Temple to offer Yeshua to Yahweh. He was awestruck, trembling as if he had seen the face of God. Tears streamed down Simeon's cheeks. These were tears of joy. The Holy Spirit had filled the old faithful believer's mind and heart.

As he handed Yosef his baby son, a woman approached. Simeon said, "This is Hannah, she is a very holy woman and a prophetess."

She had been listening discreetly to their conversation. Hannah was elderly. Her husband had died only seven years after they married. She was now 84, and had lived all those many years in Yerushlem as a widow. Hannah spent all day and night in the Temple. Never leaving, she worshiped, fasted, and prayed. At the sight of Yeshua, she broke into songs of praise:

> "Bless the LORD, my soul;
> all my being, bless his holy name!
> Bless the LORD, my soul;
> and do not forget all his gifts,
> Who pardons all your sins,
> and heals all your ills,
> Who redeems your life from the pit,
> and crowns you with mercy and compassion,
> Who fills your days with good things,
> so your youth is renewed like the eagle's." (Psalm 103:1-5)

Tears of joy streamed down Hannah's cheeks, too, as she leaned in to see Yeshua's precious little face. Until the day she died, Hannah gave thanks to God and spoke about Yeshua and Simeon's prophecy to anyone who would listen. Her passionate words brought great hope and anticipation to all who longed for Israel's redemption. A few of the elderly in the Temple who had listened to Simeon and Hannah were still alive when Yeshua took his first Passover pilgrimage to Yerushlem. They were waiting for the Messiah's triumphant reign.

Miriam and Yosef had never forgotten that day with Simeon and the devout woman who lived in the Temple. They knew Yeshua was part of God's salvation plan. But they wondered how he would save his people. Every time they returned to the Temple for Passover, they recalled the first time Yeshua entered the holy place, the day he was consecrated to Yahweh as his firstborn. And now he would return.

chapter
SIXTEEN

THE SABBATH COULDN'T HAVE COME AT A BETTER TIME. It gave Yosef a full day to rest his ankle without travel. After sundown on Saturday, the Nazarene camp prepared for an early departure the next day.

Yosef was the first to wake up on Sunday, and he hobbled around the camp, ready to hit the road. He had already said his morning prayer, washed himself, and eaten. The night before he had fashioned a crutch for himself from pieces of wood he'd stowed on the wagon. He'd bound his ankle tightly with cloth bandages. The combination of rest, elevation, and cold and warm water soaking had done wonders for the swelling and flexibility. But the ankle was still tender.

"Wake up. There's no time to waste," Yosef called to Miriam and Yeshua. "How do you feel, son?"

Yeshua wiped the sleep from his eyes and nodded. He had gone a whole night without another bad dream. Miriam spotted the crutch under Yosef's arm and shook her head.

"My husband, I don't think you should walk today, unless the doctor approves," Miriam suggested.

"I'll go see him as soon as we pack up the tent," Yosef replied. "Say your prayers, Yeshua, and let's get to work."

Miriam and Yeshua obeyed Yosef, and said their morning prayer together. Then they both washed and ate a little breakfast. It was obvious Yosef had already eaten some of the yogurt they had bought when the Sabbath ended. They also enjoyed fresh bread and some honey. Yosef had purchased it at the inn. The wheat loaves were still warm.

Throughout the camp, the excitement was palpable. For obvious reasons, the innkeeper's staff attended to the wealthy guests first, many of them purchasing the choicest lambs for their Passover sacrifice. They were the first to hit the road. The caravans took longer to assemble, as people haggled to get a decent price on the livestock. One rich man saw Yosef leaning on his crutch, and insisted he take his place in line.

"I'm Yosef, the carpenter. If you're ever in Nazareth, I would be honored to have you as a guest in my home," he responded gratefully.

"Does anything good come from Nazareth?" the rich man joked, poking fun at the small, country town.

Embarrassed, Yosef smiled and the man laughed.

"Thank you for giving me your place in line," Yosef said, as he cast his eyes downward.

"Even King David showed kindness to the lame," the man replied.

Yosef nodded respectfully. He remembered the Scripture story where David provided for a man whose feet were crippled. Meribbaal was his name and he was the grandson of the late King Saul. Yosef then answered to the rich man, the same way the disabled Meribbaal had responded to King David:

"What am I, your servant, that you should pay attention to a dead dog like me?" (2 Samuel 9:8)

Humbled, the man reached out, and touched Yosef on the shoulder in appreciation. They had shared a spiritual moment, and the rich man was rewarded for his mercy.

When Yeshua saw his father hobbling along, leading a little lamb on a tether, he ran to help him. It was painfully obvious Yosef would not be able to walk the eight or ten miles to Yerushlem, or even half the distance.

Yeshua suggested his father rest for another day.

"I'm going to see the doctor now," Yosef replied. "Otherwise, I'll never hear the end of your mother's complaining!"

Yeshua walked along with the young animal in tow. His mother was already making room for it in the wagon. Yeshua lifted him up, and the animal scurried about in the cart, his hooves knock-knock-knocking on the wooden floor. Miriam quickly tied his tether through a knothole in the side of the wagon, giving him a short leash in the corner.

By the time Yeshua had secured Mo and Mazel in the yoke, Yosef and the doctor had returned.

"I understand it's demanding work in the sun for Yeshua. But I think one more day of rest, and you will be mended enough to enjoy the Passover. But it's your decision, Yosef. Otherwise, you will not be able to climb the steps of the Temple," the doctor cautioned, making sure Miriam heard his advice.

Disappointed, Yosef nodded in agreement. "Thank you, doctor. May your journey be smooth. Shlama," he said.

Yosef insisted on paying the physician for his services. Most people on the pilgrimage provided their skills for free. But the doctor got little rest. There were many maladies to treat, wounds to cleanse, and aches and pains to medicate with balms, herbs, and other natural therapies.

Miriam was relieved that the doctor had finally convinced Yosef to rest his ankle another day. She happily went off to purchase a little more food for the day's journey. When she returned, Yeshua helped her and his father into the wagon, and they were soon positioned at the head of the caravan, ready to roll out of camp. Yosef had spent so much time in and around Yerushlem as a younger man; now he would lead the way. He was an expert on the city.

Despite his disappointment, Yosef couldn't conceal his enthusiasm. Yerushlem was a bit of a homecoming for him. It was always inspiring to be at the Temple, especially during the festival.

The road was not only jammed with pilgrims, but it was festive and noisy today. Within minutes, the traffic slowed, and the caravan moved at about half the normal pace. At this rate, it could take all day to reach the Temple Mount.

"If we hope to arrive in Yerushlem at a reasonable time, we will have to travel through lunch," Yosef shouted to the caravan behind him. Soon the message was passed along, all the way through the Nazarene contingent.

And the answer echoed back from family to family until it reverberated in Yosef's ears.

"'Let us go to the house of the LORD,'" the pilgrims chanted. (Psalm 122:1)

Miriam pulled out her lyre and began to strum the instrument. The rabbi's boy, Benjamin, joined in, beating his drum, while another man played his flute. Soon they were singing Psalms one after the other. These were Passover Psalms pilgrims had sung for centuries. They shared the exuberance any good Jew would feel, while approaching the Holy City to celebrate God's great act of mercy for his Chosen People.

They began with King David's famous song of ascents. The spiritual connection brought tears to Yeshua's eyes. Many people were crying with joy. For some, this would be their only trip to the Temple. Everyone in the caravan sang:

> *"I rejoiced when they said to me,*
> *Let us go to the house of the LORD.'*
> *And now our feet are standing*
> *within your gates, Jerusalem.*
> *Jerusalem, built as a city,*
> *walled round about.*
> *There the tribes go up,*
> *the tribes of the LORD,*
> *As it was decreed for Israel,*

to give thanks to the name of the LORD.
There are the thrones of justice,
the thrones of the house of David.

For the peace of Jerusalem pray:
'May those who love you prosper!
May peace be within your ramparts,
prosperity within your towers.'
For the sake of my brothers and friends I say,
'Peace be with you.'
For the sake of the house of the LORD, our God,
I pray for your good." (Psalm 122:2-9)

The energy was contagious and the caravan picked up speed. The music and the singing reminded everyone of their journey's purpose. With the festive mood, the drudgery of the dusty, climbing road, and the rising temperatures were quickly forgotten.

People shared food and beverages among their wagons. At lunchtime, the Nazarenes stopped just long enough to water the animals, and rest them briefly before resuming the climb toward the Temple. With each step and bend in the road, their sense of anticipation rose. The Pilgrims watched the horizon for the first sign of the Holy City. Yosef had talked to those making their first pilgrimage, and had raised their expectations with his descriptions and stories. Among the newcomers, their imaginations were racing. They envisioned the sight of the Temple with its walls adorned in gleaming gold, reflecting the sun like a beacon of faith, just as Yosef had described. And Yeshua was every bit as anxious as the other new Passover pilgrims. After all, the Temple was his heavenly Father's house.

As midafternoon approached, suddenly, there it was on the horizon, a golden glint shimmering atop the vista, above the heads of the pilgrims snaking their way up the highway to Yerushlem.

"To you I raise my eyes,
   to you enthroned in heaven,"

Yosef shouted as he stood on his crutch in the wagon. He was reciting the start of another song of ascents to the Holy City.

Then Eli, who was leading his wagon right behind Yosef's, called
out the second verse.

"Yes, like the eyes of servants
   on the hand of their masters," he sang.

Miriam began playing her lyre again, and Avigail sang with her
from her seat on the caravan:

"Like the eyes of a maid
   on the hand of her mistress,
   So our eyes are on the LORD our God,
   till we are shown favor.
   Show us favor, LORD, show us favor,
   for we have our fill of contempt," sang Yeshua.
   (Psalm 123:1-3)

All of Nazareth cheered at the sight of their destination. They were
within a mile of the city. After another few minutes, more of the
Temple and Yerushlem were visible. Now they could see the high
walls and four major roads converging.

Thanks to the wealth and power of the late King Herod the
Great, Yerushlem was one of the most impressive cities in the world.
Thanks to God, it was still a holy place for believers. For a devout
Jew, it was breathtaking.

"Stop! Stop your beasts!" shouted a Roman soldier as he thrust
his hand out in front of Yeshua. It was obvious Aramaic was not his
native language.

The soldier appeared to come out of nowhere. It was as if he'd risen right out of the road. Actually, everyone had had their eyes fixed on the hills of the Holy City, Yeshua included. They had failed to notice the Roman guard who was stationed along a curve in the road to control congestion.

"Let us pass!" shouted Eli as he walked up next to Yeshua.

"The city is overwhelmed," said the soldier, struggling to speak the language of the Jewish pilgrims. "We're controlling the traffic. Get back in line."

Another soldier took a step toward Eli to make sure he got the message. Eli was a tough old farmer and he wasn't really afraid. He made eye contact with both Romans.

"Eli! Come back here and protect your daughters," Judith shouted. She was panicked for their safety, and worried her husband would say or do something they would all regret.

The Romans and the Jew stared at each other. Two other guards stepped forward.

Now Ephraim climbed down from the wagon he was riding to support Eli. He stepped up behind him and put his hand on his shoulder. The situation was escalating.

"Your troops damaged my cart just the other day. They delayed our whole caravan," Ephraim said, shaking with anger. "Now, let us pass."

Suddenly, the caravan grew silent, as those in the front stood in their wagons to get a better view of the impending conflict.

Judith held her breath and put her arms around her daughters. She knew any one of the Roman guards could arrest Eli and Ephraim. The thought was agonizing.

Just then, Yeshua reached out, gently touched Eli's other shoulder and smiled at Ephraim. He began to chant another song of ascent in a calm, confident voice so the whole caravan could hear him.

"Had not the LORD been with us,

let Israel say,
Had not the LORD been with us,
when people rose against us,
Then they would have swallowed us alive,
for their fury blazed against us."

They could all feel the fever of the moment break. Miriam began playing her lyre and others joined in, beating drums and clapping along. Yeshua continued.

"Then the waters would have engulfed us,
the torrent overwhelmed us;
then seething water would have drowned us."

The words of the Psalm celebrated Israel's escape from oppression in Egypt. It glorified the fruit of the Lord's Passover. It reminded Eli and Ephraim why they were on the journey, and it quelled their anger. Eli nodded to Yeshua. He put his arm around Ephraim's shoulder, and the two headed back toward their carts.

Yeshua laughed as he sang on:

"Blessed is the LORD, who did not leave us
to be torn by their teeth."

At that point, the guardsmen took one step back in formation. One of the Romans noticed that traffic ahead had cleared. He turned and waved his arm, gesturing to the Nazarene caravan and those behind them to resume their travel to Yerushlem.

Yeshua tugged on the tether to alert Mo and Mazel, and they stomped and started moving. The four Romans stepped clear. Not only had the Nazarenes avoided a disastrous conflict, but also the road was now much less congested. There was an open pathway for hundreds of yards.

As the Nazarene caravan rolled past the Roman guard toward the city, Yeshua led the way and they finished their song of ascent.

> *"We escaped with our lives like a bird*
> *from the fowler's snare;*
> *the snare was broken,*
> *and we escaped.*
> *Our help is in the name of the LORD,*
> *the maker of heaven and earth." (Psalm 124:1-8)*

Several mounted Romans stood by and watched as the pilgrims traveled freely up the road. It was almost as if Yeshua had called on God to part the Red Sea, and drive back the Pharaoh and his chariots — again.

chapter
SEVENTEEN

YERUSHLEM WAS THE KING'S CITY.

The most beloved Hebrew ruler, King David, conquered the site about 1000 B.C. People had lived there at least 900 years earlier. Even ancient Egyptian records mention Rushalimum and later Urushalim.

When the mighty Joshua led the Hebrew people across the Jordan River, he conquered the Jebusites who occupied the location. But Joshua didn't remain in the city.

Hundreds of years later, King David had a decision to make. Where would he live? He wanted to unite the Hebrew people. Yerushlem was in a central location, between his loyal tribes in the south and those up north who wanted to join him.

David was a pragmatic king. To unite his nation, he drove the Jebusites out of Yerushlem, and made it his new capital. Israel was now one!

He was also a strategic thinker. Because Yerushlem sat on a very high elevation, it was easier to defend. But nothing on earth could protect its residents from a contagious plague that threatened the Israelites. David listened to the prophet, Gad, who told him how to defeat the illness that had swept the city. He must build an altar to the Lord on a threshing floor owned by a certain Jebusite in Yerushlem. Doing the honorable thing, David bought the land for a high price, 600 gold shekels. He dedicated a permanent altar and sacrificed to Yahweh. The plague ended.

Then David constructed buildings for himself and prepared a place for the Ark of the Covenant, pitching a tent to house it. It was a chest that held the two stone tablets of the Ten Commandments that Yahweh had given to Moses. This is where the Israelites stood in front of God. This was "Jerusalem, the city in which, out of all the tribes of Israel, the LORD chose to set his name." (1 Kings 14:21)

David had also wanted to build a temple on the site of the Ark, but it would be his son, Solomon, who would fulfill the plan in 960 B.C. It was a glorious place. No expense was spared to create Yahweh's house on earth. The main part of the Temple was 90 feet long, 30 feet wide, and 45 feet high. Solomon hired the best carpenters from Phoenicia to build it. Another 30,000 Israelites labored to fulfill Solomon's vision, crafting massive walls from Lebanon's majestic cedars. The timbers were free of knots and their natural aroma repelled insects. The artisans covered the walls in pure gold. Huge bronze columns at the main entrance featured carvings of pomegranates and lilies.

Solomon wanted a Temple second to none. It would symbolize the power of his nation and the God of Israel. Imagine ceremonial purification basins that held 10,000 gallons of water, weighing 30 tons! The scale of this Temple, and the quality of its materials, placed it among the wonders of the known world. But inside this manmade masterpiece was the Holy of Holies. Only the Chief Priest could enter this chamber, and that was only permitted one day each year. This was the space dedicated to the Ark of the Covenant, the law that sealed the relationship between God and his people.

However, that would not be the same Temple Yeshua would enter. In fact, when he arrived in Yerushlem at 12 years old, there would be no stone tablets in the Holy of Holies.

Tragically, some four hundred years after Solomon built the Temple, Nebuchadnezzar, king of Babylonia, destroyed the building and the Ark. Fortunately, by then, God had written his laws into the minds and onto the hearts of his people. It took nearly another century of toiling in Babylonian captivity before the Israelites returned to the Temple site. The Persian king, Cyrus the Great, gave them permission to rebuild their Temple. And they did. Theirs was a simple place that lacked the majestic gold and bronze architectural features. There were no mammoth basins for purification. But it offered the most important things. The second Temple was a reverent sanctuary dedicated to the living God of Israel. The humble Holy of Holies was still His sacred, exclusive home on earth.

It was this Temple that Herod the Great dismantled. He would erect his own colossal monument to earthly power on its foundation. Although the renovated Temple was lavish, spiritually it meant nothing more to the true believers. It was God's presence they were worshiping, not man-made adornments. In their eyes, the king could have accomplished so much more had he used his resources to help people, especially those who could not help themselves.

The Ten Commandments were God's word written by His hand. Even though they had been lost to history and war, they existed in the spirit and actions of every good Jew. Love God and love your neighbor as yourself — that was the essence of the Torah. That was God's will for His people.

And when Yeshua returned to the Temple for his first Passover, the Ark of the Covenant would be physically and spiritually restored — because He was the Word of God in the flesh. But only he and his heavenly Father and their Holy Spirit knew that. To the rest of Nazareth, he was just another boy. Even his parents didn't fully understand Yeshua's destiny. Yosef wouldn't live to see it. Miriam would have to wait another 20 years for God to reveal everything to her.

By the time the caravan approached Yerushlem's north gate, the people were nearly in a trance, absorbed by the energy of the festival and the sheer drama of the capital city. They were from a tiny town, and Yerushlem marked one of the world's quintessential intersections of political power, business, and religion. It was an international hub and a showplace.

Among the first landmarks the pilgrims spied was Antonia Fortress. The structure was one of many towers and walls that were restored after foreign sieges destroyed Yerushlem's bulwarks. Herod the Great named the prominent tower for his Roman patron, Mark Antony.

"Is that the King's palace?" Avigail shouted from her perch on the wagon.

"That's Antonia Fortress," Yosef responded. "It used to be Herod's castle. Now it's a Roman garrison. Lots of men and weapons in there. The soldiers have a powerful device, a catapult that fires great numbers of arrows and darts with a single shot!"

Yosef pointed to a fortress high above the city on a hill in the wealthy western sector. "The castle is up there," he explained.

Standing in the cart, Yosef turned to the caravan behind him, so others could hear better. Facing north, with his back to the city, he now pointed to his right.

"To the Mount of Olives!" Yosef proclaimed.

Yeshua immediately followed his father's directions and turned his beasts in the road. It was challenging because there was a mass of crisscrossing traffic. People, wagons, animals, and many, many sheep and goats were in the way.

Yeshua chuckled at the chaos. It was the best way to deal with the stress. He saw a fat woman jump down out of her cart to chase a little lamb whose tether had come loose. The woman shouted after him as she waddled among the carts. The louder she yelled, the faster the little lamb scurried to get away.

"You are a Passover lamb, little one!" the woman shouted. "Baa, baa, baa … come back to me!" The crowds quickly enveloped the round woman and her lamb. Her husband sat down, shaking his head in frustration, as people streamed past on both sides of his cart.

Roman sentries spied the commotion from towers high above. The caravan wheeled eastward around the city walls, and headed just a little farther across the Kidron Valley to the Mount of Olives. This is where Yosef and Miriam had camped every year they came to Yerushlem, except for the time they had hidden in Egypt.

For the last several Passovers, the Nazarene caravan decided to follow Yosef's suggestion to reserve a spot for their entire group in the olive grove that overlooked the city. Yosef knew the owner of the grove, Abner, from his days working in Yerushlem. Abner always kept a choice campsite for them, but it was essential they get to the mount early so they could pitch tents and set up in daylight.

As grove master, Abner was also the head of gethsemanes, or commercial oil presses. Olives and their rich, delicious oils were Yerushlem's chief export. Otherwise, the land was too dry to support many vegetables and fruit. But when it came to olives and oils, Yerushlem was blessed with the valuable emollient that oozed from its presses.

The choice olives were green, black, purple, red, and amber, and grove workers harvested them by shaking the tree branches with poles. The fruit landed on yards of cloth or fine nets spread out along the grove floor. This made gathering them easier, and helped protect the produce during efficient handling.

Israel was known for the high quality and flavor of its first press olive oil, which was hard to match. Craftsmen squeezed the fruit in a mortar, and then placed the bruised olive meats in hanging baskets so the luscious oil gently dripped into catch basins. That produced the finest results. Following the first press, the gethsemane workers generated less expensive "beaten oils" by using weights to force the remaining product from the leftover pulp. Like most women, Miriam could make cooking oil in the stone mill Yosef had made for her. The olive and its slippery, tasty byproduct lubricated life throughout the Holy Land and the Mediterranean trading circuit.

Since olives were a fall crop, the grove was a perfect place for Passover pilgrims to camp beneath the trees in the springtime.

Like all young boys on their first trip to the Holy City, Yeshua was anxious to walk the streets of Yerushlem and to visit the Temple.

But first things first. Staging the camp was critical. The Nazarenes would live there for more than one week.

As they approached Abner's land, Yosef again stood in his wagon. He let his crutch fall at his side, as he cupped his hands around his mouth and yelled.

"Abner! It's Yosef of Nazareth!"

Abner was sitting on a branch of a very old and sturdy olive tree. When he heard Yosef shout from a distance, he quickly stood up on the branch and waved, and tried to spot him climbing the terrain. He was surprised that Yosef wasn't walking, but riding atop the wagon. Abner confidently ran along the stout limb, as if it were a path, until he reached the trunk where he jumped out, grabbed another branch, swung down, and landed firmly on the ground. Abner was as comfortable climbing trees in his grove as a bird on the highest perch.

As he ran among the olive trees, Abner's tunic blew behind him. When Yosef saw him coming, he slid down out of the cart, and with his crutch under his arm, hobbled along next to Yeshua. Resting the ankle another day had reduced the swelling and tenderness, and he could move pretty well now.

"Shlama, Yosef! Welcome back to Yerushlem," Abner said as he ran up and embraced Yosef.

"Shlama, Abner. And may your entire family be blessed," Yosef replied. "This is my son, Yeshua. It's his first Passover in the Holy City."

"What a fine young boy you are, Yeshua! Welcome, welcome," Abner said.

"Shlama," Yeshua replied shyly.

"And you remember Miriam, of course?" Yosef asked as he gestured to his wife on the cart.

"Of course, of course. Welcome back, Miriam. How was your journey?" Abner asked.

"Other than Yosef spraining his ankle, and our neighbors losing their cart in a crash with the Romans, God blessed us with a very uneventful trip. Praise Adonai!" Miriam said.

"The ankle is fine," Yosef said. "The doctor insisted I rest it one more day."

By this time, other Nazarenes had gathered around. Yosef made the traditional introductions, beginning with the rabbi and his wife, and then the other elders. All those who had been walking took a seat on the ground. Those who had been riding were delighted to stand up and stretch their legs. One of Abner's workers brought buckets of water and ladles for people to drink. They could finally relax. The first half of the long journey was complete!

Abner passed around large bowls of olives preserved in salty oil. He also offered leavened bread, as Passover wouldn't start for two days, two sunsets away. The pilgrims had allowed an extra travel day in the event of problems on the road.

Passover officially began at nightfall on the fourteenth day of the ancient Hebrew month of Nissan. Dusk marked the start of the fifteenth day, and Nissan fell in mid-March to mid-April. Pilgrims took their animals to the Temple for sacrifice on the fourteenth day. That evening, the start of the fifteenth day, they would eat their Seder of unleavened bread, lamb or kid goat, and consume all of it by midnight. Today, they could still enjoy leavened bread with their olives.

It didn't take long for a spontaneous party to break out. The mood was very festive. Since they hadn't really stopped for lunch, the pilgrims pulled out the rest of their supplies and began sharing everything. They were soon having a feast in the middle of the grove, complete with wine, music, dancing, and, of course, singing Passover Psalms.

"Then our mouths were filled with laughter;
our tongues sang for joy.
Then it was said among the nations,
'The LORD had done great things for them.'"

In his excitement, Yeshua jumped up on the wagon and finished the Psalm at the top of his voice.

> *"The LORD has done great things for us;*
> *Oh, how happy we were!"*
> *(Psalm 126:2-3)*

"My, my! He really isn't shy at all," Abner exclaimed.

The Nazarenes laughed. They knew Yeshua as a fun-loving boy, especially once he got over his initial shyness. And tonight, they would all revel in a pre-Passover party, consuming most of the left-over food and beverages from their journey. There would be no travel tomorrow and plenty of time to shop and take in Yerushlem. Today, they would laugh and sing, frolic, and celebrate.

The Passover festival honored the salvation of God's Chosen People and His most glorious triumph. Somehow these nomadic tribes, the Israelites, had always escaped danger and captivity. They survived and thrived even while they were oppressed. They proclaimed it was their one God who blessed them. But how could just one God be more powerful than all the gods of Egypt or Greece or Rome? How could they continue to praise that deity, even as other nations dominated them, like the Babylonians, the Persians, or the mighty Romans?

Every good Hebrew knew that the Passover in Egypt and the rebuke of Pharaoh was a profound proof of God's love for them. Now it was only a matter of time before the Messiah would come and save His people for evermore.

Maybe it would be this Passover.

chapter
EIGHTEEN

THE PARTY IN THE OLIVE GROVE HAD ROARED LOUD
and strong, long past bedtime.

There were some fuzzy heads this morning, but most of the
Nazarenes were up before the sun. They were eager to make their
way into Yerushlem to eat breakfast, to buy provisions and special
supplies for the Seder, and most of all, to visit the Temple. That
was the reason for their five-day journey and the financial sacrifices
they had made all year to afford their Passover pilgrimage. It was all
about Yahweh, the God of Israel.

For Yeshua, this was a momentous occasion. He would set foot
in his heavenly Father's house and worship. His earthly father, Yosef,
had told him about the Temple his whole life. But now he would experience it with all his senses. The magnificent architectural shapes
and structure; world-class carvings and craftsmanship; the music
of the Levites and the voices of thousands; the aroma of incense
blended with sacrificial roasting meat; and the textures of cedar and
stone. All this awaited him.

But first, Miriam, Yosef, and Yeshua were expecting a guest. It
was John, Yeshua's cousin and Elizabeth's son, who had been born
to her in her old age. He was the same child whose birth the angel had prophesied to Miriam, when he also announced that God
would conceive Yeshua in her virgin womb. John was no ordinary

young man, either. He would fulfill the great scriptural prophecy to become a voice proclaiming in the wilderness: "… prepare the way of the LORD! Make straight in the wasteland a highway for our God!" (Isaiah 40:3)

John would be the last prophet before the Messiah.

Abner had marked the campsites with the names of each caravan. Jericho; Dan; Modein; Joppa; Masada; Capernaum; Sepphoris; Nazareth; and many more were represented on the Mount of Olives. The fabric signs helped families and friends reunite. And if someone had drunk a little too much wine, he could stumble through the camp, even at night, to find the right caravan, with the help of the markers and the light from campfires.

Yeshua sat in front of his tent, smoothing the toy boat he had carved for his cousin. He nimbly used the edge of his knife and a rough stone to refine his work. It had been more than five years since he had seen John, who was now quickly approaching 13. Miriam and Yosef had once brought John to Nazareth when they returned home after Passover. He stayed with them for a summer, and then traveled home with a family friend making the pilgrimage to Yerushlem for Succoth. John and Elizabeth lived nearby the Holy City.

Yeshua and John became fast friends that year. They shared nearly every waking moment. John even attended school with Yeshua. In fact, John grew close to Ezra, too, and the three were inseparable during his stay in Nazareth.

John had enjoyed an unusual childhood. He often played in the Temple region at his father's knee. Zechariah was a priest, so his son had special access to the Temple. Many of the priests and guards had watched the little boy grow up, praying, studying, and playing in the shadows and the nooks and corners of the holy place. John had taken scripture classes with a rabbi in the Court of Women. But now, John was no longer a child. He was a young man with an unbridled zeal for his faith.

From the moment John was old enough to understand, Zechariah had divulged a supernatural experience that had occurred in the Temple. He explained to his son how the priests had routinely drawn lots to determine who would go into the Temple and burn incense. One day, Zechariah was chosen. The people remained outside and prayed. During the ceremony, the Lord's angel, Gabriel, had appeared to Zechariah, who was terrified by the spirit.

But the angel said to him, "Do not be afraid, Zechariah, because your prayer has been heard. Your wife Elizabeth will bear you a son, and you shall name him John. And you will have joy and gladness, and many will rejoice at his birth, for he will be great in the sight of [the] Lord. He will drink neither wine nor strong drink. He will be filled with the holy Spirit even from his mother's womb, and he will turn many of the children of Israel to the Lord their God." (Luke 1:13-16)

Later, Zechariah had told John that he thought this prophecy unimaginable because Elizabeth was older and had been unable to conceive. Zechariah assumed she was infertile. He was overwhelmed by the angel's unbelievable news about the child the old couple would finally call its own.

And then the angel Gabriel added this revelation about John: "He will go before him in the spirit and power of Elijah to turn the hearts of fathers toward children and the disobedient to the understanding of the righteous, to prepare a people fit for the Lord." (Luke 1:17)

In a single moment, Zechariah learned he would become a father after many sad and childless decades. But he also came to understand that this baby boy, his only male heir, would be filled with the Holy Spirit from before birth, and become the last of God's prophets. One who would reveal the Messiah. Zechariah had asked the angel how he might believe this incredible news.

Because of his disbelief, Gabriel struck him speechless. Zechariah would not speak again until John was born and circumcised to

Yahweh. On the day of John's bris, the old priest asked for a writing tablet, and with a shaking hand inscribed, "John is his name." (Luke 1:63)

Zechariah had fulfilled the angel's command. Instantly, he could speak. God had mercy on Zechariah as a reward for his simple act of obedience. And Zechariah began to sing out in praise to the Lord. He lifted his baby son above his head, and walked around his home. Elizabeth, Miriam, and Yosef were there. All were relieved and thrilled to hear him speak again. The family was overwhelmed by God's goodness. He had chosen to work through them and their offspring. They had no idea how John and Yeshua would fulfill Yahweh's will, but they celebrated the miraculous gift of life and the promise of the Messiah. They would witness the fulfillment of God's great commitment to His people and all creation.

Then Zechariah lowered baby John, looking into his son's wide-open eyes. He held the infant in front of his face, singing in a quieter voice, almost a whisper.

> *"And you, child, will be called prophet of the Most High,*
> *for you will go before the Lord to prepare his ways,*
> *to give his people knowledge of salvation*
> *through the forgiveness of their sins,*
> *because of the tender mercy of our God*
> *by which the daybreak from on high will visit us*
> *to shine on those who sit in darkness and death's shadow,*
> *to guide our feet into the path of peace." (Luke 1:76-79)*

John never tired of hearing the story about God's amazing grace. Over the years, he grew strong. He developed a fierce love of God and a devout relationship with Him. John devoured the Scripture and was destined to be a preacher. But he'd also developed a powerful distaste for the Temple hierarchy, the Sanhedrin, the Pharisees, and Sadducees. However, it was the king of Israel who really earned

John's ire. The royal court might be responsible for remodeling the Temple, but they were shamelessly hypocritical. Herod and his sons were puppets of Caesar, even building shrines to Roman gods. These kings dishonored Yahweh and desecrated his law. Herod the Great had murdered his own wife, and had even slaughtered babies in an attempt to kill a newborn King of the Jews.

Herod's son would divorce his wife to marry his brother's spouse. These rulers flaunted their wealth with ostentatious embellishments of the Temple for all to see. This is not what God wanted of his kings and their subjects.

Years later, after his mother died, John would retreat to the wilderness to be alone with God. Then he would begin a public ministry, baptizing near Bethany east of the Jordan River, urging Israel to repent. He would openly admonish the king to prepare Israel for the coming of the Messiah.

At nearly 13, John already walked with a sense of righteousness in every step. It was not ego, but the Holy Spirit that drove him and his confidence. As he climbed up the Mount of Olives, John whistled, and then sang a Messianic Psalm, loud enough for anyone to hear.

> *"Better to take refuge in the LORD*
> *than to put one's trust in mortals.*
> *Better to take refuge in the LORD*
> *than to put one's trust in princes."*

John chanted in a deep voice as he walked in rhythm to the Psalm.

> *"The LORD, my strength and might,*
> *has become my savior." (Psalm 118:8-9, 14)*

He was already very broad shouldered and tall for his age. With his muscled build, John looked more like the son of a farmer or carpenter, than the descendant of a priest. Even his mother was from the family of Aaron, the brother of Moses, and Israel's first High Priest.

Yeshua looked up from his carving to see who was singing in the distance. He instantly recognized John's shape and mop of curly hair, as he climbed the road to the Mount of Olives. Stuffing his carving and knife into his shoulder bag, Yeshua ran to greet his cousin. He shouted to his parents, announcing John's arrival.

"My little cousin!" John bellowed as he spotted Yeshua sprinting toward him.

They both laughed as they embraced. John kidded Yeshua about being a good deal shorter than he was, even though Yeshua was only six months younger. After his recent birthday, John had begun to sprout coarse whiskers. Soon, he would officially be a member of the family of Judaism. And with that came all the spiritual responsibilities of an adult male.

"My mother will be so excited to see you," John exclaimed. "She is waiting for us at the Temple. Too tough for her to walk up the mount."

Yeshua led the way back toward their tent, but after a few hurried strides, John grabbed his arm to stop him.

"I almost forgot," John said, digging in the pouch on his belt. "My mother gave me something for you. You'll want to put it in a safe place."

He tugged at the pouch and slid it along his belt from his hip to his abdomen. He looked inside and pulled out what appeared to be a rock.

"My father saved a few of these," he said, handing the gift to Yeshua. "It's a piece from the old Temple."

When he turned the stone over in his palm, Yeshua revealed one side carved with a lily. He ran his fingertips over the ancient, worn work. He felt he was touching the fingertips of a craftsman from hundreds of years ago. The stoneworker had likely been a devout

Hebrew, delighted to be toiling at Yahweh's house and restoring the Temple that had been lost to their Babylonian conquerors. Perhaps this piece of handiwork had been tossed aside by Herod the Great to make way for his grander, earthly vision of a house of worship.

Yeshua looked up at John and grinned broadly. He closed his eyes and expressed his sheer joy.

"Where's Ezra?" John asked. "I have a piece of the Temple for him, too."

As they walked toward the tent, Yeshua explained Ezra's illness and assured John his friend would be fine.

"God's peace be with you!" Yosef said to John as the two boys approached the tent. He was seated outside and stood to embrace the young man. Miriam joined them, repeatedly hugging and kissing her kin. She felt a special closeness to John, since the angel Gabriel had foretold his birth to her, and she had stayed with her cousin Elizabeth during her pregnancy and his birth.

"How is your mother?" Miriam asked with some concern.

"She had felt so tired and old," replied John, "until the week of Passover. Mom looks forward to seeing you two every year, but this year, she's anxious to spend time with Yeshua. You are all she talks about. I left her praying in the Court of Women, and she has packed a meal for us. Even baked those honey cakes you love, Yeshua."

John gave Yeshua the other Temple stone for Ezra. The ancient artisan had carved a palm tree into it. Yeshua wrapped both pieces in a polishing cloth he took out of his bag, and nestled them inside the sack. Then he reached in and took out John's boat and handed it to his cousin.

"Impressive work, Yeshua! Is this for me?" John asked cautiously.

Yeshua nodded with a grin.

John noticed the fine detail, including the wavelike pattern around the perimeter of the boat. It rose up higher at the bow.

"The waves are clever, Yeshua," John said.

"There is the sea, great and wide!
It teems with countless beings,
living things both large and small,"
Yeshua replied with a laugh. (Psalm 104:25)

John continued the psalm:

"There ships ply their course
and Leviathan, whom you formed to play with.
All of these look to you
to give them food in due time." (Psalm 104:26-27)

"Thank you for carving this little ark for me!" John said. I will display your work in a special place, and think of you and Noah whenever I see it."

"It's wonderful to see you boys together again, but let's not keep Elizabeth waiting," Miriam urged.

The family gathered a few provisions for the day and headed to meet John's mother. Although Yosef was still limping, it would be easier to go on foot than to try to manage the donkeys through the crowds. He used a staff as the foursome headed toward the east gate of the city.

There was a massive crush of people on the road. Yerushlem was normally a busy place, but with the festival it was chaotic. Fortunately, the Temple was close to their camp. As they passed through the gate, the throng of pilgrims absorbed them. The narrow, hilly streets were choked with people. If you closed your eyes you might not be able to identify which country you were in. There were Jews from across the known world, and the air was filled with many languages, as well as the shouts of the street merchants.

"Yeshua, stay close to John. Grab hold of his belt or mine if you have to," Yosef warned.

They headed for the Valley of the Cheesemakers, the traditional merchants market in the city's lowest ravine. It was nestled in the Tyropoeon Valley.

"Fresh eggs. Sheep cheese 'n' goat cheese! Creamy milk!" shouted one vendor.

"Crisp vegetables. Cool cucumbers. The sweetest dates and figs from the oasis," a farmer yelled. "Barley and wheat! Fine flour!"

A baker stepped out of his shop carrying a huge woven basket; Passover flatbreads tumbled onto a cloth-covered table. A little girl and her mother stacked them. They sold as fast as the baker could pull them out of the oven. People grabbed hot leavened loaves off the table, juggling the bread into fabric sacks and straw baskets as it singed their fingers. This was the last day they could eat leavened bread until the end of the week of Passover.

Yeshua eyed the honey cakes.

Money was everywhere. It moved from hand to hand like water ricocheting off rocks in a babbling brook. There were coins from all over the world jingling together.

Lambs and kid goats were for sale everywhere. And souvenirs. Someone had stamped a commemorative coin for the Passover, and there were toy versions of the Pharaoh's chariots that drowned in the Red Sea. Yeshua was impressed with the handiwork. Someone had produced hundreds of them. But nothing would match the relics of the old Temple. Ezra would be mesmerized by his gift from John.

Yeshua listened to the people haggling over prices, but the merchants wouldn't budge. He'd have to share this experience with Ezra, too.

"Fine, don't buy it. The price will be double tomorrow when the Passover sacrifices begin or we'll be sold out," said a wine merchant.

Olives were everywhere. Some soaked in brine, others in oil. Some were salted to preserve them in the hot climate. People tasted the freshly pressed olive oil, licking their fingertips and rolling their eyes in delight.

Some bought food and supplies for their whole caravans. Others were slaves shopping for their masters. Still others were local people, Yerushlem families, trying to cope with the hundreds of thousands of visitors who would stay for a week. And indeed the crowds would peak in the next two days. Water was at a premium, and there were water carriers everywhere selling the precious liquid. Yosef knew he would have to stock up on supplies, but not until after they went to the Temple and visited with Elizabeth.

The Holy Family patiently pushed its way through the throngs. The foot traffic was like honey dripping from a pot, oozing slowly along the incline of an uneven shelf. Only this crowd flowed uphill toward the Temple Mount. Yeshua clutched Yosef's belt. John had a fistful of Yeshua's tunic, and Miriam held Yosef's free hand. They managed to stay together and make steady progress toward their destination.

Herod the Great had actually enlarged the Temple Mount by building a buttress into the deep valleys around it. The holy place was surrounded by enormous walls, 840 feet long on the south side, 945 feet at the north end, and more than 1,400 feet on both the east and the west. The Temple campus sprawled across and towered above more than 30 acres.

The line snaked through the city, through the Temple west wall, and up and over the viaduct. But first, everyone stopped at the south wall for a mikveh; the ritual cleansing bath every good Jew took before entering the holy place. Back in Nazareth, there was a mikveh outside the Synagogue. In fact, it had been completed before the Synagogue was built because the workers had to cleanse themselves prior to working on the building. No rabbi or member of the congregation would think about entering the Synagogue without purifying themselves and washing away their sins before God.

During Passover, hundreds of thousands of pilgrims would immerse themselves in the Temple baths. The water fed from the Gihon spring in the west wall of the Kidron Valley. There were also rain gutters along the Temple walls and structure that fed fresh water into the mikveh.

Throughout Yerushlem, there were cisterns to collect rain. But during the festival, there would never be enough clean water, even in the Temple. Thankfully, the cleansing was really intended for the soul, and not for the body.

As Yeshua and his family finally made their way near the Temple, they passed another layer of merchants. Peddlers hawked fresh garments for people who wanted something clean and new to wear for Passover.

"I know a fair moneychanger," said John as they passed the busy row of merchants. "Uriel is his name. He's a holy man who works here outside the Temple. He's on the end, right before the bath house."

If they waited to enter the Temple, they'd find a line of bankers or moneychangers in the colonnades at the entrance to the courtyards. No foreign currency could be used inside. Only Tyrian shekels were permitted. The First of God's Commandments forbade graven images. Many non-Jewish coins had people's faces or animals stamped on them. Caesar's likeness was inscribed on Roman coins. They would defile the Temple treasury; even the Romans respected this wish of the Jews.

Inside the Temple courtyard, they would find people fiercely arguing about the exchange rates. But with an endless stream of business for Passover, this was a seller's market, even for money.

"Good morning. How much do you need?" Uriel said as the family squeezed up toward his table.

Yosef fished around in his bag and took out a small leather purse. He pulled the string on it to reveal a number of coins. Fingering several of them, he placed the metal pieces on the table in front of Uriel. One was a Roman coin and another Greek. There were even a few Egyptian coins. These had been part of the savings Yosef and Miriam had acquired when they lived in Egypt with baby Yeshua.

"We will be getting many Egyptian coins during Passover. Not as valuable as they used to be. This one is very old, though," Uriel said, as he held it up to examine in the sunlight. He had an appreciation for the craftsmanship that went into minting money. "I will keep this one for myself," he said. It had some gold mixed with silver.

As he looked at the coin he saw John standing behind Yosef.

"Shlama, John. Are these friends of yours?" Uriel asked.

"Shlama, Uriel. These wonderful people are my cousins," John replied. "They come in from Nazareth for every Passover. But this is Yeshua's first trip to Yerushlem," he said, patting Yeshua's head.

"Well, welcome to Yerushlem, Yeshua!" said Uriel with a chuckle. "Nazareth will never be the same after you spend Passover here," he added. Miriam and Yosef nodded and laughed along with him.

Then Uriel quickly used his small scale and abacus to calculate the value of the money. He counted out two stacks of silver shekels.

"This is the very best I can do," Uriel said. He had taken a very small commission for the exchange.

"Thank you," said Yosef with a smile and a nod. "That's more than fair." He had a separate purse for the shekels and raked them off the table and into the leather bag.

"A blessed and joyous Passover to you, Uriel," Miriam said.

"And to you and your fine family," he replied.

Yosef looked carefully over both shoulders, as he turned to his left hip to put away both purses. He wanted to be sure no thief was waiting for a careless move. He then stuffed the leather bags in his larger shoulder bag, and double tied the cinch shut. Yosef picked up his cane that had been leaning against Uriel's table. He grabbed it with his right hand.

"Yeshua, walk on my left side, in case someone reaches for my bag," he said. "Your mother will hold John's hand. It's time for the mikveh."

The foursome moved back into the crowd and waited in line for the ritual bath. Yeshua stared at the wall above him, yearning to step inside the Temple grounds. His father eyed him, studying the boy's expression. He knew Yeshua was a special child in God's watchful eyes, but Yosef did not fully grasp Yahweh's plan for his son, nor did he know how Yeshua would fulfill the promise of the Messiah. He often wondered if his son would become a military leader and reclaim the Holy Land. Would Yeshua preach and change the hearts of the Romans and Israel's other enemies?

It was difficult to imagine how this seemingly ordinary, 12-year-old boy would save his people.

John and Miriam eyed Yeshua, too, as he took in the crowds and the magnificent structure. There were no builders today. The Temple construction had been halted for the festival because the crush of the crowd made work dangerous and nearly impossible. Yeshua was busy analyzing the magnificent craftsmanship, some of it still in progress. The human part of him was fascinated with art. But he was also peering into the eyes of the pilgrims, as they bumped and jostled each other. He watched the Chosen People, some very old, others young, with their whole lives ahead of them. Some parents looked genuinely happy, some stressed, and others simply exhausted. Only God knew their minds and hearts. There were crippled pilgrims and others with mental handicaps. Yeshua looked upon them all with understanding and a sense of divine mercy.

As he stood quietly amidst the chaos in Yerushlem, John spoke in a low voice, intended only for Miriam and Yosef.

> *"The LORD is in his holy temple;*
> *the LORD's throne is in heaven.*
> *God's eyes keep careful watch;*
> *they test the children of Adam,"* John proclaimed. (Psalm 11:4)

Overhearing this, Yeshua turned to John, and with a sigh, he closed his eyes to enjoy the moment. In his heart, he felt God's profound compassion for his Chosen People. The whole experience made him smile.

chapter
NINETEEN

THERE WERE TWO SEPARATE AREAS FOR THE
ceremonial cleansing, one for men and one for women. Modesty is a
vital Hebrew virtue. Each person kept his or her tunic on until the
last possible moment, until walking down the stairs and slipping
under the mikveh water.

Some used their garments like towels, wrapping them around
midsections to conceal breasts and bottoms. Then, as the water approached their waists, they'd slowly lift the fabric up and overhead,
handing linen tunics to family members who stood at the edge of
the bath.

Others were less bashful because they took a mikveh at Synagogue every Friday evening for the Sabbath. Most people looked
downward as they waited. When they stepped into the water, they
closed their eyes as they immersed themselves. But there were always a few waiting in line who peeked.

The Temple guards stood at the doorways to each mikveh, controlling traffic and watching for thieves who might steal clothing,
purses, sandals, or any other property left at the side of the pools by
the bathing believers.

"Yeshua, wait until I've come out before you step in," cautioned
Yosef. "Please watch my belongings, son. And look over your shoulder, too."

Being the rugged craftsman he was, Yosef made quick work of his mikveh. He removed his sandals and set down his staff. He handed Yeshua his shoulder bag and quickly dropped his tunic. As he had done thousands of times before, he very respectfully walked down the steps into the pool. Spreading his arms and legs, Yosef submerged himself under the water until the bystanders could no longer see his hair. Then he quickly came up for air, and dunked himself two more times.

John handed Yosef his tunic, as he rose from the bath and climbed the steps. Yosef prayed aloud,

"Blessed are You, God, Majestic Spirit of the Universe, Who makes us holy by embracing us in living waters." [6]

The water of the mikveh symbolically cleansed each believer of past sins, and purified him to enter the holy place.

John entered the water next and repeated the same steps.

Then Yeshua handed Yosef his bag. He gave him his cap as he slipped out of his sandals. Following his father's example, he slid off his tunic in one quick move, and walked deliberately down the steps. Then Yeshua looked upward for a moment, and paused before submerging himself in the water three times.

For John, this was a powerful experience. He knew his cousin was Yahweh's Word in the flesh. John's mother, Elizabeth, had told him the special story many, many times. Elizabeth vividly recalled how John leaped in her womb the day Miriam came to visit. Miriam was newly pregnant with Yeshua. Even before he was born, the Holy Spirit was with John, and he was aware that the unborn Yeshua was the Messiah. He proclaimed the divine presence of God from within the water in his mother's womb. There was a spiritual reconnection to that experience, as he watched his younger cousin make his first mikveh at the Temple in Yerushlem. He was witnessing the rebirth of Israel, and the Temple was its womb.

Under the water, though his eyes were closed, Yeshua could see a crowd of people in a river, and as he looked up, a pure white dove hovered overhead. He heard a voice.

"This is my beloved Son, with whom I am well pleased."
(Matthew 3:17)

He opened his eyes, and stepped out of the water, repeating the mikveh prayer solemnly. "Blessed are You, God, Majestic Spirit of the Universe, Who makes us holy by embracing us in living waters."

He lowered his head and shook the water out of his dark curls. Yosef handed Yeshua his tunic, which he slipped on over his wet body. John gave him his sandals. The two shared a smile as Yeshua finished dressing, the water dripping down his face and onto his shoulders. He shook his head again like a dog that had run through a river.

"Now we are clean," John said.

"Behold, I was born in guilt,
  in sin my mother conceived me.
  Behold, you desire true sincerity;
  and secretly you teach me wisdom," John proclaimed.
(Psalm 51:7-8)

For him, these were prophetic words from a Psalm.

Yeshua knew the verses well. And he chose an appropriate response:

"A clean heart create for me, God;
  renew within me a steadfast spirit.
  I will teach the wicked your ways,
  that sinners may return to you." (Psalm 51:12, 15)

As they slowly moved out of the bathhouse in a long line, Yosef couldn't help but admire the unique relationship Yeshua and John shared. How could they be apart for so many years, and reconnect as quickly as if they shared everyday lives? And when they recited sacred Scripture together, it felt as if they were having a conversation.

Miriam was waiting outside, basking in the hot sun, when the men stepped out of the bathhouse.

"Let's go find your mother," she said with enthusiasm. They walked along the south wall, the sand and dust sticking to their wet feet. Turning north along the western wall, toward the large viaduct, they pushed their way through to the bridge that would take them into the Temple courts. They first passed a worksite, where laborers had been building a footing for a huge staircase. When completed, it would rise above the Temple walls, carrying people to a meeting hall for the Sanhedrin, an assembly of 23 religious judges who gathered to rule on a variety of issues. But the structure wouldn't be finished for another 18 years or so. One day, as an adult, Yeshua would climb those same stairs to the Sanhedrin for a trial.

Yeshua felt tiny as he gazed up and walked past the walls. Some of the stones weighed many tons. Finally, the family reached the viaduct as the crowd slowly traversed up its rising ramp and into the colonnade.

The din of voices echoing off the stonework was deafening. Moneychangers haggled with pilgrims. And they competed with the cackle and squawk of birds. There were sheep, goats, and cattle bleating and mooing. Their owners negotiated fees for these sacrificial offerings. Some merchants exploited their customers, especially those from rural areas who were unfamiliar with big city deal making.

Yeshua shook his head at the frenzy.

John turned to him and said, "This is why I suggested visiting Uriel."

*"Blessed is the man who does not walk
in the counsel of the wicked,
Nor stand in the way of sinners,
nor sit in company with scoffers,"* Yeshua replied. (Psalm 1:1)

He was very disappointed to see intense business in a holy place, especially when people were being cheated.

They quickly exited the colonnade to avoid the gaggle of people, and entered the Court of the Gentiles. Non-Jews were permitted in here. Some of them had come to offer sacrifices to God. They had brought their own animals, or bought them in the colonnade. It was well known in Yerushlem that one of Caesar's lieutenants had once purchased 100 oxen to be burnt on the Temple's altar. Many Gentiles, who didn't understand the God of Israel, marveled at the magnificent Temple, and respected the worship of the Higher Power there.

"No foreigner may enter within the balustrade and enclosure around the Temple area. Anyone caught doing so will bear the responsibility for his own ensuing death." (Source: "Jesus and His Times," The Reader's Digest Association, Inc.)

The inscribed warning appeared in several places within the Court of the Gentiles. And the Temple guard took it seriously. Roman troops respected their authority, refusing to prevent the enforcement of Temple laws, even when Roman citizens were involved.

Many people found their families in the Court of Gentiles. But as the widow and son of a Temple priest, Elizabeth and John knew every corner of the building, and had their own special meeting place.

The Holy Family approached the railing surrounding the inner courts, the Holy of Holies and the sanctuary. They ran up the three steps to enter the Court of Women. John immediately pointed to his mother. "There she is," he proclaimed.

Elizabeth was standing in the corner outside the Chamber of Nazirites. These were people who were dedicated to God. They were forbidden to drink wine, cut their hair, or approach a dead body. Years earlier, the angel Gabriel had commanded that John should never drink wine.

Elizabeth had a basket and a bag with the small feast she had prepared for Miriam and her family. In her excitement, Miriam ran across the court toward her cousin. "Elizabeth!" she shouted. It was a familiar scene, as many pilgrims would rendezvous here on the day before the sacrifices for the Passover. The air was filled with laughter and tears of joy. Others wept when they learned that a relative had died, or was very sick or injured. Some travelers had been lost or hurt on the way to Yerushlem. There were also preachers and self-proclaimed prophets chanting or calling on Israel to repent.

In the midst of this cacophony of voices and languages from around the world, Miriam and Elizabeth vigorously embraced. Elizabeth was much older than Miriam, more than twice her age. She could have been a grandmother. But now, in Elizabeth's wrinkled face, Miriam could see the same smiling expression and youthful exuberance that had welcomed her more than a dozen years earlier. At that time, Elizabeth and Zechariah were anxiously and prayerfully expecting the birth of their son, John. He would be born less than three months later. Miriam was newly pregnant with Yeshua, when she and Hannah traveled five days to visit and assist the old couple.

On the day Miriam arrived, Elizabeth said to her, "Most blessed are you among women, and blessed is the fruit of your womb." (Luke 1:42)

Miriam remembered the words as if it were yesterday. In humility, she had knelt down in front of Elizabeth that day, overcome by the gravity of her words.

"And how does this happen to me, that the mother of my Lord should come to me?" Elizabeth had asked, pulling

Miriam up to her feet. *"For at the moment the sound of your greeting reached my ears, the infant in my womb leaped for joy. Blessed are you who believed that what was spoken to you by the Lord would be fulfilled." (Luke 1:43-45)*

Elizabeth put her hands on Miriam's shoulders and studied her cousin's face. Although more than a decade had passed since that memorable day, Elizabeth could vividly recall precisely what Miriam had said to her. She began to repeat Miriam's response word for word.

"'My soul proclaims the greatness of the Lord;
my spirit rejoices in God my savior.'"

Miriam smiled broadly and began singing quietly to her cousin. They shared this moment every year when they met at Passover.
Miriam chanted:

"'For he has looked upon his handmaid's lowliness;
behold, from now on will all ages call me blessed.
The Mighty One has done great things for me,
and holy is his name.
His mercy is from age to age
to those who fear him.
He has shown might with his arm,
dispersed the arrogant of mind and heart.
He has thrown down the rulers from their thrones
but lifted up the lowly.
The hungry he has filled with good things;
the rich he has sent away empty.
He has helped Israel his servant,
remembering his mercy,
according to his promise to our fathers,

to Abraham and to his descendants forever.'"
(Luke 1: 46-55)

Year after year, Yosef had witnessed this scene at other Passover re-unions in the Temple. Yeshua and John smiled and embraced their mothers because they knew the praise and thanksgiving involved them. Of course, Miriam and Elizabeth had told the boys about their special births many times.

But now, they were grown. And this was the first Passover they were all together, both to celebrate at the Temple, and to commem-orate the day that John had announced the arrival of the Messiah—from his mother's womb.

chapter
TWENTY

THE AROMA OF ROASTING ANIMAL FAT FILLED THE AIR within the Temple. Even though it was blended with burning incense, it was an appetizing smell. Most people could not afford to eat meat very often. Killing a sheep meant the loss of wool production. Butchering a goat meant no milk or cheese. The priests would consume some of the roasted livestock after the sacrificial offerings. The people who provided the animals for the burnt offerings also took some of the flesh. Usually, it was only the fat, the digestive tract, and kidneys that were burned in the holocaust.

Selling animals skins was a lucrative side business for the Temple priests, and the daily sacrifices provided a reliable supply throughout the year. Plus, there would be many thousands of sheep and goatskins after Passover.

On a typical day, people offered pigeons, doves, and even oxen for sacrifice. The flesh was burned to ashes on the altar. The Hebrews believed that the animal's blood belonged to God because it was the stuff of life. Priests splashed blood on the altar or smeared it on the horns of the altar. Believers made offerings to atone for sins, to thank God for healing, or to commemorate an agreement or reunion. Every day began with a priest sacrificing a lamb at dawn. He'd offer another at the end of the day. In between, priests made individual offerings on behalf of Temple visitors. On the Sabbath, only two lambs were sacrificed in the name of all the people, and pieces of the lambs were burned bit by bit to keep a constant holocaust before God. Twelve loaves of unleavened Sabbath bread, called shewbread, were also placed on a table and offered to Yahweh, along with burning incense.

Since it was Passover festival, Yosef would purchase no sacrifice until he brought his lamb to the Temple on the next day. But he did make an offering to the Temple treasury, paying his half-shekel annual dues, which were required of every observant Hebrew man. Yosef placed the donation in the Shekel Chamber.

There were 13 chests in the treasury, located in the Court of Women. Each was shaped like a larger-than-life ram's horn, or shofar. Historically, Hebrews had fashioned musical wind instruments from the horns of male sheep. In Scripture, when Joshua led the nation through the toppled walls of Jericho, there had been seven priests blowing seven shofars to signal God's divine intervention on behalf of Israel.

Yeshua was impressed with the masterful craftsmanship of the treasury. He recalled the Scripture aloud, "'Take up the ark of the covenant with seven of the priests carrying ram's horns in front of the ark of the LORD.'" (Joshua 6:6)

John nodded and added, "As the horns blew, the people began to shout. When they heard the sound of the horn, they raised a tremendous shout. The wall collapsed, and the people attacked the city straight ahead and took it." (Joshua 6:20)

Every good Jew recalled Joshua and the walls of Jericho when he looked at the Temple shofars.

Each chest in the treasury served a different purpose. Money from The Chamber of Secrets went confidentially to "poor of good family." Some private individuals used the Temple as a personal bank, depositing their wealth for safekeeping. The Levite guards maintained a watchful eye to secure the treasury.

Miriam and Elizabeth accompanied Yosef, Yeshua, and John as they walked across the Court of Women to the Nicanor Gate. Elizabeth was so pleased to see Yeshua, and kept hugging him every few minutes. He laughed about it, a little embarrassed. But only the men were permitted to climb the 15 curved steps that led to the Court of Israelites. There was one step for each of the Psalms of Ascent. The women would remain behind to talk and pray.

"Yeshua, you are stepping closer to the world of manhood, my son," Miriam proclaimed. She hugged him vigorously. A tear of joy rolled down her cheek. She reached into her bag, and pulled out a new prayer shawl she had made for him. She wrapped it across his shoulders. Yeshua was surprised to see the new linen piece.

She had worked in secret, usually when he was at school. The shawl was white with blue stripes. Shifra, the dyer, had given Miriam the indigo coloring at no charge because she admired Yeshua so much.

"Your mommy has been weaving that shawl every chance she's had," Yosef said. "I wish I had one that nice," he declared proudly.

Yeshua admired his mother's skill. He handled the fringes of the shawl delicately and thanked her with a big smile. Then he kissed Miriam on the cheek and laid his head on her shoulder for a moment. He knew just how hard she toiled every day. He took her tired, hard working hands in his and kissed them. It was clear he understood her sacrifice, and that he loved the special gift she had made for his first pilgrimage to the Temple.

Yeshua pulled the new shawl up onto his head, as he turned to climb the stairs. Yosef and John covered their heads, as well, and followed him into the Court of Israelites.

As they reached the top of the stairs and entered, they could see the high altar, decorated with a horn-shaped carving at each corner. The space was very narrow, crowded, and surprisingly noisy. Many men had brought animals for sacrifice, even though tomorrow would be a day of endless Passover holocausts. Some men prayed and chanted loudly. Others engaged in excited conversations. And then there were those who begged for the Messiah to come.

Yeshua walked the full length of the court toward the Court of the Priests. He didn't stop until he reached the edge of the narrow Court of Israelites. He looked up at the altar and the draped Holy of Holies. Then he stepped back several paces, and with his eyes closed, he bowed toward the floor and prayed. Yosef and John joined him. After a few moments of prayer, Yeshua stood straight up, but kept his eyes closed and his head bowed.

Stepping up in front of them was a Pharisee dressed in a beautiful tunic and prayer shawl. He looked up at the altar and prayed in a loud voice for all to hear. Yeshua opened his eyes and lifted his head as he listened.

"Oh, Adonai, you know I fast twice a week and give ten percent of all I earn to the Temple. Oh Adonai, I thank you that I am not like other men. So many are evildoers, adulterers, liars, robbers or thieving tax collectors," said the Pharisee. "I even give to the poor."

Behind Yeshua, a man quietly prayed. Yosef and John couldn't hear him at all. He was a tax collector. He stood at a distance from the altar, and away from the noisy crowds, well behind Yeshua. Every few moments, he struck his chest with his fist and said, "'O God, be merciful to me a sinner.'" (Luke 18:13)

Yeshua smiled when he heard the man's prayer, and closed his eyes again. He began to overhear other prayers in his head. They were the whispered words of believers in the Temple, begging the Lord for his blessings in their lives. Some were said silently in their hearts.

"Oh, Adonai, please allow my son to walk. He is so sick and has lost his strength. His mother is caring for him, but his suffering and atrophy are killing her," said an anguished father.

A farmer prayed in desperation, "Oh mighty one of Israel, my land is failing me. I cannot keep up with the pests and the animals. It is like the plagues of Egypt. Please show me your mercy, oh, Adonai. We are afraid of starving! Tell me what to do, oh, Holy One. Heal my land."

A young man prayed for a family. "Adonai, my creator. Please allow my wife, Ariel, and me to have a son. We have no children, and Ariel believes it is me who is infertile. She says all her sisters have had children, and no one in her family is barren. How can she say this, Lord? This is causing me pain, as well as my parents and her parents. It is straining our marriage. What have I done to deserve this curse, Adonai? I will repent. I will fast. I will sacrifice. Please give us at least one child. Others have so many."

Yeshua tipped his head back, as he heard prayer after prayer from the hearts of those around him. They echoed in his mind. The sheer weight of the pleading caused him to sweat. He leaned forward and prayed for all whose petitions he'd heard. He prayed for his mother and father. He thanked his heavenly Father for healing Ezra, and for blessing his good mother, Deborah. He prayed for the people of Nazareth, those in the caravan, and those who couldn't make the journey. He prayed for his grandparents, living and deceased. And he prayed for all the people of Israel. For the faces he had seen that day. He prayed that they might know God's peace by finding their way to do His will. He knew they could only find true peace by showing others the same mercy they asked of God.

And then after all his requests, Yeshua stopped to praise God for all His blessings, as he recited a Passover Psalm of thanksgiving. He said the verses loud enough for Yosef and John to hear, but no one else. They joined Yeshua in prayer, repeating the refrain with him after each line.

"Praise the LORD, for he is good;
for his mercy endures forever;
Praise the God of gods;
for his mercy endures forever;
Praise the Lord of lords;
for his mercy endures forever;"

A few men nearby could faintly hear Yeshua, Yosef, and John. They stepped up closer behind them to listen, and to silently pray along, swaying with the rhythm of the verses. Yeshua continued without turning to acknowledge them.

> "Who alone has done great wonders,
> for his mercy endures forever;
> Who skillfully made the heavens,
> for his mercy endures forever;
> Who spread the earth upon the waters,
> for his mercy endures forever;
> "Who made the great lights,
> for his mercy endures forever;
> The sun to rule the day,
> for his mercy endures forever;
> The moon and stars to rule the night,
> for his mercy endures forever;"

Now the tax collector stepped forward and prayed the refrain quietly. The other men also began to say the refrain aloud.

> "Who struck down the firstborn of Egypt,
> for his mercy endures forever;
> And led Israel from their midst,
> for his mercy endures forever;
> With mighty hand and outstretched arm,
> for his mercy endures forever;"

Then the father, the farmer, and the young husband who had been praying silently, joined the group behind Yeshua. They quietly sang the chorus with Yeshua leading the verses.

> "Who split in two the Red Sea,
> for his mercy endures forever;

And led Israel through its midst,
for his mercy endures forever;
But swept Pharaoh and his army into the Red Sea,
for his mercy endures forever;"

At this point, even the Pharisee paused to notice the group. He was impressed with Yeshua's knowledge of the Psalm. The boy recited it quietly but passionately from memory, as if he had written it himself.

"Who led the people through the desert,
for his mercy endures forever;"

When they overheard the Passover chorus, other men walked up, one by one, and joined in. But Yeshua never turned or paused; he focused on the prayer with his eyes closed and his arms and hands raised toward the heavens.

"Who struck down great kings,
for his mercy endures forever;

And made their lands a heritage,
for his mercy endures forever;
A heritage for Israel, his servant,
for his mercy endures forever.

The Lord remembered us in our low estate,
for his mercy endures forever;
Freed us from our foes,
for his mercy endures forever;
And gives bread to all flesh,
for his mercy endures forever.

Praise the God of heaven,
for his mercy endures forever." (Psalm 136: 1-9, 10-17, 21-26)

By the time they all finished the Psalm, there was a crowd of men standing behind Yeshua, Yosef, and John. The Passover imagery of the Pharaoh's defeat and Israel's freedom were exhilarating and especially relevant to the festival pilgrims. There was an air of joy and humility on their faces.

The men had been quietly praying along, and chanting the refrain behind Yeshua until the group became so large the praise became loud and strong. For a few moments, the great Temple in Yerushlem was filled with spontaneous, unselfish worship of the God of Israel. The Psalm was about thanksgiving and acknowledging Yahweh's many blessings. For a moment, they stopped asking, and instead adored the source of all goodness.

And it was a newcomer who led the worship — a confident and zealous boy from Nazareth. He had helped the group see that God was listening to their prayers. He reminded them that the Lord had repeatedly responded to the cries of Israel in glorious and profound ways. They could always trust Him to be merciful.

John looked at the men standing around. They now appeared to be revitalized, and waiting for more inspiration. He turned to Yosef and whispered in his ear, "The calf and the young lion shall browse together, with a little child to guide them." (Isaiah 11:6)

John was quoting the Messianic prophecy of Isaiah. He had just witnessed his young cousin shepherding God's people to gratitude and peace.

chapter

TWENTY-ONE

YESHUA'S HEAD WAS SPINNING WITH MEMORIES and images of his first visit to the Temple Mount. He had experienced the exhilarating crush of the Holy City overflowing with Passover pilgrims. He had seen Elizabeth and John; prayed in the Temple for the first time in his life; and enjoyed a splendid meal with his cousins and his parents in the shade of the Temple's shadows. Yeshua had shopped for supplies in the Valley of the Cheesemakers on the way back to camp, and had eaten a fresh honey cake. He'd also spent a second evening celebrating with the Nazarenes on the Mount of Olives. Yeshua slept well that night. No nightmares.

He needed no help rising early the next morning. This was the fourteenth day of Nissan, the day of the Passover sacrifice. Yeshua had butterflies in his stomach because he had waited all his young life to witness the event in Yerushlem. There was an intriguing mystery to this massive, yet solemn sacramental ritual.

According to tradition, somewhere within the Temple Mount, maybe beneath the sanctuary, was Abraham's rock. This was the sacred stone on which he had prepared to sacrifice his son, Isaac, to God — until the angel of the Lord stopped him. Abraham had been willing to obey God's command, even if it meant the death of his only son, whom he dearly loved.

Today, thousands of pilgrims would be waiting outside the Temple with lambs and kid goats to be slaughtered for their Seder. Any animal brought to the Temple was to be without blemish. Passover lambs also had to be at least eight days old, but no older than a year. Two families would share the lamb Yosef had bought. He and Eli had agreed to split the cost, which meant Avigail's family would be sharing Seder supper with them. Most pilgrims coming to the Temple for sacrifice actually represented ten or more people who would share in the festival meal, to consume every bit of the lamb or kid goat by midnight. God's law required nothing remain.

"Let's go, Yeshua," Yosef called to his son. "Don't forget, you're fasting today."

"He's almost ready," Miriam replied. Yeshua was praying in the seclusion of the tent.

The sun was barely up, but Yosef had already prayed, washed himself, and eaten his breakfast. However, every firstborn, including Yeshua, would keep a fast on the eve of Passover. Thankfully, it was a lenient fast, so he would be able to eat at lunchtime. Later, he could enjoy some of the fresh yogurt and butter they had bought the day before. But to abide by God's Passover laws, there would be no leavened bread on which to smear the butter today. Miriam warmed flat loaves over a little fire she made in a clay pot. She had also toasted some almonds. She knew how much Yeshua loved to crunch on them. He always rolled his eyes with pleasure to show his mom how good the toasted nuts tasted. She grinned and shook her head thinking about it.

When he quietly slipped out of the tent, Miriam handed Yeshua a bundle of food she'd wrapped up for lunch. He tethered it to the strap on his shoulder bag. Yosef had already filled a goatskin with water.

Miriam also gave Yeshua two pressed fruitcakes, one for him and one for his father. They were a blend of raisins and dried figs, mashed together for a quick snack that travelers and workers loved.

As he walked toward Yosef, Yeshua stretched out his hand to signal that he would manage the little lamb. Yosef was still using a walking stick, and his ankle remained a little tender. The two would walk into Yerushlem again today; it was too crowded to take the wagon or even one of the donkeys. Miriam would remain behind and begin preparations for the Seder with Judith. She gave both Yosef and Yeshua big hugs before they left for the Temple.

"Be careful. Go with Adonai!" Miriam said.

Yeshua handed his father the fruitcakes to put in his bag. The two said little as they headed down from the campsite toward the city. Their Passover lamb toddled close behind, as Yeshua kept him on a short leash. Every once in a while, he'd pat the animal's head. Yeshua felt sad that the little creature would face his death in just a few hours.

The sun was coming up fast. From the heights, they could see pilgrims pouring into Yerushlem, thousands of them leading lambs and goats. Some carried the sacrifice across their shoulders like shepherds. It was truly an impressive sight. The sound of bleating animals, blended with the voices of street vendors and pilgrims from around the world, reminded Yosef of the Tower of Babel.

"That is why it was called Babel, because there the LORD confused the speech of all the world," said Yosef.

Yeshua chuckled at the Scripture reference and nodded his head. He finished the verse, "From there the LORD scattered them over all the earth." (Genesis 11:9)

They were looking at the Chosen People from across the globe, gathered together for the great annual pilgrimage. This was a sacrifice of gratitude to God, unmatched in scale by any other. Even the Roman troops were impressed. They loved pageantry and ritual.

As they pressed their way into the city, Yeshua noticed it was slightly less crowded today. There were fewer women and children. Most knew that the solemn, mass sacrificial offering would dominate Yerushlem. It was an awe-inspiring scene, but, nonetheless serious business. The sun would be hot and the wait very long.

"Let me tell you what's going to happen here, son," said Yosef. "This is why I wanted to leave so early, but you can see everyone had the same idea.

"We will get in line at the Temple. Some will push and shove to get an advantage. But there's no point. Everybody will get into the Temple, but it won't be until the afternoon. When the priests have finished the burnt offering for the morning, they will begin opening the gates. And about one-third of the pilgrims will be allowed in. The Temple guards will keep order."

Yeshua looked up and nodded from time to time, as his father explained the Passover's community sacrifice. He was eager to learn the details.

"All those lambs will be sacrificed and flayed before the next third are allowed in," Yosef continued. "The last wave will include every-one remaining in the Temple courtyard.

"Each man will slaughter his own lamb or kid. There are many, many, many priests. Too many to count. When I cut the lamb's artery, right here in the neck, I'll drain the blood into the bowl the priest is holding. It will be a gold or silver bowl."

Yeshua's eyes widened at his father's description. The scale of it all was mindboggling. And all that blood!

"The priest will take that bowl of blood and hand it to another priest. He will hand it to another, who hands it to another, and so on. There are long lines of priests passing bowls up to the altar, where one will finally splash the blood onto the altar," Yosef ex-plained with dramatic gestures.

"Your lamb must be a year-old male and without blemish. You may take it from either the sheep or the goats. You will keep it until the fourteenth day of this month, and then, with the whole com-munity of Israel assembled, it will be slaughtered during the evening twilight," Yeshua said, quoting from the instructions God had given to Moses and Aaron before the first Passover. (Exodus 12:5-6)

"Very good, Yeshua!" said Yosef. "I can see the rabbi has really prepared you boys for your experience here. But you won't believe it 'til you see it and hear it. The Levites will be singing Psalms the whole time.

"After we kill the lamb, the priest will take a little of the fat and maybe a kidney or the guts to burn in the sacrifice. We will flay the lamb in the Temple, and then bring it home to the camp to roast for our Seder. We will tie the meat to my staff and carry it between us."

Yeshua looked at the little lamb and then at his father. Yosef could see his son felt pity for the animal. He had waited until Passover to tell Yeshua the details of the mass sacrifice, fearing he might have another nightmare.

"Yes, it's sad for this little one and the others, too," said Yosef. "But think of it this way, son, they are being sacrificed for the glory and praise of the Great One of Israel."

"For it is loyalty that I desire, not sacrifice,
  and knowledge of God rather than burnt offerings,"
Yeshua responded.
He was quoting a prophet. *(Hosea 6:6)*

For a moment, Yosef was stunned. He wasn't sure how to take Yeshua's remarks. Was it just a clever response, or was this the first sign of a young teenager testing his father? He didn't know if Yeshua was confused, or if he was suggesting that they shouldn't observe the Passover practices. After all, God had commanded that the people of Israel remember His Passover and make the sacrifice.

"This day will be a day of remembrance for you, which your future generations will celebrate with pilgrimage to the Lord; you will celebrate it as a statute forever," Yosef responded in a fatherly way. (Exodus 12:14)

Yeshua replied respectfully with precise instructions for the Passover meal: "This is how you are to eat it: with your loins girt, sandals on your feet and your staff in hand, you will eat it in a hurry. It is the Lord's Passover." (Exodus 12:11)

He knew the Scripture, and, of course, Yeshua understood God's command and would keep the Passover. But he explained to his father that the massive sacrifice seemed inhumane to the animals. Couldn't they carry the lamb and console him while they waited in line at the Temple? Could they cover his eyes and his ears, the way they put blinders on Mo and Mazel, their donkeys?

Yosef was pleasantly surprised by his son's insights and his concerns. He seemed much older than 12. Yosef couldn't remember thinking that way when he was that age.

"We will be kind to the lamb. You can carry him the whole way, and distract him until the very end," Yosef said. "Indeed, it is an intense ritual. That's why I have been explaining it — to help prepare you to witness the sacrifice. Bowl after bowl of blood is passed up to the altar, and then the empty bowls are sent back for the next wave of lamb and goat blood. Wave after wave, they'll come all day. Yeshua, you're right. I'm sure it's very frightening for the animals. They are innocent and they certainly sense the danger."

By this time, they had arrived near the outside of the Temple. Yosef and Yeshua would take turns going inside for the mikveh. One stayed with the lamb, while the other bathed. After morning Temple services, the fast of the firstborn ended, and they nibbled their lunch to pass the time during the long wait. Miriam had even packed some grass and clover from the campsite for the little lamb to eat. Yeshua cupped his hands so the animal could sip some water, as Yosef poured it from the goatskin.

Finally, in the afternoon, the crowd ahead started moving. The pilgrims and animals entered the Temple through the gate. For a moment, it looked like Yosef and Yeshua would be among the first wave. But suddenly, they heard a trumpet blast from a shofar. The gate guard blew his horn to announce the closing of the gate.

Again, Yeshua quoted a prophet. This time it was Isaiah.

"What do I care for the multitude of your sacrifices?
 says the Lord
 I have had enough of whole-burnt ram
 and fat of fatlings;
 In the blood of calves, lambs, and goats
 I find no pleasure.

"Wash yourselves clean!
 Put away your misdeeds from before my eyes;
 cease doing evil;
 learn to do good." (Isaiah 1:11, 16-17)

Yosef nodded as he, too, recalled the Scripture. Yeshua's comment got his attention. It was moments like these that reminded Yosef his son was extraordinarily different. He and Miriam could not constantly focus on Yeshua's virgin birth, or the angels that had appeared to them. How could they live normal lives, if they were always anticipating another vision or sign from God? In most ways, Yeshua was just like any other Hebrew boy. But from time to time, he was transformed.

Yeshua sat patiently outside the Temple gates holding the lamb in his arms and caressing its head. The animal had momentarily fallen asleep in his lap. Yosef studied his son's face and read the concern in his expression. He thought about the things Yeshua had said this morning, and the questions he had raised.

He realized that, indeed, God wanted more than sacrifices and ritual from his Chosen People. He wanted their hearts. Yosef recalled the refrain of the Psalm Yeshua had recited the day before in the Temple: "for his mercy endures forever." (Psalm 136:26)

He was reminded that the Passover was about God's infinite mercy and love. It was much more than a festival of national freedom and a religious tradition. It was God's example for man's behavior. He wanted His people to be merciful and loving to everyone they met.

Yosef also realized his young son was connecting thoughts he himself had never really pondered. Did the writings of Isaiah and Hosea conflict with the Passover tradition, or were they somehow intertwined? He didn't know the answer. He hadn't thought to ask the question until now. This was something he would have to discuss with the rabbi. But Yosef knew one thing for certain: Yeshua had grown up, and he was on fire with the Word of God.

Just then the guard blew the shofar again. The gates opened, and Yeshua entered the Temple with his father and their Paschal lamb.

chapter

TWENTY-TWO

ON THE WAY BACK TO THE CAMP, YESHUA CARRIED the flayed lamb across his shoulders. It hung from Yosef's walking stick. Fortunately, someone in the Temple crowd noticed Yosef was limping and offered him his staff. The generous donor was also a carpenter and mason from Yerushlem. He saw Yosef had a piece of wood over his ear, and instantly felt a sense of fellowship. It was common for tradesmen to wear a badge or icon to represent their crafts. For example, a tailor might keep a bone needle stuck prominently in his garment, or a dyer might wear a brightly colored patch of cloth. It was a calling card. Everyone was always searching for his or her next customer and paying job.

Yosef was very grateful for the man's concern and generosity, and they chatted a while about Yosef's years working on the Temple. The carpenter, named Hillel, was currently building the Sanhedrin tower of King Herod's Temple. He was enjoying his time off for the festival. It gave him a week away from working with cedar beams and stone.

Even with the help of a walking stick, Yosef hobbled a few steps behind Yeshua, so they didn't have a lot of opportunity to talk. But Yeshua had been left somewhat speechless by the bloody, mass sacrifice of thousands of lambs and goats. He was deep in thought on the return trip.

By the time they arrived at the Nazarene campsite, several others had already returned from the Temple, and the fires were quite hot. Miriam and Judith prepared their fire pit by digging a ditch in the soil and burning wood for hours. Now they tended a very intense charcoal fire. The ditch would act as an in-ground oven.

Miriam and Judith focused on cleaning the lamb with water and seasoned it with olive oil, salt, rosemary, cinnamon and other spices. Yosef and Eli pierced the meat with a spit and lowered it into the ditch. The meat rested just above the sizzling coals, and would cook well over the large, smoldering fire in the warm, late afternoon air. They would add more dried olive branches from time to time. It would take a while, but soon the heavenly aroma of all the roasting would envelop Yerushlem. Thousands and thousands of lambs and kid goats were cooking in the open air in one city. And for most people, meat was a luxury. Even the Romans had nothing to match the scale of the Passover festival.

And all across Yerushlem, women were also baking unleavened bread. The community had been eating flatbreads since the afternoon before, because every household had thrown away any leavening. At the first Passover, God had commanded that no leavening should be eaten for a week.

"For seven days no leaven may be found in your houses; for anyone, a resident alien or a native, who eats leavened food will be cut off from the community of Israel."
(Exodus 12:19)

Without fail, every year, the Chosen People kept that command during their observance of this holy feast. While the men were at Temple during the day, Miriam and the other mothers had swept out their tents and wagons, and shook out the garments and bedding to make sure they were leaven-free.

As the lamb roasted and the women prepared the other courses of the meal, Yeshua sipped some cool water and found his voice. He told his family and their Passover guests about his experience at the Temple. His mother and Judith listened politely, as if they had never before heard the event described. Avigail and her sisters hung on Yeshua's every word, and they grimaced at his report about the bowls of blood that were collected and splashed on the altar.

"And then what happened?" Avigail would ask whenever Yeshua paused. He was only too happy to fill in the details. Yeshua explained that throughout the sacrificing, the Levites sang Psalms. Musicians accompanied them on reeds, lyres, and drums. The sound of crying lambs blended with the voices and music in a chorus, the likes of which he had never heard.

Yeshua began singing as the Levites had:

> "When Israel came forth from Egypt
>   the house of Jacob from an alien people
>   Judah became God's sanctuary,
>   Israel, God's domain.
>   The sea saw and fled;
>   the Jordan turned back.
>   The mountains skipped like rams;
>   the hills, like lambs."

Miriam ran to her tent nearby to pick up her lyre. She played along as her son sang.

> "Why was it, sea, that you fled?
> Jordan, that you turned back?
> Mountains, that you skipped like rams?
> You hills, like lambs?"

As Yeshua sang the Psalm, he turned on each line, as if he were talking to the sea, the Jordan River, the mountains, and the hills.

> *"Tremble, earth, before the Lord,*
>   *before the God of Jacob,*
>   *Who turned the rock into pools of water,*
>   *flint into a flowing spring." (Psalm 114:1-8)*

The women applauded and cheered when he finished singing.

"You see, Miriam," Judith exclaimed, "this is why women don't need to enter the Temple for the sacrifice. Yeshua has brought the Temple and Adonai, Himself, to us!" She laughed joyfully. Judith genuinely admired Yeshua, and thought he'd make a wonderful husband for her daughter.

This was indeed a festive atmosphere. Before the lamb was done roasting, the sun would set and their appetites would be on fire. Every family in the camp from Nazareth would solemnly gather to eat the feast of lamb, unleavened bread, bitter herbs, endive, chicory, and wine. Jews throughout the world would partake in the feast in their homes, or wherever they were staying. And at each gathering, the youngest would ask, "Why is this night different from all other nights?"

Avigail was a little younger than Yeshua, and she had three younger sisters. So, for the first time since Yeshua could talk, he didn't ask the Passover question. It was a powerful moment for him. He was now a young man, and he had just been to the Temple in Yerushlem for the first time since shortly after his birth. Yeshua ate his Seder on the hills overlooking the Temple Mount. He was observing a holy ritual not far from the Holy of Holies. Tonight, the retelling of Israel's Exodus from Egypt would be larger than life.

At each Seder, the head of the household would repeat the story of the Exodus. Out of respect for Eli, because he was older, Yosef asked him to lead the observance.

Eli recalled the triumph of Israel at the hand of God, as if it had happened only yesterday. He spoke up as he lifted a shank bone from their Passover lamb, and proclaimed God's commands to the Israelites. They would be saved by the blood of the lamb:

"They will take some of its blood and apply it to the two doorposts and the lintel of the houses in which they eat it. "For on this same night I will go through Egypt, striking down every firstborn in the land, human being and beast alike, and executing judgment on all the gods of Egypt—I, the Lord!" Eli recited passionately.

"But for you the blood will mark the houses where you are. Seeing the blood, I will pass over you; thereby, when I strike the land of Egypt, no destructive blow will come upon you." (Exodus 12:7, 12-13)

Those houses marked with lamb or goat blood had been spared from Yahweh's justice. The God of Israel passed over them. The Egyptian homes were unmarked because they did not have a covenant with the God of Israel, nor did they hear or know His word. Their king, the Pharaoh, had defied God's merciful warnings and pleadings to let His people go. So, Yahweh brought justice on Egypt, killing each firstborn of woman and beast, to end their dominance and exploitation of His people. He set Israel free. They had been captive slaves to Egypt for 430 years. Now, Pharaoh had no power over them. He could no longer build his pyramids and his wealth on their backs.

For thousands of years, generation after generation of Israelites would tell this story to their children to commemorate the abundant love and mercy Yahweh had shown his Chosen People. Each year at Passover, fathers quoted Scripture, telling their sons, "'This is because of what the Lord did for me when I came out of Egypt.'"

"And when your son asks you later on, 'What does this mean?' you will tell him, 'With a strong hand

the Lord brought us out of Egypt, out of a house of slavery.'" (Exodus 13:8, 14)

As the night went on, Yeshua thought about his aging grandmother and his friend, Ezra, back in Nazareth. He could easily envision their Passover celebrations because he had spent so many of them in his tiny town. Wait until Ezra heard all Yeshua had seen and done in Yerushlem! He would be even more anxious to make the pilgrimage next year. Especially when he got the chance to touch the Temple relics John had given Yeshua. Ezra would want to head for Yerushlem immediately! Yeshua laughed to himself as he enjoyed the savory lamb. They would all eat their fill tonight, and then some, because Yahweh had commanded that nothing from the Seder meal go uneaten.

After dinner, all the young Nazarenes gathered at the rabbi's campfire. He told one of his favorite stories of Passover and Israel's exodus from Egypt. How Yahweh had led the people through the Egyptian desert, both day and night. By day, God appeared before the people in a pillar of cloud. By night, He was present to them in a pillar of fire, lighting the way. They traveled nonstop. The crackling campfire made his storytelling even more dramatic as the evening wind roared through the flames, and the rabbi tossed several branches on the coals.

"But the Lord hardened Pharaoh's heart," he said sternly. (Exodus 9:12)

"The great ruler of Egypt realized what he had done, in freeing our people," said the rabbi. "He was enraged!

"So he called his captains to round up 600 chariots and teams of horses, and they chased after the Chosen People into the desert. Our people were terrified that the Pharaoh would kill them. But God would show his mighty power again."

Yeshua reveled in recalling the unforgettable images of that salvation story. How Yahweh stood as a cloud between Israel and the

Egyptian army, shielding his people. How God had instructed Moses, the leader of Israel, to stretch out his hand over the sea. The great east wind had swept up the water to divide it into two standing walls of surf, one to the left and one to the right. The sea floor became a wind-blown highway to freedom. The rushing, warm air dried the sand, so the people of Israel could escape surefooted on an unlikely runway.

"The Egyptians chased our people even into the parting of the Red Sea. Even with all God's mighty power displayed before them, they sought revenge and wanted to destroy us," the rabbi explained with enthusiasm. "But then, God looked upon Pharaoh and his men through the pillars of cloud and fire, and he frustrated them. He jammed the wheels of their chariots. It was only then that they realized that God himself was fighting to protect his people. And in fear and panic they ran back toward Egypt as fast as their horses would carry them."

"And then what happened?" Avigail asked.

"Then Adonai instructed Moses to stretch out his hand over the water again," replied the rabbi. "Only this time, the walls of water crashed down upon the retreating Egyptians. On all their horses and chariots. Not one survived.

"But the sea continued to remain divided until the new nation of Israel had crossed it. We were free from Egypt for ever more!"

The kids around the campfire cheered. Some banged drums. Yeshua had closed his eyes and was imagining the entire scene. He felt badly about all those who had died. God had been merciful to Egypt, but their Pharaoh was stubborn and heartless. He would force his people to endure ten plagues, from bloody water and swarms of frogs, to diseased cattle and boils on both man and beast. Pharaoh refused to release Israel until every firstborn of Egypt had tragically died in a final plague. And even then he defied God.

Yeshua could picture the thousands of horses pulling those chariots. The powerful, majestic animals running faithfully to their deaths. They had all drowned in a sea of Pharaoh's selfishness and willfulness.

As the cheering and drumming around the fire subsided for a moment, Yeshua offered a bit of wisdom:

> *"The horse is equipped for the day of battle,*
> *but victory is the Lord's,"* he said in a strong voice.
> *(Proverbs 21:31)*

"Excellent, Yeshua!" said the rabbi. "You are correct. Nothing man or beast can do will withstand the power of the almighty."

Yeshua continued – this time with another unforgettable scene of Moses and the exodus of Israel.

> *"The Lord came down in a cloud and stood with him there and proclaimed the name, 'Lord.' So the Lord passed before him and proclaimed: The Lord, the Lord, a God gracious and merciful, slow to anger and abounding in love and fidelity, continuing his love for a thousand generations, and forgiving wickedness, rebellion, and sin; yet not declaring the guilty guiltless, but bringing punishment for their parents' wickedness on children and children's children to the third and fourth generation!"* cried Yeshua.
> *(Exodus 34:5-7)*

The youth group grew quiet. So quiet, you could hear the campfire crackle. The rabbi wasn't sure what to say. Why had Yeshua brought up that part of the exodus story?

In a single moment, Yeshua had switched the focus from the evil Egyptian Pharaoh to the hearts of the Israelites. He reminded them that they were sinners, too.

Yeshua had referred to a dramatic Scripture passage where God had appeared to Moses on the mountain. After escaping from

Egypt, the Israelites traveled through the harsh desert to the Promised Land. God called on Moses and presented him with the Ten Commandments, along with the promise to fulfill His Covenant to His people if they obeyed His laws.

In the scorching wilderness where nothing grew, God had provided His people bread from heaven, quail from the sky, and water flowing from rock. Yet, when Moses went up to the mountain to hear God's Word, the people quickly grew impatient for his return. They were anxious and began to worship a false god. They easily lost faith. Not long after Yahweh had miraculously rescued them and crushed their Egyptian enemies, the Israelites adored a handmade, golden calf.

But on this day commemorating Passover, it was easier to remember the sins of the Egyptians and Israel's triumphant escape from bondage. It was hard for the pilgrims to look into their own hearts, and to realize that God had also spared them from His wrath for their own sinful ways. In fact, just as human beings throughout all time and creation, their lives were filled with evils like envy, selfishness, and hatred. Yet, Yahweh was always both just and merciful, and He continued to bless them from generation to generation, and honor the good things they did.

For Yeshua, the Passover was more than a victory celebration or even the birth of a nation. It was not just about war, revenge or earthly slavery. It was also the beginning of a journey — a passing over of sinners through God's mercy, to freedom and salvation. Yahweh was always faithful to those who believed in Him. This journey, through His love and forgiveness, began with the Chosen People. And the Passover was part of the transformation of all sinners to true servants of the Lord.

Finally, the rabbi responded to Yeshua's comment. The boy's insights had astounded him. He was impressed. And now, the rabbi hoped to restore life to the party but also inspire his students and community. He shouted into the night.

> *"'Those who offer praise as a sacrifice honor me;*
> *I will let him whose way is steadfast*
> *look upon the salvation of God,'"* he said. *(Psalm 50:23)*

"You are a very good student, Yeshua. You have studied well," the rabbi continued thoughtfully. "Tonight, we celebrate ... and give praise to Adonai ... who saved Israel from the power of Egypt ... and continues to forgive our sins. Hallelujah!"

The boys beat their drums again and the revelry continued. Yeshua joined in, but his mind was elsewhere. It was with his heavenly Father. Yeshua wished everyone could know Him, understand Him, and love Him the way he did.

chapter
TWENTY-THREE

IN THE MORNING, MANY IN THE CAMP LUGGED HEAVY hangovers. The Seder wine had continued to flow into the night.

The Nazarenes would enjoy an endless series of parties during the week. This was also the start of the grain harvest, and Passover sparked a farming festival in Yerushlem. Some could savor their wine, but others couldn't stop drinking it.

One man in the Nazarene caravan had that problem. His name was Saul, and he was a talented potter, when he wasn't drinking too much.

Yeshua always felt badly for Saul's children, Tobiah and Shayna, and their mother, Tamar. They were often embarrassed by Saul's drinking. Their family struggled because he got behind in his work. Whenever someone talked about Saul's erratic behavior, Yeshua would change the subject and praise Saul's pottery.

Some kids could be very cruel, though. On the way home from school, they would mimic the swaying walk of a drunk as they passed Tobiah. He usually retaliated by starting a fight. One day, Yeshua and Ezra made a point of walking home with Tobiah to help shield him from the taunting. Yeshua suggested Tobiah simply ignore the cruelty and forgive it. Just let it go and give it to Adonai. The sooner he did that, the sooner the teasing would likely stop. Tobiah reluctantly followed Yeshua's advice, and after about a week, he was rewarded.

The kids stopped their bullying. But that didn't prevent the adults in the community from gossiping behind Saul's back.

Fortunately for Saul and his family, the town of Nazareth would be too busy this week to mock its alcoholic potter. Most spent time with relatives and friends who had also made the pilgrimage to Yerushlem. Yosef's family home in Bethlehem was just a few hours' walk south of the city. He took Miriam and Yeshua there to visit his nephew, Ezekiel, who was the son of Yosef's older brother, Shalom. Ezekiel's grandfather and father had both died, leaving him the family carpentry and masonry business.

Yeshua managed Mo, Mazel, and the wagon again on the busy road. Yosef had finally realized he needed to rest his healing ankle as much as possible before the long trip back to Nazareth.

While in Bethlehem, Yeshua met some relatives for the first time, including some cousins about his age. Yosef taught all the kids to play a ball game he had learned while they lived in Egypt. It was called baqet, named after the old Egyptian governor from about 2000 BC. In the time of Baqet III, girls played this ball game.

Yosef took an old goatskin, and stuffed it with grain stalks and some rags he had on the cart. Miriam sewed it shut. The cousins and some neighborhood boys and girls played for hours. There were two teams; the object of the game was to kick the ball past the other team's goal line, marked by stakes in the sand. Yeshua had a great time. He was a strong, fast runner, but his hands were more coordinated than his feet. The kids soon took off their sandals for better traction. All that kicking stirred up a lot of dust. The ball came apart several times, and the players ran home to get other materials to stuff into the old goatskin.

Yeshua wondered why his dad had never taught him the game before.

"I didn't want you to be distracted from your schoolwork," Yosef replied.

The family spent two nights with Ezekiel's family. Yosef liked to call him Zeke. Yeshua showed them some of his carving techniques. The kids convinced their parents to let them sleep on the rooftop. Truthfully, the adults were happy to get a little peace and quiet with the young people out of the small house. The cousins had a lot of fun swapping stories under the night sky, and sharing their plans for the future. They stayed up very late.

The week passed quickly. After their visit in Bethlehem, Yeshua's family traveled back to camp on the Mount of Olives. The next day, they celebrated the Sabbath in the Temple. Of course, it was much more crowded than usual, with most of the Passover pilgrims lingering in Yerushlem to enjoy the grain harvest festival among friends and family.

Yeshua, Miriam, and Yosef spent the Sabbath around the Temple with John and Elizabeth, who had come in the day before from their nearby village in Judah. After Sabbath prayers and services at the Temple, John gave Yeshua a special tour. He had grown up around the facility, tagging along with his father and watching him perform some of his priestly duties. John knew many of the Temple guards and some of the priests, so he could take certain liberties.

As they walked solemnly through the Court of Israelites, they soon encountered an old man guarding the Court of Priests.

"Good Sabbath, Ram," John said in a low voice. "This is my cousin, Yeshua, from Nazareth."

"Good Sabbath," said Yeshua.

Ram wore a stern look as he eyed Yeshua from head to foot, but it quickly melted into a broad smile. "Welcome to the Temple, Yeshua from Nazareth," he said. "Every time I see you, John, I think about your father. I miss Zechariah."

"We miss him, too, Ram," John responded.

"How is your mother?" Ram asked with concern.

"She's doing pretty well right now. We had a very good Passover visiting with Yeshua and his parents," said John. "She hasn't seen Yeshua since he was a baby!"

"So, this must be your first time to the Temple, Yeshua," said Ram. Yeshua nodded shyly.

"I'd like to show him the Court of Priests," John said. "Remember when I was little and my father used to bring me to the court?"

Ram nodded. He stepped into the Court of Priests and looked around. There was no one in sight. He came back and winked at John, then walked away into the Court of Israelites. John slipped off his sandals. Yeshua did the same. All priests went barefoot in the Temple, just as Moses had done in God's presence on the mountain. The two boys stepped over the balustrade, and entered the court, respectfully, taking only a few steps toward the altar. The stone floor felt cold and good on their feet.

A steep ramp rose up toward the altar. Only a small fire smoldered on it today, with the faint smell of lamb fat burning amidst the incense. Yeshua could see the 12 loaves of unleavened shewbread. The atmosphere was dramatically different today than it had been on Passover. The Court of Israelites was quiet, since it was late in the afternoon of the Sabbath; no one else was there. No one was allowed to offer individual sacrifices today. Even the priest on duty had stepped away. It had been an intense week with thousands of sacrifices.

John thought "Perhaps he is in the High Priest's apartment." There was a private room in the Temple, where the High Priest stayed during the week preceding the Day of Atonement.

John walked Yeshua to an area called the Chamber of Phinehas where the vestment-keeper stored the priestly robes in lockers built into the wall. They saw the lily-white, ankle-length linen tunics and the white linen hats most priests wore. The High Priest's vestments were vibrantly colorful. His hat was blue and white. Over his white tunic he wore a robe that matched the hat. The bottom was finished with tiny gold fabric bells and pomegranates. He topped his vestment with a multicolored vest that hung from his shoulders. Around his neck, the High Priest wore a purse adorned with 12 gemstones, one for each of the tribes of Israel. Centuries earlier, the

High Priest kept the Urim and Thummim in the purse. They were ceremonial objects. To Yeshua, the vestments were stunning and he was fascinated by the intricate craftsmanship and detail.

John tapped him on the shoulder to get his attention. Yeshua followed John back to the altar area, taking a few more solemn paces toward the stairs that led up to the Holy of Holies. Two colorful curtains, a double veil, covered it. The boys stood back and gazed at the drapery, which rose to the structure that soared above them. This was a sacred place, reserved exclusively for Yahweh himself. Inside, there were two cherubim, winged creatures carved from olive wood and coated in gold. They kept watch over the Ark of the Covenant that contained Yahweh's law, the commandments given to Moses. The Babylonians had stolen the original stone tablets hundreds of years earlier, but God's laws were inscribed on his people's hearts, and the scribes had copied them onto the Torah scrolls.

No one entered the hallowed room, except the High Priest, and that was only once a year, on Yom Kippur, the Day of Atonement. On that day, the entire community fasted and prayed for forgiveness. The High Priest represented all the people of Israel; he entered the Holy of Holies alone to pray for forgiveness on their behalf. But he wouldn't stay inside too long for fear that God might strike him and the nation with His wrath.

The High Priest wore special vestments, changing them often on Yom Kippur, as he washed many, many times. He bathed his entire body five times; he cleansed his hands and feet ten times. By staying in the Temple apartment, he was assured he'd avoid outside impurities. During the week before, he would study the rituals to ensure he would perform them without error. After all, he would be in God's holy space, and he must be perfect. When the day arrived, the High Priest sacrificed a young bull for his own sins and those of all the priests. He then cast lots to choose between two goats. One would later be sacrificed to Yahweh; the other would be the "scapegoat" for the community's sins.

The first time the High Priest passed the double curtains and entered the Holy of Holies, he filled the chamber with the sweet smell of burning incense to honor the Lord. He prayed for the people, invoking God's name. But he would say God's full name only three times on Yom Kippur, and then never again until the next Day of Atonement.

God had revealed his name to Moses as four Hebrew consonants, YHWH, called the Tetragrammaton. From them came the most sacred name, Yahweh. Over time, by the third century BC, this name became too holy to be uttered in Jewish society.

The second time the High Priest entered the Holy of Holies on Yom Kippur, he sprinkled the room with some of the bull's blood from his sacrifice, and prayed again for the people in God's name.

Then he would exit the chamber to sacrifice the goat he had selected earlier. At the third and final parting of the curtains, he sprinkled the chamber with the goat's blood, uttering Yahweh's name on behalf of Israel one last time.

When he left the Holy of Holies this third time, the people exhaled. They and their High Priest had survived an audience with God himself.

Now, at the altar, the High Priest would place his hands on the living goat, and on behalf of the people, make a confession of their sins, transferring them to the goat.

The people formed an aisle, and the "scapegoat" would be led through the crowd and out of Yerushlem, 12 miles into the wilderness, where it would be pushed to its death from a cliff.

When the High Priest received a signal that this sacrificial goat was dead, the ritual was over, and the celebration began. The people's sinfulness was now gone, and with renewed faith, all of Israel would attempt to do its best to live by God's law. But even though they were the Chosen People, they were not perfect. Soon, they would sin again. For a little while, though, they could enjoy being very, very close to God himself.

"John! Son of Zechariah!" Ram called in a low, stern voice.

Yeshua and John turned from the Holy of Holies, walking quickly toward Ram. As they scurried the 20 feet across the Court of Priests, the boys could hear someone climbing the stairs to the Court of Israelites. They stepped over the rail and slipped on their sandals. Just in time.

Approaching them, Ram whispered, "It's Caiaphas, the son-in-law of the High Priest!"

The old man's eyes could still identify the priest's shape across the Court of Israelites. Caiaphas was older than John and Yeshua, but he wasn't an old man. He walked with youthful vigor, a little swagger in his stride, and his head held high. As he came closer, he nodded at Ram and then recognized John, acknowledging him with a smirk. He looked up and down John's simple garments. Caiaphas had known his late father, Zechariah, quite well.

"John, are you still considering the priesthood?" he asked with a hint of sarcasm.

But John didn't respond directly. "Shlama, Caiaphas. I'm showing my cousin Yeshua the Temple. This is his first time in Yerushlem for Passover," John said. "He is from Nazareth."

Yeshua smiled and nodded respectfully to Caiaphas. "'You are a priest forever in the manner of Melchizedek,'"said Yeshua, reciting from Scripture. (Psalm 110:4)

Caiaphas was both flattered and impressed with young Yeshua's learning.

"I see something good has come from Nazareth," the priest said. He patted Yeshua on the shoulder. "But you really shouldn't be in the Court of Priests," he admonished, shaking his finger at them.

Then he took off his sandals and walked away. Obviously, he suspected John and Yeshua had been in the priestly chamber, but Caiaphas had more important things to do than report petty misdemeanors — especially those that might have occurred under the nose of an old, loyal guard. He had his eye on becoming the High Priest one day. This was an office of power and wealth. He would wait his turn, but all the while, he patiently learned the politics of Yerushlem and Rome.

Caiaphas didn't frighten John. He was keenly aware of the Roman political influence that had infected the priesthood, and he was moved to change it.

John and Yeshua thanked Ram for giving them access to the Court of Priests, and then they headed back to rejoin their family. Their rare time together was coming to an end.

John had plans for a spiritual journey, but he needed someone to care for his mother. Of course, Miriam had offered to take her back with them to Nazareth. But the long trip would be too demanding for Elizabeth. Fortunately, John had found a local family who would look in on her.

Miriam was a little troubled, but knew she had to leave this decision to God. John was old enough to be making a way for himself and his future, though he felt guilty about leaving his mother behind. Elizabeth had insisted he pursue his spiritual calling. She had reminded John many times of the angel's prophecy:

> *"He will go before him in the spirit and power of Elijah to turn the hearts of fathers toward children and the disobedient to the understanding of the righteous, to prepare a people fit for the Lord." (Luke 1:17)*

Even though John wasn't quite 13, Elizabeth knew she had to let him go; he was a man.

The Essenes, a devout Hebrew group, had invited John to join them. They were zealots who strictly adhered to Hebrew law and God's covenant. They were also rebels. They saw the Romans as evil because they occupied Yahweh's people and the land He had promised them. The Romans also worshipped idols, and ruthlessly crucified anyone they perceived to be a threat.

John had watched Israel's corrupt kings compromise their faith, allowing idolatry and all sorts of sinfulness. Their greed and lust for power caused them to honor Caesar and do his bidding. The investment in the Temple distracted the people, while they led Israel down an ungodly path. John's heart ached for the many devout Jews.

The zealots longed for a return to a land truly ruled by Yahweh's laws and real Hebrew leaders, not Roman puppets. These groups threatened the power of the Hebrew king, as well as his Roman allies and occupiers. In fact, there were a number of skirmishes during Passover week. Temple guards arrested some preachers they felt were too outspoken against the king. When supporters tried to protect them, they were all handed over to the Romans, accused of preaching against Caesar, and inciting a riot. Their punishment would be severe.

"I have to spend time in prayer," John told Yeshua. "Adonai is calling me, and I have to know what he wants me to do with my life."

Yeshua replied with advice from the Psalms:
"I will listen for what God, the LORD, has to say;
surely he will speak of peace
To his people and to his faithful." (Psalm 85:9)

"You are wise beyond your years, Yeshua. Like wisdom itself!" said John.

They embraced in the Court of Women. Yeshua understood the yearning in John's heart. John had to make more time for God in his life, and he could do that if he retreated to study with the Essenes for a little while. There was a part of Yeshua that wished he could go with John, to fast and pray in the wilderness.

"Don't worry, Cousin Miriam, I won't be far away from Mother. And after a couple months, I'll return and visit her," John promised as he embraced Miriam and Yosef.

"Go with Adonai, John," Miriam said as she held his hands. "And please send us a message about your mother."

"Your father would be very proud of you," Yosef said to John as he hugged him. "Study hard. You will make a fine priest, just like Zechariah!"

Miriam and Elizabeth held each other in a long embrace. They exchanged few words. The cousins knew this might be the last time they would see each other. As tears rolled down their cheeks, Elizabeth whispered:

> "'My soul proclaims the greatness of the Lord;
> my spirit rejoices in God my savior.'" (Luke 1:46)

John would take his mother home on a cart at sundown. In the morning, he'd depart for the Essenes' camp in Judah.

Yosef and his family made their way back to the Mount of Olives after sunset. Fortunately it was a very short trip, and they had oil lamps, which they lit at the Temple. They followed others up the hills to return to their tents. After a good rest, Yosef, Miriam, and Yeshua spent the next two days shopping for supplies in Yerushlem, and packing for the five-day return trip to Nazareth. They began by cleaning out their wagon, and washing clothing and bedding, while the festival celebration continued.

Yeshua couldn't believe his first Passover pilgrimage was almost over. He thought about Ezra and his hometown. After his amazing experiences in Yerushlem, life in the hills of Galilee would be very ordinary. He had been to the Temple, and had heard the prayers of Yahweh's people in his heart. And he could hear Yahweh's voice loudly and clearly, too. Like John, Yeshua knew he was destined to do more than inherit his father's profession. One day, he would put down his carpenter's tools to pick up a staff made of God's Word, and become a shepherd king of his people. He would lead them home, out of the valley of death to their heavenly Father.

And that new journey would begin at sunrise, in a way Yeshua's parents never expected.

TWENTY-FOUR

"SO, NEXT YEAR WILL BE A BIG YEAR FOR YOU, YESHUA!" said Abner, landlord of the olive grove and camp. "We will look forward to celebrating with you as a man at Passover."

Abner himself was getting ready to roll out of Yerushlem. He wouldn't need to harvest olives until October and November, so the end of Passover was an ideal time for his family to relax for a few days. It had been a very profitable week, with all the caravans renting space in his grove. He would simply hire two men to watch his olive trees, while he stayed with friends along the Mediterranean coast.

Yeshua, Miriam, and Yosef thanked Abner, and then left the Mount of Olives. Instead of heading directly out of town, the caravan would stop at the Temple first. This was an annual tradition for the Nazarenes. Their rabbi would cleanse himself and then enter the Temple, making an offering to ensure their safe journey, as well as their general good health and prosperity. He would buy two doves and bring them to the Court of Priests to sacrifice. Outside the Temple, the community would pray, taking one more long look at the sacred place in the early morning light.

Yosef let Yeshua lead the wagon so he could talk to Miriam.

"I think we should give Yeshua a little break for the next day or two," Yosef suggested.

"What do you mean?" Miriam asked with a smile.

"Let him travel with his friends, the rabbi, and his classmates," said Yosef. "I feel badly that he's had to do so much work on the road. He's been leading the donkeys, while I've been limping and riding around. But I've truly healed. My ankle is as good as new. Finally!" he said with relief.

Miriam trusted Yeshua. He'd done everything they asked of him, and more, without complaint. The city was crowded, but not like Passover week. This would be a good time to give him a little independence. Besides, three people sharing a wagon and a tent for three weeks could get on anyone's nerves.

"You are so wise," Miriam said, touching Yosef's face. "And I'd like some time to talk to you about Avigail and Yeshua.

"Women! How they love to plan weddings," Yosef responded as he jumped off the cart to walk next to his son.

"Yeshua, your mother and I feel you have earned some free time to spend with your friends. When the rabbi comes out of the Temple, why don't you go along with him and the other boys?"

A grin flashed across Yeshua's face. He didn't have to be asked twice to eat, or to have some fun. He handed his father the tethers to Mo and Mazel, and jumped up on the cart to grab his bag and one of the small goatskins of water. He quickly kissed Miriam and thanked her.

"We'll see you in the camp at lunchtime," his mother laughed. "Have fun, Yeshua."

He hugged his father. As Yeshua ran off, his shoulder bag and the goatskin bounced on his hip and shoulder. Yosef smiled, recalling his own boyhood energy and enthusiasm. Yeshua was excited about his new freedom and a chance to be with his buddies. The talk would make the journey seem shorter, and they'd all have plenty to share about friends and family they'd seen in Yerushlem. Yeshua could tell them about the baqet game he had played with his cousins, and how John had taken him for a private tour of the Temple.

Some of the other boys were already milling around the rabbi's wagon when Yeshua ran up, put his foot on one of the back wheels, and shouted joyfully. "Then I proclaimed a fast, there by the river of Ahava, that we might humble ourselves before our God to seek from him a safe journey for ourselves, our children, and all our possessions." (Ezra 8:21)

"Oh, that's good, Yeshua! I know that one," said Aaron, one of the schoolboys. "Wait, it'll come to me."

The boys often played this game, challenging each other to remember Scripture verses and their sources.

They took turns guessing.

"Exodus?"

"Joshua?"

"What about Isaiah?"

Finally, one of them thought he remembered. Benjamin, the rabbi's son, leaned into Yeshua's ear and whispered. He cupped his hands around his mouth, so no one else could overhear him or read his lips. Yeshua chuckled and nodded.

"I'll give you a hint," said Benjamin. "It's Yeshua's best friend."

"The book of Ezra!" Aaron shouted. "I knew it. I knew it. It was so obvious. I'll bet you missed Ezra on this trip," he said to Yeshua.

Yeshua nodded, as he poked around in his bag and pulled out the two Temple relics to show the boys. They were so busy "oohing" and "aahing" and swapping stories, they didn't notice when the rabbi walked up.

"What have you got there, Yeshua?" the rabbi asked.

Yeshua extended both hands, an ancient carving in each one. He explained that they were gifts from his cousin, John, and that John's late father, a priest, had rescued them from destruction during Herod's remodeling of the second Temple.

The rabbi ran his fingers over the stonework, smiling broadly.

"What a splendid keepsake of the old Temple, Yeshua! You will be able to pass them down to your children, and your children's children," said the rabbi.

"Ezra gets one," Benjamin exclaimed with a hint of envy.

"Now, that's a special gift for your very good friend," the rabbi said to Yeshua. He patted him on the shoulder before climbing into his wagon. The rabbi was grateful someone had taken Ezra under his wing. Left behind, kids like Ezra and Tobiah might feel hopeless if their schoolmates rejected them.

The rabbi sat atop his wagon with his wife and the rest of his family. Benjamin would manage their beasts as they left Yerushlem. His friends would tag along with him and help.

Most of the Nazarenes gathered around the rabbi. Miriam put her hand on Yeshua's shoulder. The men stood at their carts, minding their animals, but they all turned to their teacher as he rose. From atop his wagon, he stretched out his hands over his congregation and prayed.

"Lead us toward peace, emplace our footsteps toward peace, guide us toward peace, and make us reach our desired destination for life, gladness, and peace." [7]

"Amen!" said the Nazarenes as they scattered to their spots in the caravan. Within seconds, their two dozen wagons began to roll northward out of the city. The rabbi's cart was near the end of the line, so the boys waited while the other vehicles rumbled ahead.

"Can you imagine what it was like when the Israelites were leaving Egypt?" asked the rabbi. "What a mass of humanity!"

Today's journey wasn't really much different, except the Israelites weren't running away, and there were thousands of people headed in different directions. Yosef and Miriam had earned a spot near the front of the caravan. The couple had often traveled to Yerushlem and Bethlehem, and even once to Egypt, so the other Nazarenes valued their experience and insights. Yosef had become very savvy about survival on the road.

"It's a good thing we're going early because the Roman legion will be leaving at some point and heading north, too," he said to Miriam, with a sense of anticipation. His words proved prophetic.

Just after the caravan started pulling away from the Temple area toward Antonia fortress, the Romans arrived. A centurion on horseback galloped up right behind Miriam and Yosef, blocking the rest of the caravan. When Yosef stopped, the soldier shouted, "Ite! Ite! Ite!" A few understood his Latin command, "Go." He quickly caught himself, switching to Aramaic for the pilgrims. "Keep moving! The legion is marching through. In the name of Caesar, keep moving on the right side of the road." The centurion was hell-bent on preventing a traffic jam. Tens of thousands of travelers were trying to leave Yerushlem, and Caesar's legion was headed back to Rome.

The first several Nazarene carts cleared the intersection as the Romans rolled through, and turned up the road. They were forced to move, or risk being crushed by the mounted troops, their burly beasts, and heavy supply wagons. The road was barely wide enough to accommodate both the soldiers and the civilian traffic.

"We've got no choice," Yosef yelled over the sound of hooves and wheels roaring past him. "If we just stand here, that centurion may arrest us for ignoring his order."

So the group continued, staying as close as possible to the right side of the road. Other pilgrims up ahead weren't as lucky; the passing Romans simply shoved them aside, brushing and bumping many of them. After what seemed like an endless stream of wagons and mounted troops, a column of marching foot soldiers followed. They stepped in unison, armed with swords, shields, and lances.

The rest of the Nazarene caravan stopped. Fortunately, before breaking camp, the group had already decided where they'd pause for lunch, and where they'd camp at day's end. So no one was panicked about being separated. But it meant the few families leading the caravan would be more vulnerable on the road because they were now traveling in a smaller group.

The centurion waved the Nazarenes forward. "Let's go! Move! Move! Move!" As soon as he saw the first carts begin to roll, the Roman briskly turned his horse and followed the last of the marching soldiers. He galloped to the top of the column. The caravan began to gain momentum, too. All along, the rabbi had been standing in his wagon, watching the events from his spot near the rear of the line. When he sat down, it was a good sign of progress.

But before long, they stopped again. After a dozen carts rolled through the intersection, another mounted centurion cut in front of the remaining Nazarenes. This time, several Roman guards on horseback led prisoners in irons. At the back of the chain gang, one man had a wooden beam strapped across his shoulders. He struggled to keep his balance under the weight. Gaping wounds and bloody cuts covered his body. The condemned had been flogged to start his punishment.

Later, he would suffer unimaginably; his arms outstretched, his wrists nailed to the wooden crossbeam. Four soldiers would hoist the beam, and place it atop a pole. Insects would burrow into his wounds, while birds picked at his flesh. Besides the intense pain and profuse bleeding, the man would eventually suffocate, every breath a struggle. His body, exhausted from the effort, would buckle at the waist and sag against the cross. His diaphragm would strain to expand and contract his lungs. With every tortured breath, the condemned man would use his feet to push off the cross. If he managed to linger longer than the soldiers wanted, they might break his legs to hasten his death.

"It's a crucifixion!" the rabbi said as the criminals moved into full view of the caravan. "Don't watch, boys. Look away." The pilgrims gasped and hid their faces.

But Yeshua couldn't escape. When he closed his eyes, the images became more vivid and more personal. Suddenly, he felt as if he were walking behind the horses. He could see blood dripping on the ground in front of him. It seemed to flow from his head and body. There was so much blood.

When he opened his eyes, the vision stopped, and the prisoners had passed. Now, the centurion allowed east-west traffic to cross the road. Many pilgrims headed west toward the coastal towns; others were going eastward toward the Jordan River and places like Jericho. When Yeshua looked south, he could see a series of caravans stacked up behind the Nazarenes. Travelers were backed up to the east and west as well. With all the animals and wagons and foot traffic, this would take some time to clear. Maybe an hour.

The boys were bored. They leaned on the cart or sat down on the ground. Finally, two climbed into the rabbi's wagon and lay down.

Yeshua welcomed the delay. He stood gazing at the Temple complex, where thousands of craftsmen had resumed their work on the massive campus in the early morning light. They had postponed construction during Passover and the grain harvest festival. Compared to the carpentry and masonry in Nazareth, the scale of their work was very impressive. They generated plenty of noise and activity, using powerful equipment to craft large beams and fashion huge stones. Foremen shouted orders. Workers called to their helpers for tools. Many carpenters and masons hammered, sawed, and chiseled throughout the massive site. Yeshua wanted to watch them for a while.

The Romans allowed a group of laborers with a crane to cut through the intersection. A team of oxen hauled the device to the Temple on a low wagon, specially built to move it. Yeshua had never seen such a large, sophisticated mechanism.

Suddenly, he recognized Hillel, the carpenter. He had given Yosef his walking staff outside the Temple, the day before Passover. Now he was on his job, following behind the construction crane, in front of a wagon loaded with long cedar timbers.

"Hillel! Hillel!" Yeshua called as he waved to the worker in front of his position in line. But Hillel didn't hear him, and kept walking toward his Temple assignment, hauling his tools in a small cart.

Yeshua ran a few steps up the line. He stopped and quickly turned to his schoolmates to tell them his plan. He was going to catch up with a man who had helped his father. Yeshua shouted his message to the boys. But with all the noise from the construction site and the crowd, they couldn't hear him very well.

"Yeshua! Yeshua!" yelled the rabbi. But the commotion was too loud. Yeshua disappeared into the crisscrossing people and animals.

"Where's he going?" said Aaron. "Should I go get him?"

"Absolutely not!" ordered the rabbi. "You boys stay here, where we can see you."

"I think he said he's going to catch up and help his father," said Benjamin.

"He's in for a long run," the rabbi replied, shaking his head.

"He's very fast," Aaron shouted. "He'll catch them."

"Shlama!" Yeshua said, greeting Hillel as he ran up alongside him. Hillel was surprised at first, but then he remembered Yeshua's face.

"You're still here?" Hillel asked. "Is your father alright? Is that ankle healed?"

Yeshua pointed to the traffic jam. As he walked with Hillel toward the Temple, he explained how he'd gotten separated from his parents. He reached into his shoulder bag, pulling out the Temple relics. He recounted their story for Hillel.

"Be very careful with those treasures," Hillel cautioned. "So much was destroyed from the old Temple, they're pretty rare. Let me show you one of my favorites."

Reaching into his toolbox, Hillel pulled out a thick stone tile with the image of a menorah carved into it. The menorah is one of the oldest Hebrew symbols, a candleholder with seven branches. There was a real menorah in the Temple sanctuary; priests lit its seven candles each night, and then cleaned it every morning.

"I believe this piece may even date back to Solomon's Temple. I found it here when we were doing some excavation to build the foundation for the Sanhedrin tower," said Hillel.

Yeshua marveled that the image had not worn away. If Hillel was right, the piece was about 1,000 years old! The artwork had survived foreign invaders and Herod's display of power and pride.

"The LORD protects the loyal,
but repays the arrogant in full," Yeshua said. (Psalm 31: 24)

He handed the stone relic back to Hillel. Yeshua had quoted a Psalm of King David, who was Solomon's father.

"You know your Scripture!" Hillel said. "Hey, looks like the traffic is moving faster now."

Yeshua turned back toward the road. He could see the Nazarene caravan had actually moved up quite a distance, and was almost out of sight.

"Thanks!" he yelled, putting his stone icons into his shoulder bag. Yeshua waved goodbye, racing as fast as he could toward the intersection. But the traffic had already begun to blend from the various directions. Some moved from the west to the north, some from the east to the south. Suddenly, the road was congested with people, animals, and carts.

"Stubborn Hebrew mules!" yelled another centurion as he rode up on his horse into the crowd.

"You there, wait," the Roman shouted as he gestured south at an aggressive traveler. Then he turned on his horse, and pointed to the pilgrims on the east side of the intersection. "You there, you move," he commanded, waving the crowd to travel north.

"But I'm headed south past Bethlehem," one traveler complained.

"Well, not right now you're not. Head west or head north, but you're not going south, it's too backed up right now."

Every second that passed, the last of the Nazarene caravan got a little farther up the road. And the crowd that wanted to push north was pressed against those at the front of the line. Yeshua thought about running through the cross traffic, but it moved too fast. Then a column of twenty mounted Romans rushed up, forcing traffic to move east or west only. They formed a wall across those facing north.

The troops held the line to protect the flow of merchants and goods coming in from the west and the Mediterranean Sea. They had shipped their wares through trade companies in Ascalon. Caesar collected taxes on all the merchandise, so the Roman army's priority was to protect their ruler's wealth. No one would be allowed to cross until all the commercial carts and deliveries had passed. Donkeys, oxen, and camels trudged before the anxious crowd, loaded with goods to replenish Yerushlem after the Passover.

The pilgrims grew impatient. The harder they pushed toward the front of the line, the more some became claustrophobic. Several fainted. One toddler couldn't find his parents. He sat down in the road and cried. Yeshua crawled over to him, wrapping his arms around the child for protection. He crouched over the boy, while feet and legs pressed around him for what seemed like an hour. Only five minutes had actually passed. Suddenly, people started to move, ignoring him and the child in his arms. They bumped Yeshua as they trudged by. He saw nothing but sandals, garments, and dust. There wasn't any room to look up, so he closed his eyes.

Finally, he felt the pushing and shoving ease up. Then it stopped. When Yeshua opened his eyes, he could see the hooves of a horse pawing the ground right in front of him. He looked up into the morning light, and saw the silhouette of a black stallion with a Roman officer on its back. Shielding his eyes with one hand, Yeshua recognized the centurion. This was the same man who had stopped to help Ephraim and his family when Roman troops crashed into their cart on the road to Yerushlem.

"Are you alright? Is the child hurt?" asked the mounted soldier.

Yeshua picked himself up and smiled at the centurion. He helped the toddler to his feet, and told the centurion he'd found the little boy lost in the crowd, alone and crying.

"Give him to me," said the Roman, bending down from his saddle, and stretching out his arms. Yeshua lifted the child toward the soldier. The Roman hoisted the little one up and stood him on the horse's back. Then he gently kneed the stallion to walk a circle around Yeshua, who had moved to the side of the road.

"Anyone missing a child? Is this your little boy?" the soldier shouted.

The crowd continued to push by the scene. People looked up, but no one claimed the tearful toddler. They seemed obsessed to leave Yerushlem. The pilgrims were truly in a hurry to get home. Travel was expensive; they had to get back to their farms and businesses, or they could lose them. Perhaps the child's parents hadn't realized he was missing. Or maybe they were searching for him elsewhere.

The centurion lowered the sobbing boy and handed him back to Yeshua. He looked down at them with sympathy. "Take the little one to the Court of Women," the Roman said. "There are faithful widows and mothers there who come to the Temple every day. They will take care of the boy until his parents arrive." He reached into his belt and tossed down a coin as an incentive. Yeshua caught it and examined the small gold piece. Caesar's image was stamped upon it. He rubbed the surface of it with his thumb, admiring the workmanship.

Yeshua thanked the centurion for his kindness and stroked his horse on the nose. The animal nodded and the soldier smiled at Yeshua. He appreciated the valor he had shown by protecting the little boy. Maybe he was thinking of his own children back home.

The Roman turned his horse toward the crowd and trotted into the traffic. Yeshua took the little boy by his hand and headed directly for the mikveh. He cleansed himself first, and then helped the child do the same. All the while, the boy whimpered, and refused to speak when Yeshua asked his name.

As they climbed the viaduct to the Temple Mount, the walk quickly became too much for the little one. Yeshua lifted him onto his shoulders, carrying him as Yosef had done with Yeshua when he was small. After entering through the outer Temple gate, called "Beautiful," Yeshua made his way toward the Court of Women. He and his tiny passenger passed the moneychangers and the merchants hawking sacrificial animals. The toddler finally stopped crying, enjoying the ride on Yeshua's shoulders. Yeshua mimicked the sounds of the livestock to make the little one laugh.

"Coo, coo. Ba-ha-ha-ha-ha!" Yeshua thought his impression of doves and lambs was pretty good. The little boy cackled and grinned from ear to ear every time Yeshua pretended to be an animal. He walked like a pigeon and then skipped along like a little lamb. Anything to keep the toddler happy. He struggled to balance the child on his shoulders.

Approaching the Court of Women, Yeshua set the boy down and took his hand. The Court had four chambers, one in each corner: the Chamber of Lepers, the Chamber of Oils, the Chamber of Wood, and the Chamber of Nazirites. The Nicanor Gate separated the Court of Women from the Court of Israelites.

Yeshua noticed a group of women praying at the 15 semi-circular steps that led up to Nicanor Gate. He glanced down at his young companion and smiled. The little one smiled back, and then looked away, pretending to be shy. Slowly, Yeshua led him across the court toward the steps. A beggar approached them. Yeshua reached into his bag.

"Shlama," said Yeshua, handing him the Roman coin.

"Oh, thank you, thank you," said the beggar. "May Adonai bless you all the days of your life."

Yeshua nodded a quiet 'thank you' and continued on his way toward the praying women. As he drew closer, none of them noticed. He waited respectfully. Yeshua could hear their silent prayers in his head. There were fears and illnesses in their lives. Marriages that were in trouble. But these women were also grateful for God's blessings, for their children, for their husbands and homes. They were happy to be alive to talk to God in his Temple.

Finally, the little boy became bored and began whimpering again. In a calm, confident voice, Yeshua spoke to the group.

> *"'Many are the women of proven worth,*
> *but you have excelled them all.'*
> *Charm is deceptive and beauty fleeting;*
> *the woman who fears the LORD is to be praised.*
> *Acclaim her for the work of her hands,*
> *and let her deeds praise her at the city gates."*
> *(Proverbs 31:29-31)*

As he spoke, the women glanced back to see who was reciting Scripture. Finally, an older woman turned and knelt on both knees in front of the little boy. She dried his tears with her apron. Reaching into her pocket, she pulled out a few raisins and gave them to the little one. Immediately, he stopped crying and began stuffing the treats in his mouth. Yeshua and the women laughed.

"He's very hungry! Is this your brother?" the woman asked.

Yeshua shook his head. He explained who he was, and how he'd found the boy in the street. How a centurion had suggested Yeshua bring him to the Court of Women, where he'd find someone to care for the child.

"The Gentile gave you good advice, Yeshua," the woman replied. "We'll be here for another hour and we'll see that he's safe. After that, there are a few old grandmas who live here and pray day and night. They will protect him. We'll see that he's fed. You can go now. Don't worry; he'll be fine."

"Thank you. Shlama," said Yeshua as he waved goodbye to the toddler. He bent down and kissed him on the forehead.

But where would Yeshua go now? As he walked away from the women, for the first time he stopped to think about himself. Yeshua realized it would be very hard to catch up with the caravan. The Nazarenes were easily an hour up the road. He could try to make good time, but the highway was congested and traveling alone would be risky. He knew his father, Yosef, would expect him to be smarter than that.

Just then, Yeshua felt a tug on his shoulder. When he spun around, he saw it was the beggar he had met a little earlier. He had untied Yeshua's bag and had his hand in it. He wasn't really a beggar at all, but a pickpocket.

The man started to run, but Yeshua grabbed him by the arm. He reached into his bag with the other hand, and pulled out a few coins. He put them in the thief's hand.

The man looked at the coins and then up at Yeshua's face. Yeshua let go of his wrist. The pickpocket blushed, momentarily embarrassed. Not only had Yeshua caught him, but he was also willing to share more of his money. He couldn't understand the gesture, but he knew how it made him feel.

"I can't help myself," said the thief. "This is how I live."

"You are indeed accursed," said Yeshua.
"For you, the whole nation, rob me.
Bring the whole tithe
into the storehouse,
That there may be food in my house.
Put me to the test, says the LORD of hosts,
And see if I do not open the floodgates of heaven for you,
and pour down upon you blessing without measure!" he added.
(Malachi 3:9-11)

The thief remembered the Scripture. He looked down at the coins again and gave them back to Yeshua. He pulled up his tunic and reached into his own purse, hidden under his cloak. Taking out some coins, he said, "I promise, I'll go to the moneychangers, and I'll bring shekels to donate to the Temple treasury. I will tithe and try to change my life." His eyes watered.

Yeshua could see he was sincere, so he told the thief, "'Do not be afraid, for God has come only to test you and put the fear of him upon you so you do not sin.'" (Exodus 20:20)

This was the statement Moses had made to the Israelites, just after they had received the Ten Commandments.

The thief smiled at Yeshua and quickly walked away. He was profoundly grateful for his kindness. Yeshua could have hollered for the guard and had him arrested. They would have found all he had stolen, and would have thrown him in their jail. Yeshua had saved him from their wrath. He had also touched his heart and soul.

Yeshua knew his earthly father had been right. Yerushlem was a dangerous place for a young boy to be alone. Even in the Temple, someone had tried to rob him and he had only been there a short while. He heard Yosef's words loudly and clearly in his head:

"Promise me, Yeshua, that if something goes wrong, or you get lost while we're in Yerushlem, no matter who tries to persuade you, you will not go home with them unless you know the person well. There are people there who could steal you and sell you into slavery. You would be worth 2,000 denarii as a slave. They'd kidnap you and ship you off to another part of the world, and we'd never see you again."

Yeshua sat down in the court and thought hard for a moment. He could try to find his cousin, Elizabeth, but he didn't really know where her house was. He could travel south to Bethlehem, back to the home of his cousin Zeke. But that would take half a day. What if his parents had returned to the Temple to look for him while he was gone? They'd panic if they couldn't find him.

He had met Ram, the Temple guard, and Hillel, the carpenter, as well as Uriel, the moneychanger. But he certainly didn't know them well enough to ask for lodging in their homes.

Gazing up at the majestic architecture around him, Yeshua realized that the one he knew best in Yerushlem was his heavenly Father.

Yeshua would be safest in the Temple, his Father's house. He would stay there until Miriam and Yosef found him. And besides, there was so much of Yahweh's work he could do in Yerushlem. There were hungry people here, starving for God's Word.

TWENTY-FIVE

THE NAZARENE CARAVAN FOUND THE GOING SLOW
on the way back to Galilee. Not only was there a lot of traffic, but
the day was hotter, too. And not everyone was an experienced traveler. The group had been split into three smaller caravans by the
Roman traffic cops and the morning's delays.

Yosef and Miriam had made very good time in the lead group,
but all the while Miriam was a little nervous about Yeshua.

"I would just feel better if I could see their wagon," she said.
"Maybe we should stop and wait for them."

"Miriam! Have you any idea how long we'll wait? Besides, I
thought you trusted Yeshua, and had faith in Adonai," Yosef responded in frustration. "He's with the rabbi and his school friends. We'll
see them at lunch. And if not, they'll certainly catch up by nightfall."

Miriam was a little embarrassed, as she nodded in agreement.

"I understand, Yosef, but what if something happens to them?
Let's say the rabbi's wagon breaks down. We'd never know it," she
said, her voice rising.

"Then Yeshua will repair the wagon. They've got the right man
for the job," Yosef replied.

Yosef paused to think about what he'd just said. He'd never referred to Yeshua as a man before. Indeed, their son would soon be
13, and he had already demonstrated he was very responsible. He

had really stepped up on this Passover pilgrimage. Yosef smiled confidently and assured Miriam they had taught Yeshua how to take care of himself.

As Yosef looked back to the south, it was obvious they had begun their descent from Yerushlem. Now the view of the road behind was more limited. On the way up to the Holy City, a pilgrim could look over his shoulder and see miles of travelers at times. Climbing the rising terrain provided a great rearward perspective. But since they were now descending away from the city, they didn't have a bird's-eye view of the traffic behind them. The road was either flat or it sloped downward in front of them.

There were many wagons and walkers right on their heels, making it difficult to see past them. People pushed hard in the hot sun to make up for the morning's delays. It seemed everyone had decided to leave Yerushlem on the same day at the same time. Even though some pilgrims had departed earlier in the week, the Sabbath fell right at the end of the grain harvest festival this year. Most visitors took an extra couple of days after their day of rest in order to stock up on travel supplies and pack. They weren't allowed to purchase goods on the Sabbath, so they delayed their departure until Tuesday, after Passover ended. That would give the Nazarenes four whole days to travel north, before the next Sabbath arrived at sunset on Friday. God willing, they'd keep the Lord's Day in the wilderness of the familiar Jezreel Valley, and then arrive home on Sunday in time for lunch.

Meanwhile, the rabbi and his contingent made pretty good time. With all the young boys taking turns leading his beasts, there was plenty of energy in the third segment of the caravan.

"Maybe we can catch up with Yeshua at lunch," Aaron exclaimed as he skipped alongside the wagon.

"I can't see his wagon from up here," said the rabbi from his perch on the cart. "There's too much traffic, but don't worry, boys. If all else fails, we'll see Yeshua and his family tonight."

Lunch was still a couple hours off. Yeshua was already hungry. He'd had a very busy morning so far. There was nothing to eat in his shoulder bag, so he took a long slow drink of water from his goatskin. It would have to do until he went outside to buy something. He didn't want to exit the Temple or he'd have to bathe again before entering. He'd wait until later in the day.

Fortunately, Yeshua had some money. Not only did he still have most of his savings, but his cousins, Elizabeth and Ezekiel, had also given him coins for the journey home. He was very grateful. He'd need to make his money last until Miriam and Yosef found him. He decided he'd feel less hungry if he stopped thinking about food. He would fast until lunch on behalf of all those people who were starving or unhealthy because they couldn't afford to eat well.

Yeshua sat down, closed his eyes, and leaned on a pillar to say a brief prayer for the poor. Almost immediately, he heard a small, sobbing voice behind him.

"Dear Lord, I cannot marry this man. Please, please help my father see I do not love him," a young woman pleaded.

Yeshua opened his eyes and quietly listened.

"It would be better to die now, than to spend a lifetime with someone I don't love," she cried. "I can't have his children. I love Asher. He will always have my heart. Almighty Adonai, please help me."

There was a very serious, desperate tone in her voice that grabbed Yeshua's attention.

He said to her, "Thus says the LORD:
Cease your cries of weeping,
hold back your tears!" (Jeremiah 31:16)

The young woman froze with fear. She thought she had found a safe hiding place in the Temple, where no one could hear her. Yeshua continued.

"Honor your father and your mother, as the LORD, your God, has commanded you, that you may have a long life and that you may prosper in the land the LORD your God is giving you," he said in a soothing voice. (Deuteronomy 5:16)

The girl was startled. She didn't know what to do next. Perhaps it was someone she knew. She wondered whom the voice belonged to.

Yeshua slowly turned his head in her direction. He whispered, "Do not judge from his appearance or from his lofty stature … God does not see as a mortal, who sees the appearance. The LORD looks into the heart." (1 Samuel 16:7)

The remark provoked the young woman to speak. Was he suggesting that she was a superficial person, infatuated with a handsome young man? She was insulted.

"Excuse me, but I love Asher for his heart. I know his heart, and he's a generous and good man," she replied. "I barely know this older man my father wants me to marry." She caught herself, realizing she didn't even know who was listening.

"Call to me, and I will answer you; I will tell you great things beyond the reach of your knowledge," Yeshua said. (Jeremiah 33:3)

The young woman was startled by the wisdom of his quick response from Scripture. She peered around the corner of the pillar, surprised to see someone younger. From the thin hairs on his face, she could tell Yeshua was still a kid. She was only 14 years old herself.

"I don't know you at all. Who are you?" she asked.

Yeshua introduced himself and explained he was on a pilgrimage from Nazareth.

"What makes you so wise then?" she scoffed.

"For the spirit of God made me,
the breath of the Almighty keeps me alive," replied Yeshua.
(Job 33:4)

"He made me too, but what could you possibly know about an arranged marriage ... about my situation?" she pressed.

Yeshua paused and said,

"For I know well the plans I have in mind for you—[says the LORD]—plans for your welfare and not for woe, so as to give you a future of hope. When you call me, and come and pray to me, I will listen to you. When you look for me, you will find me. Yes, when you seek me with all your heart." (Jeremiah 29: 11-13)

The Scripture passage calmed the young woman. A slight smile cracked the corners of her mouth. Her anger and fear faded.

"Your rabbi in Nazareth must love you. You're probably his top student!" she said.

Yeshua blushed and lowered his head.

"I appreciate your advice, but I have been praying, and I'm not getting any answers," she said.

Yeshua replied,

"But as for me, I will look to the LORD,
I will wait for God my savior;
my God will hear me!" (Micah 7:7)

The young woman nodded. "I know I need to talk to my father. But I can't find the courage to tell him what I feel," she confessed. "He'll be very angry. He won't let me even talk to Asher."

Yeshua paused and then slid toward her on the Temple floor.

"There is an appointed time for everything,
and a time for every affair under the heavens.
... a time to be silent, and a time to speak," he whispered.
(Ecclesiastes 3:1,7)

She was struck by the clarity of the Scripture she had heard all her life. In her heart, she knew Yeshua was right. If she had an issue, she had to find the courage to respectfully tell her father. And then she had to live with the consequences. Ultimately, she would obey her father, but if she told him how she felt, there was hope. There was a chance he would allow her to marry Asher instead.

"You are so wise for a kid, Yeshua," she said drying her tears. "I've been rude to you. My name is Zilpah. Thank you for your kindness. You've made me feel better."

Yeshua smiled at Zilpah and humbly said,

> *"'Give thanks to the LORD for he is good,*
> *his mercy endures forever!'" (Psalm 107:1)*

Zilpah smiled back in agreement. Now she knew what she had to do. She stood up and walked away confidently praising God for His wisdom and for answering her prayers.

It was a joyful moment for Yeshua, too. He was relieved he could help the young woman escape her despair.

"Are you Yeshua from Nazareth?"

Yeshua turned and looked up to see who had spoken. "Yes, I am," he answered. An adult couple stood over him, so Yeshua immediately jumped to his feet, out of respect.

"Oh, thank you for protecting our son! Adonai, be praised," said the woman. She was holding the little boy Yeshua had rescued from the crowded Yerushlem street.

Yeshua could see the Temple women across the court waving to him and smiling. They had obviously told the boy's parents about Yeshua's good deed. He waved back, and then put his hand on the little boy's knee and said:

> *"Certainly sons are a gift from the LORD,*
> *the fruit of the womb, a reward." (Psalm 127:3)*

"Indeed! Indeed!" exclaimed the boy's father. "Here, please take all that we have." He reached into his purse and pulled out all his traveling money. "We have no other way of repaying you for our son's life!"

Yeshua looked at the handful of coins. He could certainly use some of the money, but he knew his parents would be returning for him sooner or later. He refused the reward, and suggested the couple give the money to someone who was needy. Perhaps someone in their village, a widow or an orphan.

The little boy stretched his arms out toward Yeshua.

"He likes you!" said the toddler's father. "He's usually afraid of strangers, especially men. His name is Noam."

Yeshua took Noam in his arms and hugged him. He pretended to be a dove, bobbing his head back and forth. "Coo-coo-coo!" chortled Yeshua. The little boy giggled. They were all laughing as Yeshua handed the toddler back to his mother.

"There is a widow in Antipatris where we live. She has a daughter. We could give her the money and tell her it is from you, Yeshua," declared the boy's mother.

> *"She reaches out her hands to the poor,*
> *and extends her arms to the needy,"* Yeshua said.
> *(Proverbs 31:20)*

He was very pleased with the family's decision, and flattered they would make the donation in his name. Talking about the widow and her child made him think of Deborah and his buddy, Ezra. He missed them very much, especially now that he was alone.

The couple embraced Yeshua and promised to pray for him. Just as they were ready to leave, the father turned and asked, "Will you at least let us buy you something to eat? It's time for lunch. Come. Join us!"

Yeshua happily agreed. It had already been quite a day for him, on his own in Yerushlem. And he had worked hard, doing his Father's will, with both words and deeds.

chapter TWENTY-SIX

THE BREAD WAS FRESH AND THE GOAT CHEESE smooth and creamy. The salty olives blended wonderfully.

"Don't talk too much, boys. Eat. Eat. We need to make up some time so we can catch the others," the rabbi told his students. His wife, Dara, scurried about, serving a roadside lunch for her family and their guests. The boys had a lot of energy, but they had burned it up frolicking on the road. The group had to stop sooner for lunch because a few boys were getting dehydrated from running around in the hot sun. There was little shade to be found. Dara had insisted her husband stop their little caravan, so the boys could eat and drink their fill. The last thing she wanted to do was return these young men to their parents exhausted and sickly.

Up the road, Yosef and Miriam had parked at the caravan's lunch destination, a popular turn-off near the town of Gabaon. Their contingent of the Nazarene caravan made the destination by noon, about six hours after sunrise. A half hour later, the second group arrived.

"Have any of you seen the rabbi's wagon? Are they close to catching up? Shouldn't we wait for them?" Miriam asked those who had just arrived.

"I think they've already stopped for lunch. For a while, I could see them on some of the turns, way back in the line," said Reuben, the town's beekeeper. "But I haven't seen them in the last hour or so.

There was lots of traffic. I really think we should keep going. We can wait for them at camp tonight, near Shiloh."

"I'll be happy to wait here, if it makes you feel better," said Ethan, the town tailor. "I'll wait another hour and then if I don't see them, I'll head south to look for them. I can make better time." Ethan rode a donkey. Unburdened by a wagon, he could move much faster, and if he had to travel against traffic, he could squeeze by more easily.

"Maybe I should stay here with you," Yosef suggested to Ethan.

"No!" Miriam protested. "I don't need to lose my husband and my son in the same day. Besides, no one knows these roads better than you do, Yosef. And you promised to navigate for the caravan."

The whole group was quiet for an awkward moment. Yosef put his hand on Miriam's. "You haven't lost your son," he assured her. "He's just delayed. Reuben said he'd spotted their wagon, and I'm sure the rabbi and Dara have their hands full with all the boys. They're young and strong. They'll make it to Shiloh. It may be after dark, but the rabbi's also a very experienced traveler. And who is closer to Adonai than the rabbi?"

The Nazarenes laughed in agreement. Yosef had a nice way of defusing tense moments. So, it was decided. Ethan would stay; the rest of the group would head for the inn near Shiloh. The second group ate and drank quickly, so they wouldn't hold up the other travelers. They stretched their legs and watered their beasts. Shimon, a young farmer, volunteered to accompany Ethan. He had moved to Nazareth to help his brother and his wife with their farm. He was 17 and not yet betrothed.

"Thank you, Ethan and Shimon, for making this sacrifice," Miriam said as she packed up the lunch supplies. "May Adonai repay you every day for the rest of your lives."

Everyone could tell she was anxious about Yeshua. Many of the other mothers were also concerned about their sons. But Miriam had a unique reason to feel uneasy. She remembered Simeon's

prophecy about Yeshua in the Temple, when he was just over a
month old:

> *"Behold, this child is destined for the fall and rise of many
> in Israel, and to be a sign that will be contradicted (and
> you yourself a sword will pierce) so that the thoughts of
> many hearts may be revealed." (Luke 2: 34-35)*

Usually, Miriam wasn't a worrier. She trusted God. But she was always waiting for the pain of the blade that would wound her deeply.
Could this be it? She wouldn't know until nighttime. She figured
Yeshua and the other boys would soon join them. Miriam promised
herself she would focus on the road ahead, and leave her son and his
companions in God's hands. It was time to let him grow up.

"Be sure to take plenty of squab! Eat, eat, Yeshua," the grateful father urged. Yeshua, Noam, and his parents enjoyed a freshly grilled
lunch at an inn, not far from the Temple. This was a rare treat for
Yeshua. Eating meat was one thing, but poultry was special. His
parents rarely killed a chicken. Eggs were too valuable. The grateful
family splurged and bought roasted dove to thank Yeshua for res-
cuing their son.

Yeshua savored his share of the bird, some warm bread, and olive
oil. The water he drank was cool and fresh, and he enjoyed some
pomegranate.

> *"Then the LORD will guide you always*
> *and satisfy your thirst in parched places,*
> *will give strength to your bones*
> *And you shall be like a watered garden,*
> *like a flowing spring whose waters never fail." (Isaiah*
> *58:11)*

He was very grateful for the delicious meal. The young couple appreciated his wisdom, and relished the sight of Yeshua finishing his food. They imagined their little boy in about ten years, and laughed about all they would experience along the way as he grew up. Yeshua played with the toddler a little, and then offered sincere thanks and farewell. It was fun having a "little brother" for a few hours. He left the family with a blessing.

> *"The LORD let his face shine upon you, and be gracious to you! The LORD look upon you kindly and give you peace!"*
> (Numbers 6:25-26)

The young couple was touched by his prayer. They assumed they would never again see this marvelous young man who had rescued their son. Yeshua headed back to the Temple without telling them he'd been left behind. He'd only said he was waiting for his parents to pick him up.

As he walked toward the mikveh, Yeshua ran into some of Yerushlem's street people. There were the beggars and the lame, the ha-aretz or "people of the land." Some were blind. Others suffered from mental illness and disabilities. Most people walked right by them, without even a look or a nod. Occasionally, someone would give them alms, but realistically, there were too many people for one person to help. Most helped no one.

Yeshua's heart ached at the sight. During Passover, the ha-aretz had been driven away by the overwhelming crowds, not to mention the Temple guards' desire to keep everything looking perfect for the festival. But today, Yerushlem was back to routine business, and that included plenty of thievery and other crimes.

Suddenly, someone snatched Yeshua's shoulder bag. A barefoot kid in a raggedy tunic ran past the street people, carrying the stolen property. Yeshua instinctively began chasing him. All his money, his new prayer shawl, his carving knife, and the Temple relics from his cousin, John, were in that bag. Yeshua was faster than the thief, and he quickly closed in on him. As they raced along the wall near the mikveh, the thief tripped. Actually, Uriel, the moneychanger, had seen him coming with Yeshua in pursuit, and he knew something wasn't right. He stuck out his foot, and the thief stumbled to the ground. Yeshua had his man, and grabbed hold of his tunic.

Uriel jumped up from his table and stomped his foot on the strap of the shoulder bag. He yanked it out of the thief's hand.

"You grumpy old crook! That's my bag!" yelled the young thief.

Out of breath, Yeshua quickly explained to Uriel that he'd been robbed. The old moneychanger had dealt with his share of con artists. All the while, he kept one eye on his table, but his money was safe in a belt tied snuggly across his waist.

"Oh, I don't need the wisdom and knowledge of Solomon to judge this dilemma," laughed Uriel. "If it's your bag, tell me what's inside."

"My money!" said the thief as he picked himself up off the ground and tried to snatch the bag again. He almost succeeded, but Yeshua still had a fistful of his tunic.

Uriel looked inside the bag, smiled and turned to Yeshua. "What do you say is inside your bag?"

Yeshua described the contents in detail, right down to the carving on the Temple icons. As he mentioned each item, Uriel held them up mockingly in front of the thief. He handed everything to Yeshua, who proceeded to open the bag. Then Yeshua gave a coin to the thief, while Uriel firmly held onto the bandit's garment.

"Are you serious?" asked Uriel in shock. The thief was incredulous himself.

Yeshua replied,

"Merciful and gracious is the LORD,
  slow to anger, abounding in mercy.
  He has not dealt with us as our sins merit."
  (Psalm 103: 8,10)

"Are you sure you don't want me to call the Temple guard?" Uriel asked, still holding onto the young purse-snatcher.

Yeshua shook his head. Uriel shrugged his shoulders in disbelief.

"Well, at least we got your bag back," he said.

Yeshua thanked the honest moneychanger, and insisted the kid explain why he had stolen his bag. The thief felt obliged to respond, since Yeshua had paid him. The two boys walked while they talked.

"I'm broke. If you hadn't chased me, I would've just taken the money and dropped the bag," he said matter-of-factly. "I live on the streets, cuz my house is no place to be. My dad's a drunk, and I got tired of him slapping me around, so I left. I grew up here in Yerushlem. Once in a while, I stop by to see my mother and my sister and grab something to eat. But the drunk is still there, so I don't like to stay. I hate that old man!"

"For the Lord sets a father in honor over his children
and confirms a mother's authority over her sons," Yeshua replied.
(Sirach 3:2)

"That's easy for you to say," snapped the young thief. "I don't see any scars like this on your face." He pulled off his cap to show Yeshua a long crease across the top of his forehead. "Have you ever had a wine jug broken over your skull? Do you get blamed for everything that goes wrong in your house?"

"Wine is arrogant, strong drink is riotous;
none who are intoxicated by them are wise," Yeshua replied.
(Proverbs 20:1)

"Exactly. Do you know how many times he promised my mother and us he'd quit? I wish he were dead!" the thief said.

"Do not glory in your father's disgrace,
for that is no glory to you!" said Yeshua.
"… be steadfast in honoring your father;
do not grieve him as long as he lives.
Even if his mind fails, be considerate of him;

do not revile him because you are in your prime.
Kindness to a father will not be forgotten;
it will serve as a sin offering—it will take lasting root."
  (Sirach 3:10, 12-14)

"My old man is out of his mind already. How am I supposed to feel sorry for someone who beats me? We've tried everything to help him. We hid the wine. I've even poured out his wine. That's when he broke the jug over my head," the young man explained. "I worry about my mom and my sister; they won't leave him. And they're running out of money, cuz he's drinkin' it. My mom spins wool all night to make money. She's skin and bones. I don't know how long she can last."

"Do not worry about tomorrow; tomorrow will take care of itself," Yeshua advised. (Matthew 6:34)

"It makes me crazy!" exclaimed the boy. "I think about it all the time, but I can't figure out how to save them. How do I fix it?"

"Trust in the LORD with all your heart,
  on your own intelligence do not rely,'" urged Yeshua.
"In all your ways be mindful of him,
  and he will make straight your paths." (Proverbs 3:5-6)

The young thief hung his head. He was exhausted from spilling his guts to Yeshua. It was obvious he was obsessed with his problems, and he was ashamed of them.

After listening intently, Yeshua finally introduced himself. He explained he had friends back in Nazareth, Tobiah and Shayna, whose father was a great potter, but also an alcoholic. Once the young thief heard about Yeshua's friends, he opened up even more. His name was Daniel, and he was only 11. His father was a day laborer at the Temple construction site. He had been a gifted mason, but his drinking made him so unreliable that he'd lost his job. Now he worked for friends who occasionally hired him as a helper.

"My old man isn't working today," Daniel explained. "I usually avoid the Temple whenever he's on the job. If he catches me stealing, he'll beat me up, right on the street in front of everyone."

Yeshua put his head in his hands. He felt sorry for the whole family. He could see Daniel had become as crazy as his father. Yeshua told Daniel he should stop worrying about his father's drinking, and concentrate on changing his own life.

> *"Trust in the LORD and do good*
> *that you may dwell in the land and live secure,"* said Yeshua.
> *"Refrain from anger; abandon wrath;*
> *do not be provoked; it brings only harm." (Psalm 37: 3, 8)*

Daniel slowly began to understand the wisdom in Yeshua's advice. It was true. The more he had tried to control his father's drinking, the worse his life had become.

"That makes sense," Daniel replied. "But Yeshua, I'm afraid to go back home and live with my father."

Yeshua told Daniel that wherever he chose to live, he needed to stop stealing, and find a way to help his mother make ends meet. Then Yeshua had an idea. He took Daniel and began to search for Hillel among the craftsmen around the Temple. He knew he was working on the tower that would hold the Sanhedrin meeting room.

"I thought you left with your caravan!" Hillel said with surprise, as Yeshua and Daniel approached him. Hillel continued his carpentry while Yeshua shared his unfortunate travel story. He explained how the Romans had blocked the road north, and that he'd found a little boy lost in the crowd. Now, he was waiting for his own parents to return. Then Yeshua introduced Hillel to Daniel, and asked if he knew anyone who might be able to hire the lad.

"I could use someone as a runner every day," said Hillel. "We're cutting these big cedar beams, and it helps to have someone run the cord up and back to measure, or chase down tools. Even fetch water when I'm thirsty."

"Well, Yeshua knows I'm a pretty good runner," Daniel replied. He and Yeshua laughed loudly. "But Yeshua is faster! He caught me."

Hillel wasn't sure what they were talking about, but it was obvious the boys had become friends. "Alright. Come back tomorrow at sunrise, and we'll see how the first day goes," Hillel offered. "Get plenty of rest tonight because I'm going to run you tomorrow. And if you own a pair of sandals, wear them. You'll cut your feet around here."

The boys thanked the craftsman several times before departing. Hillel thought Yeshua might be spending the night with Daniel, so he didn't offer him a bed in his home. He watched the boys walk away. There was a skip in Daniel's step now. He held his head high. Yeshua stopped from time to time, picking up a chunk of scrap wood and stuffing it into the bag on his waist.

Daniel decided to go home after all. He wanted to tell his mother and sister the good news about his job offer. He had newfound courage, thanks to Yeshua.

"I can deal with my dad for one night," Daniel said.

"Those who respect their father will live a long life;
those who obey the Lord honor their mother," said Yeshua.
(Sirach 3:6)

The boys made plans to see each other the next day.

As the sun reached for the horizon, Ethan and Shimon were hustling up the road with the rabbi and the last of the caravan. They all knew Yeshua was missing, and they wanted to get to Shiloh before dark. Benjamin, Aaron, and the other boys were panicked that their friend might be in trouble, but they didn't dare turn back to find him. Brigands might attack them on the open road at night.

"Don't worry, boys; we have lamps, torches and plenty of oil," said Dara, the rabbi's wife. "If we have to, we'll stop and make a quick fire to light them." Dara and the rabbi concealed their anxiety. They dreaded the thought of facing Yosef and Miriam to tell them Yeshua was lost.

The rest of the Nazarene camp had already arrived at the inn near Shiloh. They had set up camp and were preparing to eat. But Miriam and Yosef had no appetite, despite the fact they had spent the day traveling 20 miles from Yerushlem. Yosef had walked the distance, leading their wagon.

Back in the Holy City, Yeshua stood in the golden light, the hour before sunset, watching the colors as they reflected off the Temple. It was awe-inspiring. He was a little hungry, but he decided he'd better get off the streets and into the courtyards before dark. He slipped into the mikveh and said his prayer under the water. He was preparing to spend the night alone in the Temple with his heavenly Father. This would be the first night on his own, far away from his mom and dad.

Yeshua hoped they were safe and said a prayer for them. He knew his heavenly Father was watching his family. He loves all His children.

TWENTY-SEVEN

MIRIAM BUSIED HERSELF BY BUILDING A FIRE and preparing supper. She included portions for Yeshua, Shimon, and Ethan. The mother in her imagined her son would run up any moment to give her an exuberant hug and a kiss, and tell her about his day on the road with friends. But she was also very anxious. There was still no sign of the third leg of the Nazarene caravan, and it was getting late. The rabbi and his contingent were an hour behind. Wherever they were, Miriam hoped they all were safe.

After quickly watering Mo and Mazel, Yosef bought some wine from the innkeeper to help him and Miriam relax. This might be a long, tense evening while they waited for word from the caravan.

When he approached their tent, Yosef quietly settled in and sat in the opening. Miriam left the fire and joined him. Both the sun and moon were in the sky, and they made for a beautiful evening. There was a warm breeze that waved the fabric in the many tents at the roadside inn.

Yosef and Miriam washed up in a basin and prayed. Then he offered her wine from the goatskin. She took some. They ate slowly without speaking. Similar scenes were repeated in the other tents where parents were also troubled about their sons. The whole caravan was uneasy about the rabbi, his family, and several other Nazarenes who had not yet arrived.

Miriam knew the campers would welcome a little music after a long, sweaty, confusing day. She strummed her lyre. Yosef closed his eyes, trying to enjoy her music and the soothing breeze. Miriam began to sing a Psalm:

> *"Because you have the LORD for your refuge*
> *and have made the Most High your stronghold,*
> *No evil shall befall you,*
> *no affliction come near your tent.*
> *For he commands his angels with regard to you,*
> *to guard you wherever you go.*
> *With their hands they shall support you,*
> *lest you strike your foot against a stone.*
> *You can tread upon the asp and the viper,*
> *trample the lion and the dragon." (Psalm 91: 9-13)*

Yosef could hear the tears in her voice. He put his arm around her, and she rested her head on his shoulder, still strumming the harp. One of the mothers in the caravan was so worried about her missing son she became physically ill. The doctor gave her a tea made from mint mixed with rue. It seemed to calm her.

"I see them! They're coming!" shouted Ephraim. He had climbed atop the roof of the inn for a better view of the road. As soon as he hollered his announcement, everyone in the caravan jumped up in anticipation. Yosef and a few of the men lit torches at the campfires, and headed a hundred yards or so back up the road. Indeed, they could see five wagons in the distance. The sun was nearly down, but its orange glow illuminated the sky. It was a glorious sight to the Nazarenes who were anxious about their friends and families.

When they spotted the torches, several in the caravan waved. The campers cheered as they became more confident that the silhouettes in the distance belonged to people from their village. Ethan led the way, riding solo on his donkey.

Miriam paused to thank God and all the mothers embraced. They, too, ran up the road. A few of the elders remained by the fires to watch their campsite. Experienced travelers knew they should never take safety and security for granted.

It seemed like an eternity for the wagons to cover the last half-mile. But soon enough, the Nazarenes could identify the rabbi seated atop his wagon and neighbors on the four other carts. Shimon had taken over managing the rabbi's wagon. Dara and Benjamin sat next to the rabbi.

One by one, the mothers called to their sons as they spotted them aboard the wagon in the distance.

"Aaron!"

"Tobiah!"

"Boaz!"

"Ira!"

The boys stood and waved back.

"Yeshua!" shouted Miriam. But there was no sign of him. The other parents could sense the tension in Yosef and Miriam. Finally, the pilgrims engulfed the rabbi's wagon as it arrived. Yosef walked around all the other wagons, looking for Yeshua with torch held high. But he simply wasn't with the last group of travelers.

Before Yosef or Miriam could speak, the rabbi jumped off his seat and took Miriam's hand. "I am so sorry, but I don't have good news for you," he said. "We all thought Yeshua was with you — until Ethan and Shimon told us you thought he was still with us."

Miriam bowed her head and sobbed. Yosef came running up to her. "When did you last see him?" Yosef said, begging for any information.

"We were standing in the line, backed up in Yerushlem," replied the rabbi. "The Roman guard came on horseback and blocked the road for a caravan of merchants. Next thing, Yeshua was running off toward the front of the line. I called to him, but he kept running. It was really noisy, and I figured he just couldn't hear me. Seemed like he suddenly decided not to wait for traffic to clear. We thought he was running around the roadblock to catch up with you and Miriam. He disappeared into the crowd. That was the last time we saw him."

"He shouted something like, 'I'm going to catch up and help my father,'" Benjamin chimed in. "I couldn't hear everything he said."

"Uhhhhh, Yeshua." Miriam groaned. This was every mother's worst nightmare. Yosef held her close. Soon several other mothers huddled around.

"So, for all we know, he may still be in Yerushlem!" Yosef said.

The rabbi and Dara nodded. They were mortified. Dara was actually a distant relative of Miriam's. She hugged Dara and whispered in her ear.

"It's not your fault," Miriam said as she composed herself. "Please do not blame yourselves. Yeshua can be very independent."

"I don't think he's on the road. He promised me he wouldn't go or stay with anyone he doesn't know," Yosef explained, trying to sound optimistic. "My guess is he got held up by the Roman guard in all the traffic, and then missed his ride with you. He probably made his way to my nephew's home in Bethlehem. It's only a half-day's walk. We visited them during the festival."

"So he knows them well. That makes sense," said Shimon. "I'll go with you, Yosef. We'll find him."

"Shimon and Ethan, please come to our tent. I have supper ready for you, and after you rest a while, we can pack up and head back to Yerushlem," said Miriam.

"No, no, no, no, no, no!" exclaimed Yosef. "We must all get a night's rest. We'll make much better time in daylight. Besides, it's too dangerous. By tomorrow, most pilgrims will have left Yerushlem, so the road will be clearer."

"Your husband is wise, Miriam," the rabbi consoled. "You have the heart of a mother; he has the mind of a father."

Miriam was grateful for the rabbi's advice. She welcomed Shimon and Ethan to their tent, while Yosef watered Ethan's donkey.

Miriam quietly served the men supper and the remaining wine. Ethan would stay with them, since he had not had time to pitch his tent, and it was now dark. Shimon headed over to spend the night with his brother and sister-in-law. Both men had volunteered to accompany Miriam and Yosef on the return trip. When Yosef tried to discourage them, the rabbi insisted that they travel together for safety. He even offered his son, Benjamin.

"We'll be honored to have Benjamin join us," Miriam said. "You're so good to help us, Benjamin." Miriam knew the rabbi and Dara felt responsible for Yeshua's disappearance, even though it wasn't their fault. Accepting Benjamin's assistance would help relieve their anxiety.

She also knew her son. Yeshua would never have disobeyed the rabbi. Something must have prevented him from rejoining the group. What could it have been? Had Yeshua been duped by a criminal or a slave trader? The thought was painful.

Sympathetic neighbors stopped by throughout the evening, offering encouragement and optimism along with food and supplies the search party would need on its hunt for Yeshua. The sandal maker took their sandals and repaired them by the campfire. The doctor brought herbs, some splints, and bandages. Others left kindling and offered oil and spare lamps. Everyone felt connected in the crisis. Most had known Yeshua since he was a little boy, when the family first arrived in Nazareth from Egypt. He was truly loved. No one would sleep well that night.

The crescent moon was bright, casting long shadows from the rooftop to the ground. The Temple seemed a magical place at night. Even then, it buzzed with activity. Temple guards marched, while others stood chatting at their posts. A dozen sentries secured the treasury, and several archers watched from the towers and the rooftop of the Holy of Holies. They were poised to respond to any disturbance.

Torches and lamps lit many areas, but there were vast corridors and structures in shadow. People hid in the darkness — beggars, devout Hebrews, some who never left the Temple, even pilgrims who would decide to spend the night in prayer. The guard did its best to secure the campus and kick out the ha-aretz, but it was nearly impossible because of the scale of the Temple. Some of the watchmen took pity on the homeless, and looked the other way.

Yeshua found a covered area adjacent to the Court of Women. It was a corridor lined with pillars that ran alongside the open court. He leaned against the wall and used his shoulder bag for a pillow. Yeshua had slipped his right arm through the strap. If someone tried to snatch his bag, he'd find a feisty young man attached to it. Yeshua would definitely wake up. His hair was still wet from the mikveh, but he had no towel.

After saying his evening prayer, Yeshua looked out into the court, watching the shadows move against the masonry. Whenever a guard walked along the adjacent roof, the moon cast an elongated silhouette across the court. Yeshua could hear the sounds of the city reverberating off the walls and towers of the Temple. He could smell the aromas of Yerushlem, as the wind swirled around the corridors and courts. Torches and lamps flickered in the gusts.

The scene reminded Yeshua of the words from one of his favorite Psalms:

> *"You who dwell in the shelter of the Most High,*
> *who abide in the shade of the Almighty,*
> *Say to the LORD, "My refuge and fortress,*
> *my God in whom I trust."*
> *He will rescue you from the fowler's snare,*
> *from the destroying plague,*
> *He will shelter you with his pinions,*
> *and under his wings you may take refuge;*
> *his faithfulness is a protecting shield.*
> *You shall not fear the terror of the night*
> *nor the arrow that flies by day." (Psalm 91: 1-5)*

With eyes tightly closed attempting to sleep, Miriam could feel the salty tears roll down her face, across her sun-chafed skin onto the corners of her mouth. Yosef stirred next to her. She couldn't sleep, but she tried to be extra quiet because Ethan was sharing their tent.

"Where was Yeshua?" she wondered. "Was he sick or injured and in pain? Would he be forever lost to her and Yosef? Was this the sword that would pierce her?"

Miriam didn't know the answers, but she vividly remembered what Yosef had told her more than a dozen years ago — when the angel Gabriel appeared to him in a dream. The angel had proclaimed: "She will bear a son and you are to name him [Yeshua], because he will save his people from their sins."(Matthew 1:21)

She was confident Yahweh would protect Yeshua. After all, He had a very specific, significant plan for her son. She trusted God, but still, the unknown was almost unbearable. "This must be how parents feel when their children die," she thought. "Or when they suffer severe illness." Somehow, she and Yosef finally managed to get some sleep.

The cavernous Temple grew cold in the night air. When he first sat down, Yeshua could feel the warm stone against his body. Eventually, the hewn rock released the heat it had absorbed all day. The evening breezes caused Yeshua to pull his knees up closer to his chest. He wrapped his arms around them as a chill shook his body.

Yeshua looked down at his feet, and followed the path of an insect as it bumped into the edge of his sandal, then turned in another direction on the stone floor. He felt a little bit like that tiny bug on a journey in a mammoth world. Yeshua had just begun to experience living alone in the enormous Temple in Yerushlem, and sleeping in His heavenly Father's house.

chapter
TWENTY-EIGHT

THERE WAS HEAVY DEW EVERYWHERE. BENJAMIN jogged across the campsite at the inn. Miriam and Yosef had all but finished loading their wagon. Shimon and Ethan were tossing their bags aboard as Benjamin walked up.

"Good morning," Yosef said. "You can put your things up here in the corner. Climb aboard, son, and make yourself comfortable."

Benjamin's parents weren't far behind, nor were most of the other Nazarenes. The whole caravan had awakened before sunrise, and gathered around Miriam and Yosef to support them. The other young boys encouraged Benjamin. They wanted to join the search for Yeshua.

Dara had urged the rabbi to send their son with Yeshua's family. As a mother, she knew how Miriam would feel. Benjamin's youthful voice and outgoing personality might distract her from constant worries about Yeshua. Plus, he was capable and strong, and he could help the men on the journey. It was also good for the rabbi's son to set an unselfish example, and to help families in need.

Yosef had awakened the innkeeper very early to buy extra supplies. With Ethan riding a third animal, the group had a little insurance in case Mo or Mazel pulled up lame or sick. Shimon could lead the wagon if Yosef reinjured his ankle, or he could help him if their wagon needed repair.

When the search party was ready to depart, the rabbi placed his hand on Yosef's shoulder, and he led the villagers in prayer. He concluded with a verse from a Psalm of David.

> *"Even though I walk through the valley of the shadow of death,*
> *I will fear no evil, for you are with me;*
> *your rod and your staff comfort me. (Psalm 23:4)*

"Thank you, rabbi," Yosef said as he embraced him. After a flurry of good-bye hugs, the search party rolled south onto the road toward Yerushlem. Riding his donkey, Ethan trotted up ahead a short distance. As things got busier during the day, he could monitor traffic and warn Yosef of any oncoming problems. The early start would allow them to enjoy a few hours of cooler temperatures. Hopefully, they'd move at a fast pace. Because Yosef was convinced Yeshua was with his relatives in Bethlehem, they would head directly there. If they wanted to make the city of David by nightfall, they needed a quick start.

"Why don't you lie down, Benjamin?" Miriam suggested. "It's early, child." Benjamin had promised his mother he would be very obedient, so he obliged her, curling up in the corner of the wagon on a woven mat and resting his head on his sack.

The morning air was chilly. The soft blanket that landed on his shoulders was very welcome. Yeshua opened his eyes to see who had covered him. It was a man with his hood pulled over his head. Yeshua got up quickly to thank the man. He walked up behind the stranger, touching his arm to get his attention. The man turned to Yeshua and revealed his face. There were blemishes from some affliction that had healed.

Yeshua realized that in the dark, he'd chosen a spot to sleep near the Chamber of Lepers. The man had come to the Temple to be declared clean by a priest. Then he could purify himself in the mikveh and enter the Court of Israelites. There he would offer a burnt sacrifice for the many years he had spent away from service to the Lord.

Unclean, unhealed lepers were outcasts. They were not allowed inside the walls of the city, let alone the Temple.

"Don't worry, I am clean," said the man. "God has healed me!"

"... your faith has saved you," said Yeshua. *"Go show yourself to the priests." (Luke 17:19,14)*

"They are on the altar sacrificing the morning offering," replied the leper. "I'll wait here in the chamber. I've been here all night. I traveled in yesterday from outside the city, but I didn't arrive until after dark. By the way, my name is Oren."

Yeshua could smell lamb fat burning on the altar. His stomach growled. He introduced himself and accompanied Oren to the Chamber of Lepers. Yeshua had no fear about catching the terrible disease. He thanked Oren for covering him with the blanket.

"I was so excited, I couldn't sleep anyway," said Oren. "So, when I saw you sleeping on the stone without a mat, I knew you were cold."

"Whoever cares for the poor lends to the LORD,
who will pay back the sum in full," Yeshua replied.
(Proverbs 19:17)

Just then, a priest came down from the steps of the Nicanor Gate toward the Chamber of Lepers. Yeshua recognized him from his tour of the Temple with John. As Caiaphas, the High Priest's son-in-law, approached Oren, he eyed Yeshua's face. The Nazarene looked familiar to him.

"Take off your hood, and don't come too close," Caiaphas said to the leper. "You're a fool to stand near a leper in the chamber," he admonished Yeshua. "I have not yet determined him to be clean."

Out of respect for Caiaphas, Yeshua backed away from the chamber, but he could see inside. Caiaphas walked around Oren looking at his head, face, and neck. When he saw the faint blemishes from the sores that had once ravaged the leper, he leaned in slightly for a better, but cautious look.

"Remove your tunic," Caiaphas ordered. Oren slipped off his garment and draped it over his arm. It was obvious the leper had been healed. Now, Caiaphas felt safe to step in and make a closer examination.

Priests were like Temple dermatologists. The Scripture gave them the responsibility for making sure people afflicted with all skin diseases were clean. Over time, they learned to identify a wide variety of skin ailments, and they discovered effective remedies — from baths and poultices, to herbs and ointments. Doctors learned from the priests.

But the Temple clergy were also interested in spiritual healing. They believed sin caused leprosy and other diseases that left flesh unclean, well below the skin's surface. Hebrews saw lepers as sinners, outcasts with corrupted bodies and souls.

"You may return to give sacrifice in the Temple. The Lord has been merciful to you," declared Caiaphas.

"Oh, thank you! Praise the Almighty!" shouted Oren. He began to cry.

"Purify yourself in the mikveh and clean your garments before you return," Caiaphas ordered.

"I'll buy a new tunic today," Oren replied.

"And repent for the sins that caused your disease. Foul language and failure to speak out against evil afflict the leper. Arrogance is the seed of leprosy!" Caiaphas proclaimed.

Oren nodded humbly. Caiaphas turned on his heels, and proudly walked out the chamber, looking at Yeshua as he passed him. He turned back to Oren and snapped, "Repay the Lord with your tithing to the Temple treasury. Give him your first fruits."

Yeshua watched Caiaphas stomp off, and then he looked to see Oren's reaction. The healed man stood numb, shaken by the priest's unmerciful criticism after what had been a joyful verdict. Yeshua smiled. Stretching out his arms, he prayed for Oren in a loud voice.

*"I praise you, LORD, for you raised me up
and did not let my enemies rejoice over me.
O LORD, my God,
I cried out to you for help and you healed me.
LORD, you brought my soul up from Sheol;
you let me live, from going down to the pit.*

*Sing praise to the LORD, you faithful;
give thanks to his holy memory!" (Psalm 30:2-5)*

"Praise his holy name!" Oren shouted as he threw his arms into the air and jumped with excitement.

Yeshua and Oren laughed loudly. Oren put his tunic back over his body. He knew he'd have to wash it or destroy it because it was also considered unclean. Yeshua returned Oren's blanket and they walked out of the Temple together. The aroma of burning sacrifices had piqued Yeshua's appetite, and he was anxious to buy something to eat.

The sun burned brightly in the Holy Land that day, and the search party was now beginning the steep climb again toward Yerushlem. They had taken a break to switch roles. Yosef was now resting aboard the wagon, and Shimon was the cursor, leading Mo and Mazel down the path. By swapping cursors every hour or two they hoped to travel faster. When Ethan needed rest, they could tie his beast, Hasna, to the back of the wagon. Shimon was almost jogging with the animals. He was young and strong and used to managing beasts from behind a plow. The search party was making very good time.

"Here comes a caravan!" shouted Ethan. A fast moving team of merchants on camels carried products from Egypt to the north. As they roared by, some of the camels bleated and bellowed. Intimidated, Mo abruptly turned his head toward the noise, but Shimon wasn't ready for his quick movement. He lost his balance and fell. Fortunately, he wasn't seriously hurt, but his fall spooked the two donkeys, and they ran along the shoulder of the road. Benjamin awoke in the back of the wagon, and Yosef and Miriam grabbed hold of their perch to make sure they didn't tumble to the ground. The animals were out of control.

"Whoa! Whoa!" Yosef yelled. "Mo! Mazel! Whoa!" As soon as Ethan heard Yosef, he turned his animal and ran back toward the wagon, hoping the beasts would stop as he galloped up in front of them. But it was too late. The front right wheel hit a large stone, jarring it loose at the axle. The wheel wobbled badly as the donkeys continued to run. When Ethan rode up on Hasna, the tandem finally slowed down. Yosef jumped off his seat and quickly grabbed the tethers. Shimon had picked himself up and had run up behind them.

"Don't worry, Miriam!" Yosef said. "I can fix this. Yeshua and I fix wagons like this all the time." He paused, realizing how much he missed his son.

"I'll help," said Benjamin as he stood up in the wagon.

"Good idea," Miriam said encouragingly. "Yosef, what can Benjamin do?"

"Grab my tools, they're in the back in that box," Yosef replied.

Within a few minutes, Miriam and the men were all standing on the side of the road, and pitching in to help the craftsman. Miriam unhitched Mo and Mazel, and held them by their bridles to keep them calm. Benjamin crawled under the wagon to retrieve the spare wheel Yosef kept lashed to the bottom. Benjamin untied it. With Ethan's help, he hauled out the wheel. The jarring crash had damaged the hub of the right front wheel. Swapping wheels would be much faster than repairing the hub.

Shimon, Ethan, and Benjamin helped Yosef lift one corner of the wagon, just enough to remove the damaged wheel and slide on the new one. While Yosef and Shimon worked to secure the wheel, Benjamin helped Ethan stow the broken one under the wagon. The process took about a half hour.

They decided to quickly eat an early lunch, and water the animals before continuing. Shimon insisted he would manage the beasts again. He had experienced their personalities, and would be on guard for a quick jolt of curiosity or skittishness.

Although brief, lunch was delicious. Miriam had purchased fresh dates and figs at the inn the night before. They went well with the yogurt, raw honey, and bread they had.

The barley loaves had been fresh yesterday, but day-old bread was all Yeshua could afford in the Yerushlem market today. He was in the Valley of the Cheesemakers, at the bakery where his family had shopped during the Passover festival. He had no idea how long it would take his parents to find him. To stretch his money, Yeshua decided to eat a light breakfast, skip lunch, and then buy a larger meal at dinner. The day-old loaf was cheap. He bought some water to refill his goatskin.

Yeshua couldn't help but notice the stack of honey cakes the baker's daughter had just put on the outdoor table. The sweet aroma made his mouth water. The girl looked at Yeshua and smiled. He shyly smiled back. Everywhere Yeshua turned, something smelled amazing and looked tantalizing. Sizzling lamb; creamy goat and sheep cheese; fresh fish; hot lentil soup; crisp nuts; salty olives; ripe cucumbers and onions. He nibbled on his barley loaf as he passed all the delightful foods, straight from farms or the sea.

As Yeshua turned a corner back toward the Temple, he wandered down the Street of Butchers. Here, merchants trimmed meat for those who could afford the price. Average folks and the poor ate very little meat. That helped to make Passover a very special occasion, in addition to its spiritual importance. Beggars commonly panhandled in this district, hoping to find generous rich men who would give them a coin or a morsel of food. Dogs scrounged for scraps and bones, but they were typically kept for soup making. Nothing was wasted.

Here, all the meats were Kosher, meaning they were butchered according to the laws in the Torah. There were rabbis and devout

Jews in this business district, making sure the merchants followed the scriptural rules for food preparation and purity.

As he passed the first shop, Yeshua noticed a few slaughtered lambs and goats hanging above and behind the counter. Well-dressed shoppers carefully selected custom cuts of meat. The door to the shop was open. Yeshua stopped to peer inside. There was nothing quite like this in Nazareth. As he turned to continue his stroll, Yeshua spotted a tiny old woman sitting in the shadow behind the open shop door; she held a small wooden bowl for alms. Though she was sickly and her clothing was worn, she smiled at Yeshua. He smiled back at her as he walked by. Suddenly, he turned around and quickly sat down next to her.

"Are you a beggar, too?" the woman asked.

Yeshua said nothing. He grinned and took the loaf in his hands and broke off the piece where he had bitten. He gave the remaining larger chunk to the woman. It filled her small hand.

Her eyes grew bright, and she smiled so broadly that she opened her mouth. Yeshua could now see she had no teeth. He poured some water from his goatskin into her bowl. The woman dipped the bread in the water to soften it so she could chew it more easily. She closed her eyes, enjoying the barley loaf. Clearly, she was very hungry. Yeshua sat and ate his remaining bread with her.

After a few mouthfuls, the woman looked up at Yeshua with satisfaction. She whispered to him.

"God rained manna upon them for food …

Man ate the bread of the angels." (Psalm 78:24,25)

"They ate and were well filled;

he gave them what they had craved," Yeshua replied, quoting from the same Psalm. (Psalm 78:29)

"What is your name?" she asked.

"Yeshua, from Nazareth."

"May Adonai bless you, Yeshua from Nazareth!" she said. "My name is Leah."

"Shlama, Leah," he said to the beggar. He stood up to continue on his way along the Street of Butchers. A dog began to follow him, sniffing his tunic. But before he could take more than a few steps, Yeshua heard a voice from behind him.

"I saw what you did. I saw you," said the stranger, pointing to the beggar woman a few feet away.

Yeshua turned to see who had spoken. He was eye to eye with a very handsomely dressed foreigner. The tattoos on the man's hands and one on his face told Yeshua he was a Gentile.

"My master would approve if I gave you something," said the man. He was apparently a slave.

"I saw the way you shared your bread with the old woman," the man added. He reached into his full satchel, and handed Yeshua a fresh loaf of leavened wheat bread and a honey cake.

Yeshua instinctively accepted the gifts, and asked the slave to identify his master.

"I can't tell you who he is. He would prefer to make an anonymous gift," the man responded. "He is wealthy and can well afford to buy more."

Yeshua thanked him, and told him how much he loved the honey cakes his mother made him. He asked the slave where he was born.

"I am from Corinth. It's a very long story, but I worked on a merchant ship and ended up in Yerushlem," he explained. "I was broke, so I sold myself into slavery. I have only two more years to serve." His Aramaic was quite good and his accent was slight.

Yeshua recalled Yosef's warnings about slave traders. How he might be kidnapped and sold to the highest bidder.

"Where are you staying?" the slave asked. Yeshua felt uneasy about the question. Why was he asking that? He didn't even know Yeshua's name or why he was in Yerushlem.

"Come, and you will see," Yeshua answered as he put the baked goods in his shoulder bag. (John 1:39)

The slave followed Yeshua through the Street of Butchers and back through the Valley of the Cheesemakers. Yerushlem was filled with morning shoppers. Although the festival was over, hundreds of thousands of people were still in the Holy City.

As the Corinthian slave quietly walked behind Yeshua, he finally said, "My name is Lycus. I have lived here five years, and have been working for a wonderful master. I never imagined myself a servant."

Yeshua politely introduced himself, but didn't tell Lycus where he lived or anything else.

"You seem to really know your way around, Yeshua," Lycus said. "I was that way in Corinth. What a rich port! Money, goods, wonderful food and drink. Have you ever been to sea?"

Yeshua turned and smiled, shaking his head, as he continued to work his way through the crowded streets.

"Ten years ago, I began working shipping vessels," Lycus explained. "Huge sailing ships. We mostly carried wines, olive oils, fine wools, and fabrics. Free travel was one of the big benefits; plus, we got to eat very well, and there was always plenty of good wine. I had a woman in every port we visited. Alexandria. Ostia near Rome. Cadiz. Nicaea. Rhegium. Tyre. Have you ever been to any of those places?"

Yeshua turned and smiled. He mentioned he had been to Egypt as a young child, as he continued to lead Lycus through the crowded streets.

"I survived some serious storms at sea. I can't tell you how many times I thought the ship was going over on its side," Lycus yelled over the noisy street traffic. "You can't even imagine what it's like to climb a ship's mast in a windstorm. Try fixing the sail on the yard. It's like flying! I could tell you some unbelievable stories. I made good money too," he added. "Best time of my life. A party in every port town."

As they approached the Temple, the slave could see where they were headed.

"I've never been here," he said.

Yeshua turned to him, smiled and continued to make his way through the foot traffic. When they arrived at the Temple, Yeshua took the ritual bath. Lycus waited outside the mikveh. Then, the Greek slave and the young Nazarene climbed the stairs of Herod's Temple together. When they entered the Court of Gentiles, Yeshua pointed to the sign that warned visitors that only Israelites were permitted to go any farther. The slave looked all around the court. He appeared to be amazed at the diversity of people and the majesty of the structure.

"You live here?" the slave asked.

Yeshua explained he was waiting for his parents to meet him in the Temple.

"I do not know your God," said the slave. "But your king is building him a sensational palace. We have impressive temples in Corinth, but nothing that compares to this. Do you think your God hears my prayers?"

Yeshua laughed and proudly responded by singing a Psalm.

"May God be gracious to us and bless us;
may his face shine upon us.

So shall your way be known upon the earth,
your victory among all the nations.
May the peoples praise you, God;
may all the peoples praise you!

May the nations be glad and rejoice;
for you judge the peoples with fairness,
you guide the nations upon the earth.

May the peoples praise you, God;
may all the peoples praise you!

The earth has yielded its harvest;
God, our God, blesses us.
May God bless us still;
that the ends of the earth may revere him." (Psalm 67:2-8)

Lycus applauded when Yeshua finished his chanting. "Then I will pray to him, too," said the slave. "My master has never before encouraged me to worship his Hebrew God."

> *"The LORD is near to all who call upon him,*
> *to all who call upon him in truth,"* Yeshua replied.
> *(Psalm 145:18)*

He thanked Lycus for his generosity, and once more, asked him to thank his master for the baked goods.

Then Yeshua turned toward the Court of Women.

"Perhaps you would like to meet my master," he called to Yeshua. "You could thank him in person."

Yeshua kept walking.

"My master has a magnificent home, and I'm sure he would pay to listen to you chant your prayers the way you did," said the slave, running up behind him. "He only has daughters, no sons of his own."

Yeshua walked faster. He knew this man was tempting him, so he did his best to avoid him. But Lycus grabbed his tunic.

"Perhaps you would like to join us for dinner. My master has exotic concubines in his home. Some from Egypt and Persia, and even one Hebrew woman from Yerushlem. And they dance."

"Yeshua!" How are you today?" The voice of Ram, the old Temple guard, boomed from behind him. Yeshua was relieved to see him.

When he saw Ram, Lycus immediately let go of Yeshua's garment. Yeshua smiled at Ram. Then turning to the slave, Yeshua quoted Scripture:

> *"My son, should sinners entice you,*
> *do not go if they say, 'Come along with us!*
> *Let us lie in wait for blood,*
> *unprovoked, let us trap the innocent;'*

My son, do not walk in the way with them,
hold back your foot from their path!
'But whoever obeys me dwells in security,
in peace, without fear of harm.'" (Proverbs 1:10-11, 15 and 33)

This was sage advice from the wise old King Solomon. Hearing it, Ram realized that the slave wasn't Yeshua's friend. He eyed Lycus' tattoos. Then Ram pointed to a sign outside the Court of Women. He read it aloud, "No foreigner may enter within the balustrade and enclosure around the Temple area. Anyone caught doing so will bear the responsibility for his own ensuing death!"[8]

The slave quickly turned on his heels, exiting the Temple without another word.

Yeshua thanked Ram for protecting him. The old guard was surprised to see he was still in Yerushlem. Yeshua explained that he was waiting for his parents to pick him up, and that he'd stopped in the Valley of the Cheesemakers for something to eat, when Lycus approached him.

"Young man, there are a lot of treacherous troublemakers in a big city like this," Ram cautioned. "It's a very alluring place, but avoid the markets. Stay as close to the Temple as you can while you're waiting. We have our share of evil doers, but at least the guard is here."

Before Ram could press Yeshua for details on his parents' whereabouts, the Nazarene thanked him again and headed for the Court of Women.

Miriam and Yosef sat aboard the wagon, and did their best not to obsess about Yeshua, where he might be, and what he might be doing. Miriam found the strength to pick up her lyre and strum it on the way. Benjamin drummed the bottom of a large, heavy wooden bowl she had brought. The music helped everyone feel better. It was almost as if the animals kept time as they stepped briskly down the road. Miriam began to sing.

> *"You formed my inmost being;*
> *you knit me in my mother's womb.*
> *I praise you, because I am wonderfully made;*
> *wonderful are your works!*
> *My very self you know.*
> *My bones are not hidden from you,*
> *When I was being made in secret,*
> *fashioned in the depths of the earth.*
> *Your eyes saw me unformed;*
> *in your book all are written down;*
> *my days were shaped, before one came to be.*
> *How precious to me are your designs, O God;*
> *how vast the sum of them!*
> *Were I to count them, they would outnumber the sands;*
> *when I complete them, still you are with me.*
> *Probe me, God, know my heart;*
> *try me, know my thoughts." (Psalm 139: 13-18, 23-24)*

Yosef put his hand on Miriam's shoulder as she played. He understood the pain she felt. After all, she had carried Yeshua in her womb. No other human relationship was as close. He admired her ability to remain faithful, and to always find joy in the trials of their lives. And they had experienced a few with their son, including escaping to Egypt to save baby Yeshua from a maniacal king. God's way was hard, but Miriam knew in her heart it was the right way. She was convinced Yeshua was in his heavenly Father's care.

Miriam had been an only child. Many times, she had talked about her mother, Hannah, and how much Yeshua meant as her only grandchild. Hannah and Yeshua had enjoyed a unique relationship. Those thoughts also weighed heavily on her mind throughout the day on the road. Miriam and Yosef had been blessed with such a marvelous son, and now they had lost him. How could they have let that happen? The couple couldn't travel fast enough to calm their worst fears.

The sun in the clear sky marked the time as past noon. With the three men taking turns leading the wagon, the search party was more confident they could reach Bethlehem today. It might be after dark, but Yosef knew the town well enough to find Ezekiel's home. He hoped his hunch about Yeshua was right. This was the only place that made sense to Yosef, even though he had some doubts. Elizabeth's home was closer, but Yeshua hadn't been there. He could certainly ask guards at the Temple for directions. Someone would remember Zechariah and could tell Yeshua how to find his home. But Elizabeth was old and feeble. Wouldn't Yeshua be more inclined to spend time with Ezekiel's children? For Miriam's sake, Yosef pretended to be calm. But inside he prayed desperately for his only son. It made him think of the story of Abraham and Isaac.

"... God put Abraham to the test and said to him: Abraham! 'Here I am!' he replied. Then God said: Take your son Isaac, your only one, whom you love, and go to the land of Moriah. There offer him up as a burnt offering on one of the heights that I will point out to you. (Genesis 22:1-2)

"What did Adonai want from Abraham?" asked the local rabbi from Yerushlem. He was teaching a group of young men in the Court of Women at the Temple. Yeshua stood off to the side and listened.

"He wanted to see if Abraham would sacrifice the things he loved the most," replied one pupil.

"Good answer!" replied the rabbi.

"To do what is right and just
is more acceptable to the LORD than sacrifice," said Yeshua, *reciting the Proverb. (Proverbs 21:3).*

The rabbi and his whole group turned to see who had spoken. The students were very surprised to discover it was someone their own age.

The rabbi continued. "And so, did Abraham sacrifice his son to the Lord?"

"No, the angel stopped him, before he was about to kill Isaac with a knife and burn him on the altar," another student replied.

"For it is loyalty that I desire, not sacrifice,
and knowledge of God rather than burnt offerings,"
Yeshua exclaimed. *(Hosea 6:6)*

Again, the rabbi turned to Yeshua. He was impressed by his ability to quote Scripture, but unhappy about the interruptions. "Why don't you join us, young man?" he asked. "You seem to have the answers."

Yeshua stepped toward the group, and smiled at the other boys as he sat down to join them.

"Tell us your name," the rabbi commanded.

"Yeshua."

"Well, Yeshua, welcome. "But perhaps you would like to reconsider your last remark. If God does not want sacrifice, why then did he provide Abraham with a ram to kill instead of his son, Isaac?" The rabbi smiled broadly and looked to the whole group.

Yeshua paused and replied respectfully, quoting Samuel.

"But Samuel said:

'Does the LORD delight in burnt offerings and sacrifices
as much as in obedience to the LORD's command?
Obedience is better than sacrifice,
to listen, better than the fat of rams.'" *(1 Samuel 15:22)*

The rabbi blushed. Yeshua continued.

"He the LORD, is our God
whose judgments reach through all the earth.
He remembers forever his covenant,
the word he commanded for a thousand generations,
Which he made with Abraham,
and swore to Isaac,

He brought his people out with joy,
his chosen ones with shouts of triumph.
He gave them the lands of the nations,
they took possession of the wealth of the peoples ..."

Yeshua paused to get their attention, and stood up to emphasize the essence of God's covenant with Israel.

"That they might keep his statutes
and observe his teachings.
Hallelujah!" Yeshua exclaimed. *(Psalm 105: 7-9, 43-45)*

The rabbi was stunned. Yeshua had taught the lesson. It was indeed about obeying God, and trusting in His unconditional love, rather than simply sacrificing to appease Him.

"You are right, Yeshua. To keep our covenant with Adonai, we must obey Him first and foremost," the rabbi acknowledged. But Yeshua wasn't finished:

"It was not because you are more numerous than all the
peoples that the LORD set his heart on you and chose
you; for you are really the smallest of all peoples. It was
because the LORD loved you and because of his fidelity
to the oath he had sworn to your ancestors, that the
LORD brought you out with a strong hand and redeemed
you from the house of slavery, from the hand of Pharaoh,
king of Egypt. (Deuteronomy 7: 7-8)

> "Therefore, you shall love the LORD, your God, with your
> whole heart, and with your whole being, and with your
> whole strength." (Deuteronomy 6:5)

Other teachers and scribes quietly observed the scene in the Court of Women. They were astonished at this 12-year-old student who spoke with such fire and passion. They wondered why he felt such confidence, such authority. At times it seemed like God Himself was speaking through Yeshua in a new way. They didn't realize He was.

TWENTY-NINE

THE MID AFTERNOON SUN WAS BRIGHT AND HOT, and there was barely enough water to drink. Hillel and his helper Daniel took a short break. Hillel had gotten extra water from the water carrier, who lugged it in an animal skin on his back.

"Drink slowly, Daniel!" Hillel cautioned. "If you drink too fast, you'll feel bloated and sick."

Suddenly, Yeshua arrived, jumping up to walk along a narrow cedar beam that was balanced on two stone supports. He shouted like a foreman, barking an order as he tiptoed along the wood column. He pointed dramatically in every direction.

"'Moreover, you have available workers, stonecutters, masons, carpenters, and experts in every craft, without number, skilled with gold, silver, bronze, and iron. Set to work, therefore, and the LORD be with you!'" (1 Chronicles 22:15-16)

Hillel and Daniel laughed; they were happy to see Yeshua. The old carpenter recognized his words — King David had spoken them to his son Solomon, commissioning him to build the first Temple in Yerushlem.

"Well done, Yeshua!" said Hillel. "Those are inspiring words on a scorching day like this."

Yeshua added a blessing for Daniel, as if he were David speaking to Solomon.

> *"'Now, my son, the LORD be with you, and may you succeed in building the house of the LORD your God, as he has said you shall.'" (1 Chronicles, 22:11)*

"We're having great success. Daniel's been working hard and learning fast," said Hillel, as he got up to continue his project. "In fact, Yeshua, you've come along at the perfect time. I could use another pair of hands to hold this beam while I plane it. Actually, you boys can each sit or stand on top of the beam; your weight will help hold it in place."

Sitting on the solid board for more than 12 hours was worse than walking, especially as the search party climbed the bumpy road toward Yerushlem. The faster a wagon rolled, the worse the vibrations. In fact, most travelers moderated their pace for a smoother ride. But Miriam and Yosef set comfort aside today. They were searching for their son.

Because of the higher speeds, the ride was so rough that Benjamin chose to walk for hours at a time. Yosef was now at the helm managing Mo and Mazel; Shimon and Miriam were aboard the wagon. Ethan continued to ride ahead as an advance man, warning them to avoid any obstacles. Sometimes rocks and debris littered the trail. They did everything they could to prevent another mishap and delay.

From his perch on the wagon, Shimon passed time by firing stones with his slingshot. He aimed at large boulders, brush, and trees along the road. He was quite a good shot. As a farmer, he had often used his weapon to scare away predators that pursued his livestock. Shepherds protected their flocks in the open wilderness the same way.

"Good one!" laughed Benjamin, as Shimon nailed a branch at the top of a mustard tree. A flock of birds scattered every which way in the air and reconvened in the sky. "You've got the aim of David!" Benjamin added.

Miriam shook her head and laughed. The story of David, the shepherd boy, was also one of Yeshua's favorite Scripture lessons. With his slingshot and a single stone, David had miraculously struck down the giant, Goliath, the invincible Philistine warrior. This spared the Israelites a devastating defeat. Every Hebrew boy loved the tale and wanted a slingshot of his own. Yeshua often sat on the roof at home, playing games with his slingshot. He and Ezra would fire stones at small wooden targets Yosef had made for them. Sometimes Miriam would give them a broken clay pot to use, or Tobiah would bring pottery scraps from his father's shop. Ezra was actually the best marksman.

"If only Ezra had been able to come along on the pilgrimage to Yerushlem, maybe Yeshua would be with them right now," Miriam thought. She looked at Benjamin walking along the road, chuckling as Ethan continued to hit most of his targets. He reminded her so much of her son. She missed his laugh and his generous hugs and kisses at all times of the day. How could she lose her son?

Miriam knew she would have to leave Yeshua in Yahweh's hands, and trust that God would help them find their son. She prayed quietly to the Lord:

"I have wandered like a lost sheep;
seek out your servant,
for I do not forget your commandments." (Psalm 119:176)

The wagon lurched to a stop. Yeshua and Daniel helped Hillel load his tools on the cart. He took them home each evening to safeguard them.

"Thank you, boys," Hillel said. "Here's your day's wages." He handed Daniel two coins. Yeshua also received a coin because he had finished planing the beam for the carpenter. The torrid sun had taken its toll on the old craftsman, and he was grateful for another pair of experienced hands.

Yeshua tried to give him back the money, but Hillel insisted he had earned it. "I don't work for free, and you shouldn't either, Yeshua."

"Yeshua, let's go have some fun!" Daniel exclaimed. "We can buy some cheap wine. I know a place where Roman guards throw dice every night. They've let me join their game. One time I doubled my money!"

"Where there are great riches, there are also many to devour them," Yeshua replied. "Sleep is sweet to the laborer, whether there is little or much to eat; but the abundance of the rich allows them no sleep." (Ecclesiastes 5:10,11)

"He's right, Daniel. You take your wages to your mother and before long, she'll be able to quit working at night," Hillel said. "Besides, you need to rest. I'll expect to see you at dawn. Good night, boys."

"Shlama," said Yeshua.

"Thanks. See you tomorrow," said Daniel as he put the coins in a pouch on his belt. He felt good about himself after working hard for a full day. He hadn't stolen anything today.

"Yeshua, thanks for setting me up with Hillel. He's fun to work with," Daniel said. "I know that on the days my father is sober, he'll be proud that I'm learning something about his building craft."

Yeshua pointed to the Temple. "Remember then the LORD, your God, for he is the one who gives you the power to get wealth," he said. (Deuteronomy 8:18)

Daniel nodded his head and followed Yeshua. He would join him to pray in the Temple. But first, they bought dried fish, lentils, and juicy pomegranates from street merchants who were packing up for the day. They also bought salt and water. Daniel purchased a little honey for his mother.

Yeshua and Daniel sat down outside the Temple to clean up and savor their meal. The winds cooled and the sun set. Golden shafts lit their way to the mikveh. After bathing, they headed up the ramp and into the Temple courts with a few other stragglers. Some came to say evening prayers; it was the only time they could afford to be away from their homes or jobs. Others looked for shelter for the night.

As they entered the Temple precinct and passed its mighty walls, Yosef faced an important decision. Should they continue in the darkness to Bethlehem for a few more hours, or should they find a place to stay in Yerushlem and have supper? They could always camp again in the Garden of Gethsemane on the Mount of Olives.

He knew he didn't have to ask Miriam her opinion. She would vote to continue. After all, she and Yosef had traveled to Bethlehem the night Yeshua was born, and had found a place to stay in a stable.

"Let's keep going," Ethan said. "You know the way, it's your home town."

"I agree," Shimon chimed in.

"Let's find Yeshua!" Benjamin shouted from his perch on the wagon. Miriam gave him a hug and the group continued to roll along with Yosef as the cursor. Shimon walked up ahead with an oil lamp, alongside Ethan. They had stopped earlier to make a fire and light lamps. But Ethan and Shimon were only a few paces ahead of the wagon, as the sunlight grew dim and the sky grey. Yosef was really the navigator now.

South of Yerushlem, they slowed down because of the coming darkness. They hadn't passed anyone in the last 15 minutes or so. Ethan whistled a tune in the dark. It was eerie and yet exhilarating to journey at night with the stars and the moon lighting the way.

"Sistere!" a voice shouted from behind. At first, Yosef thought it was a Roman soldier urging them to "halt" in Latin. But when Yosef turned around, he discovered two men in black, wearing hoods.

They had sneaked up from the roadside. One grabbed Yosef from behind and put a blade to his throat. Miriam screamed.

"Give us all your money," said the other thief in Aramaic. He carried a club and held out a sack to collect the ransom. The brigand first approached Ethan and Shimon. Each man reached for his purse. Shimon opened the satchel on his belt and handed everything over. Actually, he had hidden a larger stash of coins under his tunic. Ethan had concealed his real purse under Hasna's saddle. He climbed down from his donkey, ready to hand the thief the purse cinched at his waist.

"Keep your distance!" the robber shouted, when Ethan leaned toward him to drop his purse in the sack.

As the crook stepped back with the loot, Ethan yanked hard on Hasna's saddle strap. She kicked, sending the robber flying. His hip throbbed. The sudden impact and pain left him breathless.

At that instant, Yosef instinctively spun around, grabbing the hand of the other criminal. As the two men struggled for the knife, they bumped along the wagon. Benjamin stood up and slammed the heavy wooden bowl over the robber's head. Not a second later, a rock from Shimon's slingshot stung the thief's side. The blows stunned the man just long enough for Yosef to disarm him.

Ethan grabbed the bag of loot and the club that lay on the ground. Frustrated and confused, the two criminals limped into the night.

"If a thief is caught in the act of housebreaking and beaten to death, there is no bloodguilt involved," Benjamin proclaimed, quoting Scripture atop the wagon. (Exodus 22:1)

The search party managed to laugh about the foiled robbery, and the two sorry thieves were left to lick their wounds.

"They didn't know what they were getting into," Shimon chuckled. "Hasna's kick and Benjamin with his mighty bowl!"

"Praise the Lord you were all with us!" Miriam exclaimed.

"And bless His Holy name!" said Daniel as he and Yeshua finished their prayers in the Court of Israelites. He was grateful for the opportunity to clean up his life, and earn some money to help his family.

"I should go," said Daniel. "I have to be up early."

"Shlama," said Yeshua as he hugged his friend.

"I'll bring you a honey cake in the morning," Daniel promised. "My mom bakes great."

Yeshua laughed as he watched Daniel walk briskly down the steps of the Nicanor Gate and into the moonlit Court of Women. He wasn't worried about his new friend because he was a wily character, and he knew the streets of Yerushlem. Anyway, Daniel didn't have far to go to make it home safely.

At the mention of the honey cake, Yeshua thought about his mother and father and the rest of his family and friends in Nazareth. Truthfully, he had expected to see them by now. Had they broken down? Were they sick or injured? Those concerns spun around his head as he leaned against a pillar. If his parents didn't arrive tomorrow, Yeshua was going to have to find a job. He was running out of money, and he needed to buy things, like a mat and blanket for sleeping. It would be another long night on the cold, stone floor. He reached into his bag and pulled out his knife and a chunk of wood. A little carving would help him pass the time and make him sleepy.

Yeshua smiled to himself, and looked up at the starry sky above the court. Then he whispered,

"Better one day in your courts
   than a thousand elsewhere." (Psalm 84:10)

In his heart, he could feel his heavenly Father smiling back at him.

chapter

THIRTY

EZEKIEL JUMPED UP FROM HIS MAT AS HE HEARD a knock at the door. It was very late. The small fire in the hearth had burned down to a warm, faint orange glow. He wrapped himself in his blanket and went to the door.

"Who is it?" he asked in a low voice, so as not to wake his entire family.

"Zeke, it's Yosef and Miriam!" Yosef replied.

When the door opened, the moonlight illuminated the entryway. Behind Ezekiel, Yosef could see a shadowy figure. One of Zeke's sons had awakened, too.

"What's wrong, Uncle?" asked Ezekiel, lighting a lamp in the outer room. "Come in, come in."

Those were not the words Miriam and Yosef were hoping to hear. Immediately, they knew Yeshua was not inside.

"We're searching for Yeshua! He's been missing for two days," Yosef explained.

Soon the entire search party was in the home. Zeke's wife, Freda, scurried about the inner room, feeding her guests. They hadn't eaten anything since their midday meal. The children sat around and watched their visitors gobble cheese, grapes and wine. Freda ran to a neighbor's home to borrow a few loaves of bread. But Miriam was worried sick and ate nothing.

The kids were wide-eyed as Yosef relayed the story of the attempted robbery. Benjamin was the hero. There would be no more traveling tonight. Freda and Zeke prepared mats and blankets for all their guests in the outer room. They said their prayers and lay down to rest. Yosef held Miriam as she quietly sobbed against his shoulder.

"We'll find him, we'll find him," he assured her.

"Where?" Miriam whimpered. "Yerushlem is enormous. "Where is he sleeping? What's he been eating? What if he's sick or injured? I'm so afraid we'll never see him again."

"Zeke knows dozens of carpenters in Yerushlem working on the Temple. And they know more people. We will search until we find him," said Yosef. "Now, my wife, we have to get some sleep! Yeshua would want you to rest."

As he rolled over on the floor, Yeshua was dreaming. He had fallen asleep carving and thinking about the day's lesson in the Temple about Abraham's obedience. He had complied with God in everything, even when Yahweh asked him to sacrifice his only son, Isaac. Abraham dutifully placed his child on the altar, atop a pile of timbers. Just as he was about to cut Isaac's throat and light the fire to sacrifice him, an angel of the Lord appeared. He stopped Abraham, sparing Isaac. In the end, Abraham sacrificed a ram that was caught in a nearby thicket.

Yeshua's mind drifted from Abraham, Isaac, and the ram to his Passover memories. He relived the mass slaughter of lambs he had witnessed with Yosef. The rivers of blood again ran in the Temple, and dripped from the altar. Suddenly, when he followed the blood with his eyes, he could see it landing near the people standing below. Some laughed and jeered. Yeshua recognized his mother in the crowd, and she cried while blood fell at her feet. When he looked back up at the altar, he could see his arms outstretched, draped across the top of it. He was the sacrifice.

"Wake up! You're dreaming! Wake up!" said Ram. Yeshua opened his eyes. Sweat soaked his tunic, and he shivered from the cold. Ram tossed a blanket over him. "I saw you enter the Temple last night when I was leaving for home. I knew you'd need this."

Yeshua thanked him for the blanket and for waking him from his nightmare.

"You were talking in your sleep and shouting for your mother," Ram explained. "If your parents don't come for you today, you're coming home with me tonight."

Yeshua resisted, explaining that he'd promised his father he wouldn't stay with strangers in Yerushlem. If he were lost or separated from his caravan, he could only go with someone he knew quite well.

"Then what about your cousin's family? Why not stay at old Zechariah's home?" Ram replied. "I can take you there."

Yeshua nodded. If his parents didn't arrive by nightfall, he would accompany Ram and visit cousin Elizabeth.

Miriam and Yosef were already on the road from Bethlehem with the search party. Ezekiel had left for Yerushlem about ten minutes ahead of them. The plan was for Zeke to arrive early at the Temple. He would spread the word that Yeshua was missing, to the carpenters, masons, and their crews. Ethan and Shimon would accompany Miriam and Yosef for a while, and then take a side trip to Elizabeth's home. This way, they could see if Yeshua was staying there. At noon, everyone would meet up in Yerushlem outside the Temple's Beautiful Gate. If they hadn't located Yeshua, they would split up to scour the city some more. Miriam would remain at the gate. Anyone who found Yeshua would immediately return to her.

Meanwhile, in the morning traffic, the search party would need three to four hours to hustle from Bethlehem to Yerushlem. As they approached the Holy City, the traffic would get heavier. In the congestion, accidents and delays were common. Wagons lost wheels, animals came up lame, and merchants spilled their wares in the road.

The sun rose over the Temple, and Yeshua sat in the shadows and the chilly morning air, wrapped in his borrowed blanket. Hillel was unloading his tools when Daniel ran up with a package.

"Quick! Let's eat them while they're hot!" Daniel exclaimed. "My mom's honey cakes straight from the oven."

Daniel unwrapped the cloth to reveal three freshly baked treats. The men inhaled the aroma and shared the sweets. Yeshua cupped the cake in his hands, and savored the smell for a while before biting into the soft dough. He was just as happy for the warmth as he was for the food.

"I will send an angel before you to a land flowing with milk and honey. " said Yeshua. (Exodus 33:2-3)

"Mmmm!" he said as he ate it, rolling his eyes.

"I wish my mom could hear you say that," Daniel said.

"Delicious! Thank you, Daniel. Now let's get to work," urged Hillel as he took another bite. Very quickly, he explained the day's task the foreman had assigned him. Yeshua licked his sticky finger-tips, and then took out his knife and carving work. While the construction crews labored, he continued to diligently craft the piece he had started before his nightmare. The early morning air was filled with noise — hammering, sawing, and stonecutting. Some of the men sang or whistled.

Yeshua looked up from his carving and considered working on the Temple. Yosef had taught him so many skills; he could certainly get a job on one of the crews. There were thousands and thousands of craftsmen working for King Herod. Yeshua's hands were gifted, and he had already proven his efficiency to Hillel. Yeshua could support himself while he waited for his parents. If they didn't arrive today, he'd send them a message with a traveler, and stay with Elizabeth while earning a living. He daydreamed about his plans as he shaped the wooden piece with his knife. He was almost finished.

"What's that you're carving, young man?"

Yeshua looked up to discover Caiaphas standing over him.

"I hope it's not a graven image in violation of the law," said the priest sternly.

Yeshua smiled and politely stood up, handing the carving to the priest. Caiaphas turned it over in his hands and was surprised to find a simple cross. The deeply cut lines made the shape stand out from the background in three dimensions. Yeshua had crafted the chunk of wood into a perfect square. He had positioned the cross on a diagonal.

"Hmmm," said Caiaphas with a puzzled look. He handed the piece back to Yeshua, and walked toward the Temple viaduct without another word. There was a time when High Priests were true spiritual leaders, decedents of Aaron, the brother of Moses. But over the centuries, kings had corrupted the inherited position, and had sometimes appointed political cronies who had no priestly lineage. This arrangement made the High Priest's title a realistic goal for Caiaphas, who was a shrewd politician.

Hillel looked up from his sawing, sweat dripping from his brow, as Yeshua tossed the carving to Daniel. He and Hillel examined the work.

"Fine piece of carving," Yeshua!" said Hillel. "If you want, I'll find a place to nail it inside the Sanhedrin tower. There will be a piece of you in the Temple."

Yeshua nodded his head in appreciation, and he headed toward the mikveh.

The cold water pouring over his head was just what Yosef needed. He was dripping with perspiration, having walked as fast as he could, pulling Mo and Mazel along the road. Benjamin handed him a towel.

"Thank you, Benjamin. So, Shimon, you will find Elizabeth in the third house in from the road on the left," said Yosef, water dripping down his face and beard.

"If she's not there, she may be at her neighbor's," said Miriam. "They are looking after her while John is away. Ask for the town smith, named Uzzi."

"We'll find Elizabeth and hopefully, Yeshua," said Ethan.

"Go with Adonai," Miriam shouted.

Shimon ran alongside Ethan, up the road toward Elizabeth's village. They were less than an hour from the Temple district, but Miriam and Yosef couldn't afford to wait. They planned to retrace their steps and talk to Uriel, the moneychanger, and the other merchants they had met during Passover festival week. Perhaps one of them had seen Yeshua. It was a long shot, but a place to start.

Miriam tried to remain hopeful, but each passing hour made everyone feel more desperate. Benjamin had grown quiet, wishing he had something to say to change the mood. Yosef was normally calm, but today he moved with a sense of urgency, and that only made Miriam more anxious.

As soon as Shimon and Ethan departed, Yosef smacked Mo on the hindquarter and yelled.

"Yeshua! It's good to see you again," said the local rabbi. He had spotted the young man on his way into the Temple.

"I'm hoping you will join us for class again today. I've spread the word about your knowledge of the Scripture. We'll have some scholars and scribes joining us in a little while," the rabbi explained.

"Then every scribe who has been instructed in the kingdom of heaven is like the head of a household who brings from his storeroom both the new and the old," replied Yeshua. (Matthew 13:52)

"Well said," the rabbi acknowledged. "What a wonderful analogy. Then I'll look for you in the court in an hour."

"Yeshua's not here," said Elizabeth. She sat in her courtyard churning butter, her old hands gnarled with arthritis. "I wish I could go with you to search for him, but I would only slow you down. At least let me pour you some cold well water and give you some food to take with you," she offered. Shimon and Ethan were grateful for her hospitality, but they were all crestfallen. They would have to give Miriam and Yosef more bad news, although they hadn't really expected to find Yeshua with Elizabeth.

"Excuse me, do you remember us? We bought bread from you a number of times during Passover week," said Yosef.

"You and a million other people," the baker laughed. "Really, sir, how could I possibly remember you?"

"Maybe you remember our son," said Miriam. "He loves honey cakes, and he was always complimenting your stack of cakes. We can't find him."

"I've seen thousands ..."

"I remember him!" said the baker's daughter, interrupting her father. "He was here yesterday and he bought some day-old bread. He spent so much time looking at the honey cakes, I felt sorry for him. I almost gave him a cake when my father turned his back."

The baker gave his daughter a piercing look. "Well, did you see where he went?" he asked.

"He walked toward the Street of Butchers," said the girl.

"Thank you so much!" Miriam said joyfully. Now, she was confident Yeshua was alive.

"Gather round, gather round," barked the Temple foreman near the Sanhedrin tower. "We have a carpenter who needs your help."

The craftsmen stepped over to the foreman, huddling around him. Zeke finished tying up his animal, and then turned to the group.

"My cousin is missing. He was left behind after Passover," he explained. "He's 12 years old, very bright boy, and a little short for his age. Carries a shoulder bag. Loves to carve. His name is Yeshua."

Zeke repeated this speech a dozen times as he worked his way around the Temple. There were so many carpenters and apprentices on the job. He knew many of the foremen, but it still took time to make his way through the construction sites scattered around the building. The sun was nearly straight overhead now.

Miriam and Yosef had retraced their steps through the Valley of the Cheesemakers, stopping at the merchants where they had bought wine, cheese, fruit, nuts, and salt. No one had seen Yeshua. But then they spoke to the water carrier.

"Yes, I remember you. I saw your boy just last night!" the man said as he filled two goatskins for a customer. "He was with a street kid. I see the other kid all the time, running around here."

"Thank you!" Miriam exclaimed. It was another good sign Yeshua was safe. But what was he doing running the streets of Yerushlem?

Meanwhile, Ethan and Shimon had arrived in the city. Ethan visited the fabric and garment merchants. Shimon stopped at many farmers' stalls, describing Yeshua. No one had seen him. Their effort was a little like searching a farm to find a rooster's feather on a windy day. And that tiny feather had blown into a huge, open barn called Yerushlem, which brimmed with laborers and produce from around the world.

"All the choicest first fruits of every kind and all the best of your offerings of every kind shall belong to the priests; the best of your dough you shall also give to the priests to bring a blessing upon your house," the student said, reading from his tablet in the Temple. (Ezekiel 44:30)

The Scripture class had gathered in the Court of Women. Yeshua walked up to join the group just in time.

"Very good, very good job," the rabbi said. "And we have the priest Caiaphas with us today. Perhaps someday he will be the High Priest."

Caiaphas pretended to be humbled by the compliment.

"Who wants to explain the reading as we know it from God's law?" asked the rabbi. "You may use your own words."

When no one responded, Yeshua raised his hand, and the rabbi recognized him with a smile. "Yes, Yeshua?"

"Give and gifts will be given to you; a good measure, packed together, shaken down, and overflowing, will be poured into your lap. For the measure with which you measure will in return be measured out to you," Yeshua said. (Luke 6:38)

"Very interesting way to look at that Scripture," the rabbi remarked. "Yes, God does return blessings abundantly. But what about the rule of tithing ten percent? That is the law."

Yeshua paused and then responded, "Hypocrites ... they pay tithes of mint and dill and cummin, and have neglected the weightier things of the law: judgment and mercy and fidelity. [But] these they should have done, without neglecting the others."(Matthew 23:23)

"I'll go to the moneychanger next and then up to the Mount of Olives," said Yosef. "Maybe he's staying up there. We camped there, and he knows the men watching the grove for Abner."

"Good idea. I'll continue working my way through the crews around the building," Zeke said.

"Most of these farmers have kids with them. I'll talk to them; maybe they've seen Yeshua," Shimon reasoned. "They can help get the word out to the community."

"I can ride Hasna through the neighborhoods," said Ethan. "Let's meet back here at sundown. Don't worry, Miriam, we're going to find Yeshua, and you're going to grow old with him at your side," he added to comfort her.

A woman, bent with arthritis, her face wrinkled by the sun, slowly walked up to the Temple treasury, and dropped a tiny amount into one of the shofars. Yeshua singled her out as an example among the people making their donations in the Court of Women.

He turned back to the Scripture study group and said, "I tell you truly, this poor widow put in more than all the rest; for those others have all made offerings from their surplus wealth, but she, from her poverty, has offered her whole livelihood." (Luke 21:3-4)

A few coins fell to the ground. Uriel, the moneychanger, bent down to pick them up, and put them in his purse.

"Shlama," said Yosef as he walked up to Uriel's table. "Do you remember me? My wife's cousin is John, the son of Elizabeth. She's Zechariah's widow. We did business with you last week."

"Of course!" said Uriel. "I'm surprised you're still here. I saw your son the other day."

"You did? That's wonderful news!" Yosef shouted with excitement. "Have you seen him today?"

"No, sorry I haven't," said Uriel. "He was with a kid who tried to steal his bag. I couldn't convince him to turn the thief over to the Temple guard, but they went off together. I haven't seen him for two days."

Yosef was stunned. What kind of people was Yeshua spending time with in Yerushlem?

"If you do bump into my son, please tell him his parents are looking for him. His mother is waiting at the Beautiful Gate. His name is Yeshua. We're from Nazareth."

"I remember, I remember," said Uriel.

"I saw your son, too" said a voice coming from the shadow of Uriel's table. It was the beggar woman, Leah, who had met Yeshua outside the butcher shop. Uriel allowed her to beg near his table. She was seated on the ground at his feet.

Yosef crouched down to talk to her and dropped a coin in her bowl.

"When did you see him?" he asked.

"It was yesterday morning. He gave me his bread and some water outside the butcher shop," she replied. "He's a sweet young man."

"Where did he go? Do you have any idea?" said Yosef, begging for information.

"He went off with a tattooed Gentile," she replied. "He was a Greek slave. The man gave him a loaf of bread and a honey cake. He talked about his generous master, and then they walked off together.

Yeshua was going to show him where he was staying. I heard their whole conversation," she added.

"A slave!" Yosef thought. This was his worst nightmare. What if the man had kidnapped Yeshua, and had sold him into service? On the other hand, just yesterday the water carrier had seen Yeshua hanging out with a street kid. Maybe he was also a slave, and they had escaped. Yosef's mind ran wild with possibilities.

"Thank you, thank you," said Yosef as he raced toward the Street of Butchers. He couldn't bear the thought of telling Miriam that Yeshua had gone off with a tattooed Gentile slave. He just had to find him.

Yosef prayed as he ran along the Temple walls. He would give away all he had to find Yeshua, and not have to tell Miriam what he knew. He stopped in every butcher shop to ask about Yeshua. "Have you seen my son?" But no one remembered him. He decided to try the Street of Ironsmiths, before he ran up to the Mount of Olives. Now he was running out of ideas. The search had taken all afternoon. "How could God do this to Miriam and me, when our son was destined to save his people?" Yosef thought. He was angry and confused, but desperately clung to his faith. He felt like his life and his family were slipping away.

"Then the LORD, your God, will generously increase your un-dertakings, the fruit of your womb, the offspring of your livestock, and the produce of your soil; for the LORD, your God, will again take delight in your prosperity, just as he took delight in your an-cestors', because you   will … because you will do what?" asked the rabbi. (Deuteronomy 30:9-10)

For a moment, no one responded. "Who knows the rest of the Scripture verse? Who knows what God wants from us?" quizzed the rabbi. "God will take delight in your prosperity because …?"

A boy jumped up and yelled, "Because you will obey the voice of the LORD, your God, keeping the commandments and statutes that are written in this book of the law, when you return to the

LORD, your God, with your whole heart and your whole being." (Deuteronomy 30:10)

Caiaphas applauded the boy and the rabbi blushed. "Extraordinary! Yes, God will bless us with wealth, family, and health if we follow his laws," he said.

"To the letter," added Caiaphas. "Do not let this book of the law depart from your lips. Recite it by day and by night, that you may carefully observe all that is written in it; then you will attain your goal; then you will succeed." (Joshua 1:8)

The priest continued:

"The wealth of the rich is their strong fortress;

the ruin of the poor is their poverty." (Proverbs 10:15)

Then Yeshua asked respectfully, "What profit is there for one to gain the whole world and forfeit his life? (Mark 8:36)

"If someone who has worldly means sees a brother in need and refuses him compassion, how can the love of God remain in him?" (1 John 3:17)

There was silence. Some of the older scribes and scholars listened and nodded approval at his questions. The devout women who lived in the court had also been listening with great appreciation to the lively discussion of God's word. They marveled at Yeshua's profound insights.

After a long pause, Yeshua continued, "No one can serve two masters. He will either hate one and love the other, or be devoted to one and despise the other. You cannot serve God and wealth." (Matthew 6:24)

Caiaphas stared at Yeshua from the back of the group. How could this young boy be so confident about interpreting the Word of God?

"Yeshua!" exclaimed Hillel.

"Yes! You know him?" shouted Zeke, standing among a crowd of carpenters at the Sanhedrin Tower. The shadows from the structure were long and dark, as the sun was now low in the sky.

"I had breakfast with him today," laughed Hillel. "He's been living in the Temple. Daniel! Come here."

Obediently, Daniel ran over to his boss. Hillel quickly explained that Zeke was searching for Yeshua, to reunite him with his family.

"Where do you think he is?" asked Zeke.

"My guess, he's in the Temple," replied Daniel. "He's my friend, and I'd bet my day's wages on it."

Zeke thanked the men, and quickly headed toward the Beautiful Gate to share the good news with Miriam.

"Yeshua is in Yerushlem! People have seen him today!" Ezekiel shouted to Miriam as he galloped up to her on his donkey.

"Oh, how my soul praises Adonai!" laughed Miriam. "I can't wait to tell Yosef. But how will we find Yeshua?"

"I talked to a carpenter's helper who said he bets Yeshua is in the Temple!" exclaimed Zeke breathlessly.

"The Temple?" said Miriam. "Thank God, he's someplace safe. He could be in the Court of Gentiles, the Court of Women, or the Court of Israelites. And it will soon be dark."

"Let's go find him," urged Zeke.

"No! We can't leave Benjamin alone, and if Yosef returns and finds no one here, then he'll think something's happened to us," Miriam explained.

"Why don't you go, Zeke?" Benjamin suggested.

"Good idea!" Miriam and Zeke said in unison.

Zeke got off his mule and tied him to Yosef's wagon. Now Miriam and Benjamin had three animals and a wagon to manage near the busy Temple Gate. Zeke ran toward the mikveh. He would have to cleanse himself before entering the Temple.

"Hypocrites ... they cleanse the outside of cup and dish, but inside they are full of plunder and self-indulgence," Yeshua explained, discussing the laws of purification. "... cleanse first the inside of the cup, so that the outside also may be clean." (Matthew 23:25-26)

The rabbi was so captivated he was speechless. He would love to have Yeshua as a student every day, because he challenged everyone to think about his faith, and not just recite answers from memory. The class and even the adults were glued to the discussion.

But when the rabbi looked at Caiaphas, he could see the priest was fuming, despite his always-calm exterior. Caiaphas noticed the older scribes and scholars nodding in agreement with the young Nazarene. He was hesitant about scolding Yeshua for his boldness, and searched his mind for a politically safe response. He didn't want any influential Israelites complaining to the High Priest, Annas.

The older, devout men and women seemed mesmerized by Yeshua. This was the kind of message faithful and compassionate Israelites had been longing to hear. They were aching for the Messiah and his healing words of humility, wisdom, and charitable love.

"Yes, Yeshua, God knows our hearts inside and out," Caiaphas acknowledged. "We can hide nothing from him." And then he turned to the senior faithful and quoted Scripture with a wink and a smile.

"As the book of Job says:

Does not the ear judge words
as the mouth tastes food?
So with old age is wisdom,
and with length of days understanding." (Job 12:12)

"Our elders know God from a lifetime of experience and devotion," he added, trying to indulge his audience.

All eyes were now on the young Nazarene.

"Does not Wisdom call,
and Understanding raise her voice?" asked Yeshua.

"'The LORD begot me, the beginning of his works,
the forerunner of his deeds of long ago;
From of old I was formed,

at the first, before the earth.
When there were no deeps I was brought forth,
when there were no fountains or springs of water;
Before the mountains were settled into place,
before the hills, I was brought forth;
When the earth and the fields were not yet made,
nor the first clods of the world.
When he established the heavens, there was I,
when he marked out the vault over the face of the deep;
When he made firm the skies above,
when he fixed fast the springs of the deep;
When he set for the sea its limit,
so that the waters should not transgress his command;
When he fixed the foundations of earth,
then was I beside him as artisan;
I was his delight day by day,
playing before him all the while,
Playing over the whole of his earth,
having my delight with human beings.'"
(Proverbs 8: 1, 22-31)

Yeshua walked around the room while he quoted the powerful Scripture on wisdom and eternity. Everyone there felt as if he were talking about himself in some way. It was obvious he knew God. The rabbi and the priest were numb. But what could they say? He was right and his Scripture was flawless.

Yeshua captivated the students. Someone their own age was leading the debate about Yahweh's law, and what He wanted from His people.

Yeshua looked at his smiling Temple classmates, and he smiled back, quoting Isaiah the prophet:

"Learn to do good.
Make justice your aim: redress the wronged,

hear the orphan's plea, defend the widow." (Isaiah 1:17)

"You won't believe what I just heard!" shouted Ezekiel joyfully, as he nearly ran into Yosef on his way to the mikveh. Yosef had been racing to reach Miriam before nightfall.

"I have terrible news," said Yosef out of breath. "Yeshua was seen in the company of a Greek slave. He may have been kidnapped. Or maybe he's running for his life."

"When?" Zeke snapped.

"Sometime yesterday," said Yosef.

"Then he's safe!" Zeke replied. "A carpenter and his apprentice had breakfast with him this morning. They believe he's in the Temple right now."

"Oh, Adonai be praised," said Yosef, falling to his knees. He was overwhelmed by God's mercy. "We need to tell Miriam!"

"She already knows and is waiting for you," Zeke shouted, as Yosef stood up and ran toward the Beautiful Gate. God had heard their prayers. Together, they scrambled to get Miriam. Finally, Yeshua's weary parents headed for the mikveh, and then inside the Temple to find their son.

"One thing I ask of the LORD;
this I seek:
To dwell in the LORD's house
all the days of my life,
To gaze on the LORD's beauty,
to visit his temple," chanted Yeshua. (Psalm 27:4)

As the sun set, Miriam and Yosef entered the Court of Women. It had been three days since they'd seen their son. The Scripture class had ended, and Yeshua sat with a small group of elders. A woman played a lyre, accompanying Yeshua. The young rabbi, the older scribes, and devout women enjoyed the moment as he sang in a soft, sweet voice.

> *"For God will hide me in his shelter*
> *in time of trouble,*
> *He will conceal me in the cover of his tent;*
> *and set me high upon a rock.*
> *Even now my head is held high*
> *above my enemies on every side!*
> *I will offer in his tent*
> *sacrifices with shouts of joy;*
> *I will sing and chant praise to the LORD." (Psalm 27:5-6)*

When Yeshua finished, his mother and father ran up and wrapped their arms around him. Miriam sobbed with joy. "Son, why have you done this to us? she asked. "Your father and I have been looking for you with great anxiety." (Luke 2:48)

"Why were you looking for me? Yeshua replied tenderly. "Did you not know that I must be in my Father's house?" (Luke 2:49)

He kissed his mother's hands, and then looked up at his father with a smile. Yeshua's response surprised everyone, including his parents. Miriam shook her head and smiled through her tears. She thought to herself, "Someday, God will give us complete understanding of His son."

Yeshua said goodbye to the people in the court and left the Temple, arm in arm with his parents. Ram spotted them and waved. "I'll see you next year at Passover, God willing," the old guard yelled.

Yeshua waved back. Hillel and Daniel were waiting outside. He stopped to give each a hug, and thanked them for their friendship. Then he joined Miriam and Yosef, Zeke, Ethan, Shimon, and Benjamin for a long meal. He spent the evening telling them what he'd done for the last three days.

The next morning, the six Nazarene travelers headed home, where Yeshua would continue to be an obedient son, and to grow in wisdom and stature before his heavenly Father and his neighbors.

During the long trip to Nazareth, Yeshua and Benjamin sat on the side of the wagon, enjoying the journey. Yosef and Shimon took turns leading Mo and Mazel all the way, while Ethan rode alongside on Hasna.

A half-day outside Yerushlem, they passed the Roman centurion and his troops. The soldiers were taking lunch alongside the road. Their handsome officer dismounted from his muscular black steed. Yeshua waved to him from the wagon, and the centurion recognized him. The Roman smiled and yelled, "Shlama," as he waved back.

"Pax!" Yeshua shouted to the centurion, the word for "peace" in Latin, the Roman's native language.

Miriam strummed her lyre most of the way home, but she didn't sing. She was too busy contemplating the entire Passover experience. She wanted to remember it, understanding that it was part of God's special plan for her son. She'd keep these memories and others tucked away in her heart.

Miriam knew Yeshua had changed profoundly during those three days he'd spent at the Temple — in his Father's house. And she suspected Yerushlem and the world would never be the same.

ACKNOWLEDGMENTS

Many people taught me about the Holy Scripture — from my mother and father, to my teachers — including nuns, priests, and spiritual advisors. I'm grateful to them all. I'm also blessed to have a patient, Christian wife, Ellen K. Stepien. My darling is always willing to review my writing, and offer ideas, support, and constructive criticism. Her advice on this book was priceless.

But for me, this novel would not have been possible without the power of the Internet to quickly search key words and phrases, and to discover Scripture passages and history.

Equally important was an extraordinary historical reference, "Jesus and His Times," published in 1987 by The Reader's Digest Association, Inc. It is a remarkably well-researched book, exploring first century life in the Holy Land and Jewish history. This invaluable resource helped me craft a realistic story about 12-year-old Jesus Christ and his family's Passover pilgrimage to Jerusalem. Thanks to Fr. Joseph "Bernie" Marquis for recommending "Jesus and His Times," and for his endless support and friendship. Thanks also to Fr. Gerard "Gerry" Battersby for reading my first draft, and encouraging me to continue my spiritual journey.

Finally, a special thank you to my talented friend and neighbor, renowned artist, Gary Ciccarelli. He generously donated his services, and designed a captivating book cover for the first edition.

And praise God for His many blessings.

ABOUT THE AUTHOR

As a journalist, Chris Stepien has spent his career asking tough questions and telling intriguing stories.

He worked as a television producer-director and writer for the American Broadcasting Company (ABC). From 1979 to 1987, while at WXYZ-TV, Detroit, he won six Emmy® Awards, as well as many other honors for documentaries, sports and celebrity specials, and children's programming. Stepien left broadcasting to co-found Adventure, Inc., a successful Detroit-based video/film production company. He created award-winning communications for Fortune 500 companies like General Motors and Ford Motor Company for nearly nine years. Since 1996, Stepien has crafted marketing and advertising for global clients, as writer-creative director and owner of Stepien Creative Services, Inc.

A lifelong metro Detroiter and Catholic, Stepien attended parochial schools and was an altar boy. He and his wife, Ellen, have two adult sons, Alex and Mike. Chris and Ellen are Vincentians, active members of the Society of St. Vincent de Paul (SVdP). Stepien, a former SVdP conference president, is currently lay spiritual advisor to a group of Vincentians in Dearborn, Michigan. Their core mission is to respond to the needs of poor families in the surrounding community, visit them in their homes, and provide financial assistance, guidance, friendship, and hope.

Bible studies, spiritual exercises, and praying the rosary inspired the author to write this novel about preteen Jesus. Stepien relied on his love of God and his passion for visual storytelling to help shape this account of the boy Messiah and His Passover pilgrimage. The author's experiences serving the needy and children of alcoholics were very influential as well.

SHARE YOUR THOUGHTS

This title is available as part of our book program for as little as $2 per copy. To purchase more copies of *THREE DAYS: The Search for the Boy Messiah*, please visit:

DynamicCatholic.com
Be Bold. Be Catholic.®

If you have questions or feedback for the author, would like more information about his speaking engagements, or would like to invite him to speak at an event that you are hosting, please contact:

Email: threedayssearch@gmail.com

For more information, please visit:

www.TheBoyMessiah.com
Twitter: @ThreeDaysSearch
Facebook: ThreeDaysSearch

Share ***Three Days*** with everyone in your parish for as little as $2 a copy.

Order today at **DynamicCatholic.com**.
Shipping and handling included with bulk order.

ENDNOTES

1) Ronald L. Eisenberg, *The JPS Guide to Jewish Traditions*. PA: Jewish
   Publication Society, 2004; "Prayer Kriat Sh'ma" The American-Israeli
   Cooperative Enterprise
   http://www.jewishvirtuallibrary.org/jsource/Judaism/bedtime.html

2 Lois Tverberg & Bruce Okkema, "Thinking Hebraically About God's Creation."
   En-Gedi Resource Center.
   http://www.egrc.net/articles/director/articles_director_0505.html

3) Rabbi Simkha Weintraub, "Mi Sheberakh: May the One Who Blessed." *My
   Jewish Learning.*
   http://www.myjewishlearning.com/texts/Liturgy_and_Prayers/Siddur_
   Prayer_Book/Torah_Service/Prayer_for_he_Sick.shtml

4) Daniel B. Wallace, "Passover in the Time of Jesus." *Bible.org.*
   http://bible.org/article/passover-time-jesus

5) Tracey R. Rich, "The Jewish Sabbath." *Judaism 101.*
   http://www.religionfacts.com/judaism/holidays/shabbat.htm

6) "Immersion in the Mikveh." *Mayyim Hayyim.*
   http://www.mayyimhayyim.org/Immersion-in-the-Mikveh

7) "Holidays and Rituals – Tefilat HaDerech-Traveler's Prayer." *Hillel International*
   http://www.hillel.org/jewish/archives/text-studies

8) The Reader's Digest Association, Inc., *Jesus and His Times*, (1987) p. 132

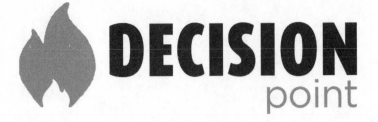

NOTES

NOTES

NOTES

NOTES

NOTES

NOTES

THE
DYNAMIC CATHOLIC
INSTITUTE

[MISSION]

To re-energize the Catholic Church
in America by developing world-class
resources that inspire people to
rediscover the genius of Catholicism.

[VISION]

To be the innovative leader in the
New Evangelization helping Catholics
and their parishes become
the-best-version-of-themselves.

DynamicCatholic.com
Be Bold. Be Catholic.®

The Dynamic Catholic Institute
5081 Olympic Blvd • Erlanger • KY • 41018
Phone: 859-980-7900
info@DynamicCatholic.com